for GCSE

Book F2 part B

PATHFINDER EDITION

PUBLISHED BY THE PRESS SYNDICATE OF THE UNIVERSITY OF CAMBRIDGE
The Pitt Building, Trumpington Street, Cambridge, United Kingdom

CAMBRIDGE UNIVERSITY PRESS
The Edinburgh Building, Cambridge CB2 2RU, UK
40 West 20th Street, New York, NY 10011-4211, USA
477 Williamstown Road, Port Melbourne, VIC 3207, Australia
Ruiz de Alarcón 13, 28014 Madrid, Spain
Dock House, The Waterfront, Cape Town 8001, South Africa

http://www.cambridge.org

© The School Mathematics Project 2002
First published 2002

Printed in Italy by Rotolito Lombarda
*Typeface* Minion   *System* QuarkXPress®

A catalogue record for this book is available from the British Library.

ISBN 0 521 01295 3   paperback

Typesetting and technical illustrations by The School Mathematics Project
Illustration on page 32 by David Parkins
Photographs on page 17 by David Cassell, page 134 by John King
and page 136 by John White

**Acknowledgements**

The authors and publishers are grateful to the following Examination Boards
for permission to reproduce questions from past examination papers:

| | |
|---|---|
| AQA(NEAB) | Assessment and Qualifications Alliance |
| AQA(SEG) | Assessment and Qualifications Alliance |
| Edexcel | Edexcel Foundation |
| OCR | Oxford, Cambridge and RSA Examinations |
| WJEC | Welsh Joint Education Committee |

Euro coins on page 29 © European Communities 1995–2002, from
The European Union On-Line
Map on page 130 includes mapping data licensed from Ordnance Survey with the permission of
the Controller of Her Majesty's Stationery Office, © Crown copyright. All rights reserved. Licence No. 100001679.

NOTICE TO TEACHERS
It is illegal to reproduce any part of this work in material form (including
photocopying and electronic storage) except under the following circumstances:
(i) where you are abiding by a licence granted to your school or institution by the
Copyright Licensing Agency;
(ii) where no such licence exists, or where you wish to exceed the terms of a licence, and
you have gained the written permission of Cambridge University Press;
(iii) where you are allowed to reproduce without permission under the provisions of
Chapter 3 of the Copyright, Designs and Patents Act 1988.

# Contents

| | | |
|---|---|---|
| 18 | Patchwork | 4 |
| 19 | Cuboids | 13 |
| 20 | Sequences | 21 |
| 21 | More circle facts | 26 |
| 22 | Travel | 34 |
| 23 | Looking at data | 47 |
| 24 | Enlargement | 57 |
| 25 | Calculating with fractions 1 | 62 |
| 26 | Substitution | 71 |
| | Review 3 | 79 |
| 27 | Probability | 81 |
| 28 | Using a calculator 2 | 90 |
| 29 | Transformations | 94 |
| 30 | Calculating with decimals 2 | 106 |
| 31 | The solution is clear | 112 |
| 32 | Calculating with fractions 2 | 118 |
| 33 | Constructions | 125 |
| 34 | Navigation | 130 |
| 35 | Percentage calculations 2 | 139 |
| 36 | Conversion graphs | 147 |
| | Review 4 | 151 |

# 18 Patchwork

You will
- work out a fraction of a shape in its simplest form
- find the area of squares and right-angled triangles
- find lines of reflection symmetry and orders of rotation symmetry
- complete designs given details of their reflection or rotation symmetry
- work with angles in a right angle, on a straight line, round a point and in a triangle

## A Fractions

This patchwork cushion cover is made from black, grey and white squares.

There are 16 equal squares so each square is $\frac{1}{16}$ of the cushion cover.

There are 4 white squares so $\frac{4}{16}$ of the cover is white.

In its simplest form $\frac{4}{16} = \frac{1}{4}$ (÷ 4).

**A1** What fraction of the cushion cover above is
(a) grey  (b) black

**A2** What fraction of each design below is grey?
Give each answer in its simplest form.

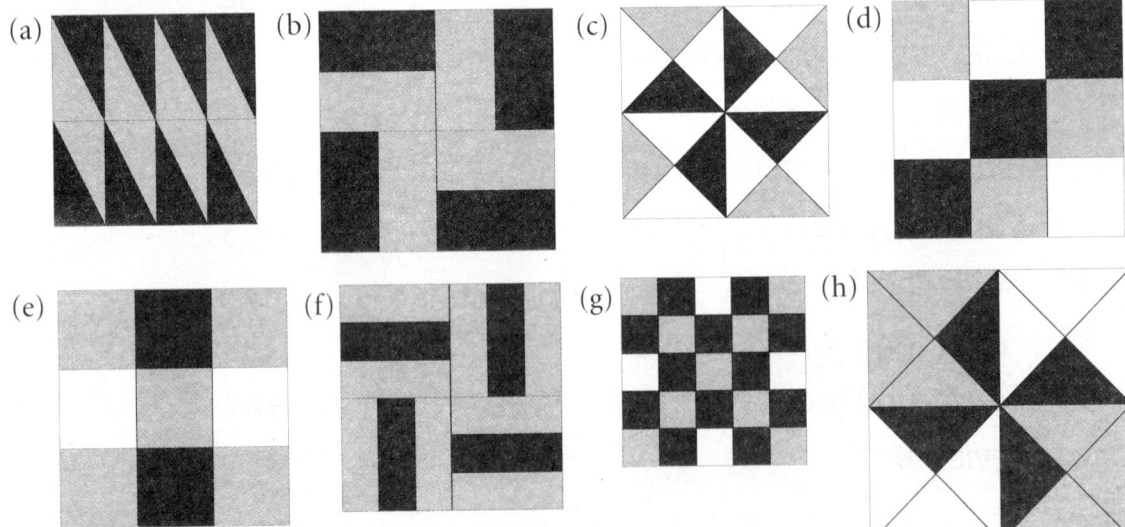

**A3** Design your own patchwork cushion cover where $\frac{1}{2}$ of the design is grey.

4 • 18 Patchwork

## B  Block designs

Patchwork quilters often use the 'block' method.
They make square designs called blocks and join them to make a whole quilt.
Some blocks have special names.
This one is called 'Hovering hawks'.

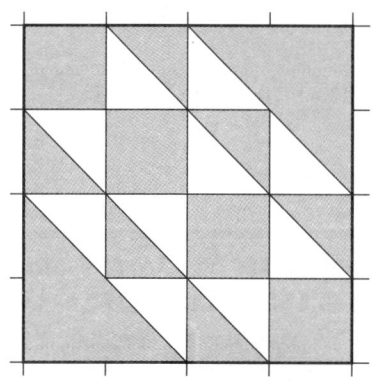

- What fraction of this block is grey?
- What fraction is white?

**B1** (a) Make a copy of the 'Shoo-fly' block.
  (b) What fraction of the block is black?
  (c) What fraction is white?

**B2** Jane is making a square quilt using 16 'Shoo-fly' blocks.
  (a) How many black squares will she use?
  (b) How many black triangles will she use?
  (c) What fraction of the quilt is black?
  (d) The whole quilt measures 144 cm by 144 cm.
    What is the size of each block?

Shoo-fly

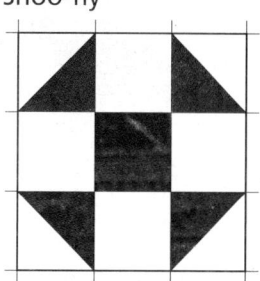

Evening star

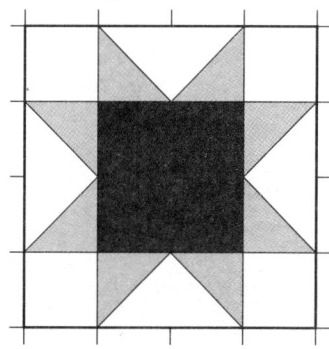

**B3** (a) Make a copy of the 'Evening star' block.
  (b) What fraction of the block is black?
  (c) What fraction is grey?
  (d) What fraction is white?

**B4** Josh is making a quilt using 12 'Evening star' blocks.
  (a) How many white squares will he use?
  (b) How many grey triangles will he use?
  (c) The whole quilt measures 160 cm by 120 cm and the blocks are arranged in four rows of three.
    What is the size of each black square piece?

**B5** (a) Make a copy of the 'Crosses and losses' block.

(b) What fraction of the block is white?

(c) What fraction is grey?

(d) What fraction is black?

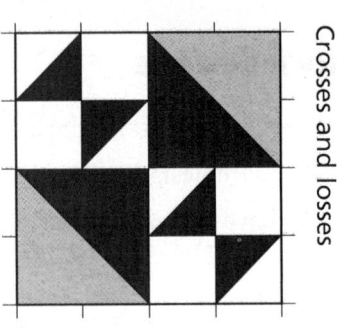
Crosses and losses

**B6** Fiona makes a 'Crosses and losses' block. Her white square pieces are 4 cm by 4 cm.

Find the area in square centimetres of each

(a) white square  (b) small black triangle  (c) grey triangle

## C  Symmetry

This block has two lines of symmetry and rotation symmetry of order **2**.

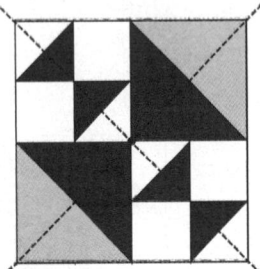

This design turns to fit onto itself in **2** different positions.

This block has no lines of symmetry but rotation symmetry of order **4**.

This design turns to fit onto itself in **4** different positions.

**C1** (a) How many lines of symmetry does this block have?

(b) What is its order of rotation symmetry?

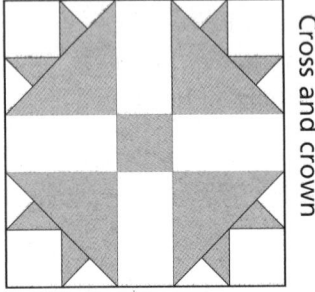
Cross and crown

**C2** Some blocks are on sheet P157.
Mark any lines of symmetry and any centre of rotation on each block.
Write the order of rotation symmetry under each one.

**C3** Complete each block on sheet P158.

**C4** Design blocks of your own with

(a) 4 lines of symmetry and order of rotation symmetry 4

(b) no lines of symmetry and order of rotation symmetry 4

## D By degrees

- What different shapes can you find in the 'LeMoyne star' block?
- What different types of angle can you find?
- How many degrees are in each angle?

LeMoyne star

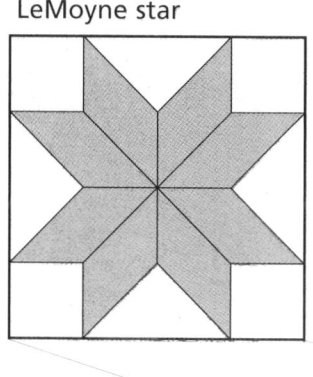
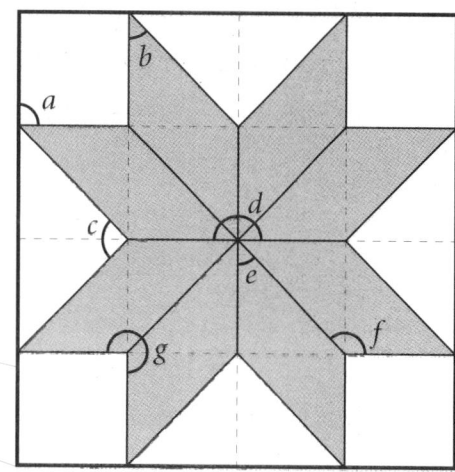

**D1** (a) Work out the size of each angle marked in the 'Weathervane' block.
  (b) Which of the marked angles are obtuse?
  (c) How many right angles are there in one of the dark grey shapes?
  (d) How many pieces in this block are light grey right-angled triangles?

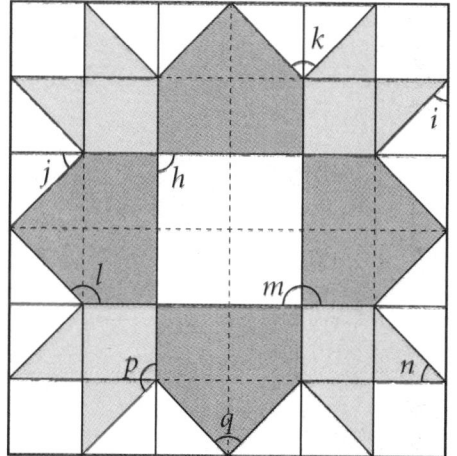

Weathervane

**D2** (a) Work out the size of each angle marked in the 'Bear's tracks' block.
  (b) Which of these angles are reflex?

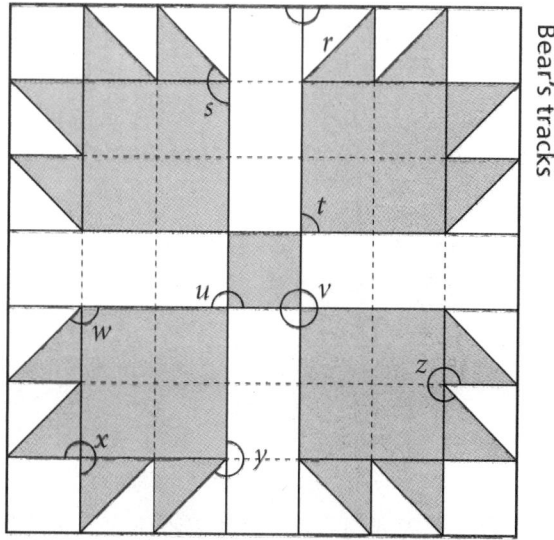

Bear's tracks

18 Patchwork • 7

## E  *It all adds up*

These are parts of patchwork cushion covers.

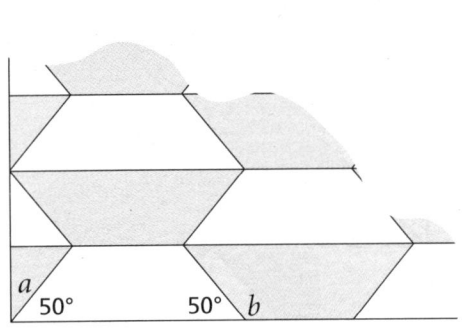
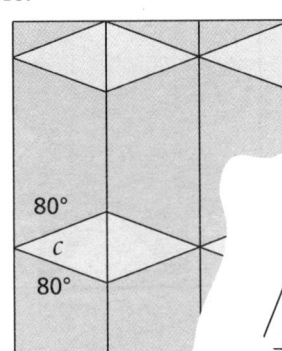
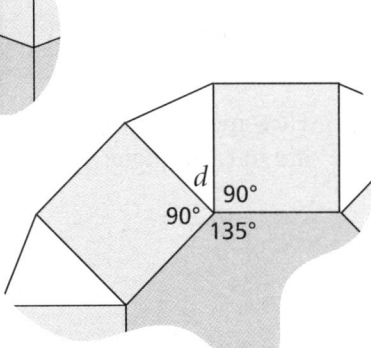

- What size are angles *a*, *b*, *c* and *d*?

**E1** Work out the size of each angle marked with a letter.

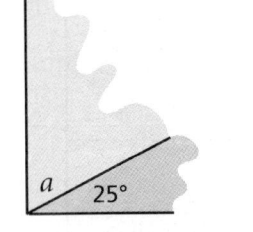
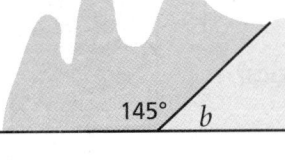
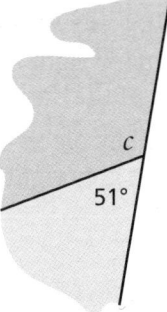

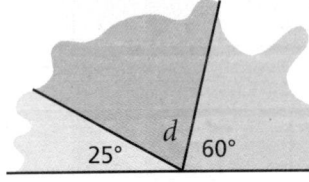
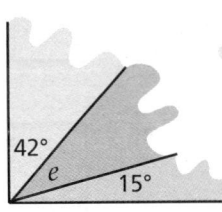
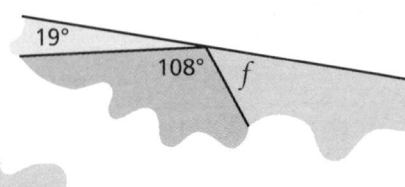

**E2** Work out the size of each angle marked with a letter.

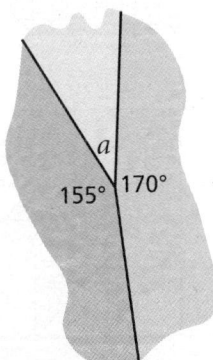
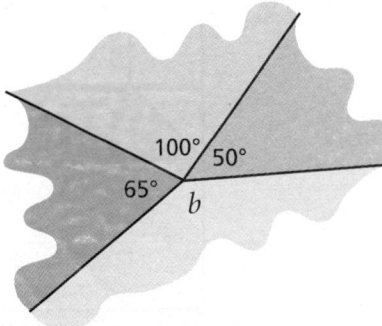
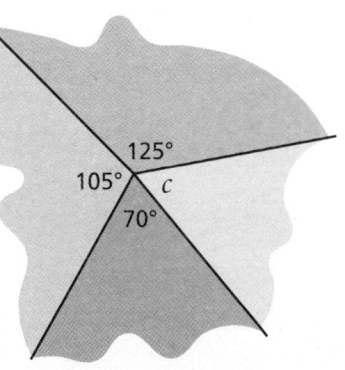

8 • 18 Patchwork

**E3** Calculate each marked angle in the 'Guiding star' block.

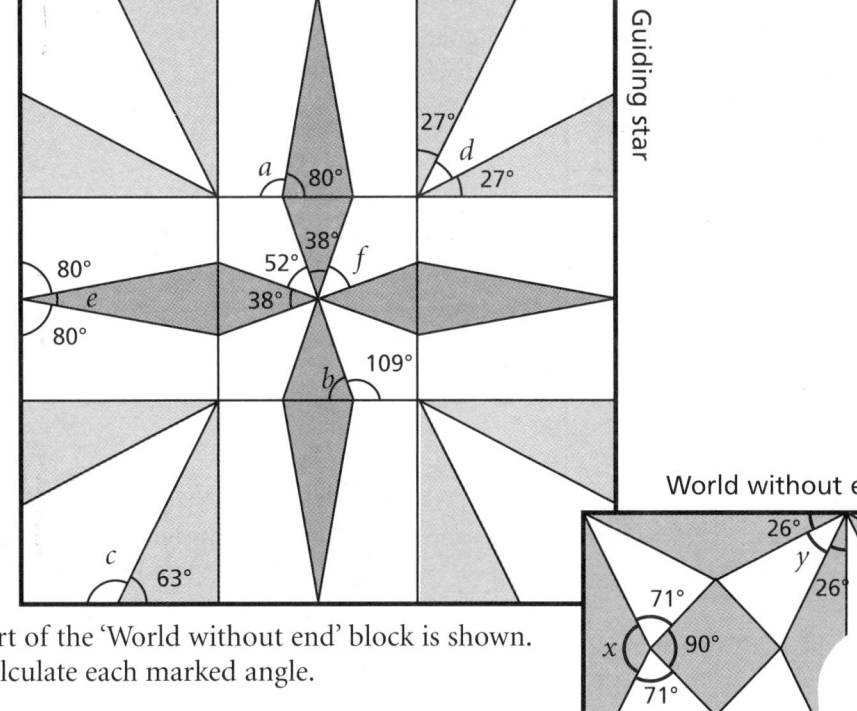

**E4** Part of the 'World without end' block is shown. Calculate each marked angle.

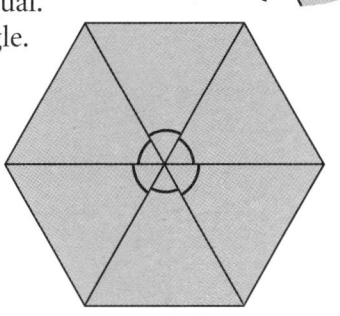

**E5** The angles shown here are equal. Work out the size of each angle.

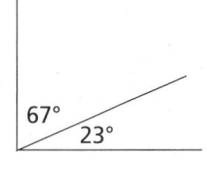

| Angles in a right angle add up to 90°. | Angles on a straight line add up to 180°. | Angles round a point add up to 360°. |
|---|---|---|
| 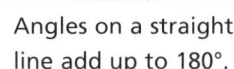 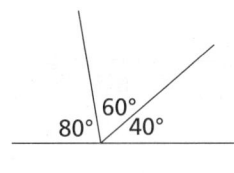 23° + 67° = 90° | 40° + 60° + 80° = 180° | 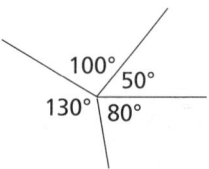 100° + 130° + 80° + 50° = 360° |

18 Patchwork • 9

# F Triangles

The border of this cushion is made from triangular pieces.
All the triangles are the same shape and size.

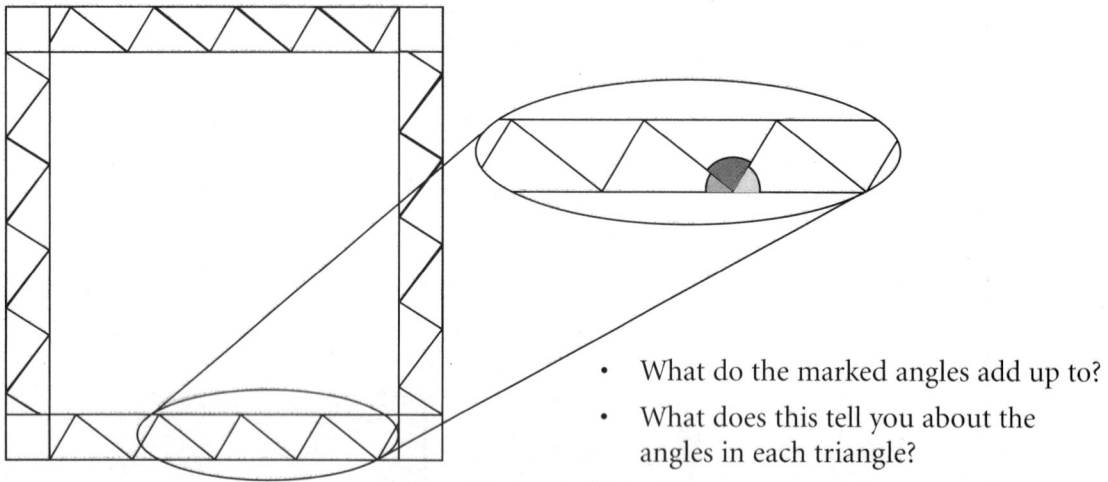

- What do the marked angles add up to?
- What does this tell you about the angles in each triangle?

**F1** Work out the size of each angle marked with a letter.

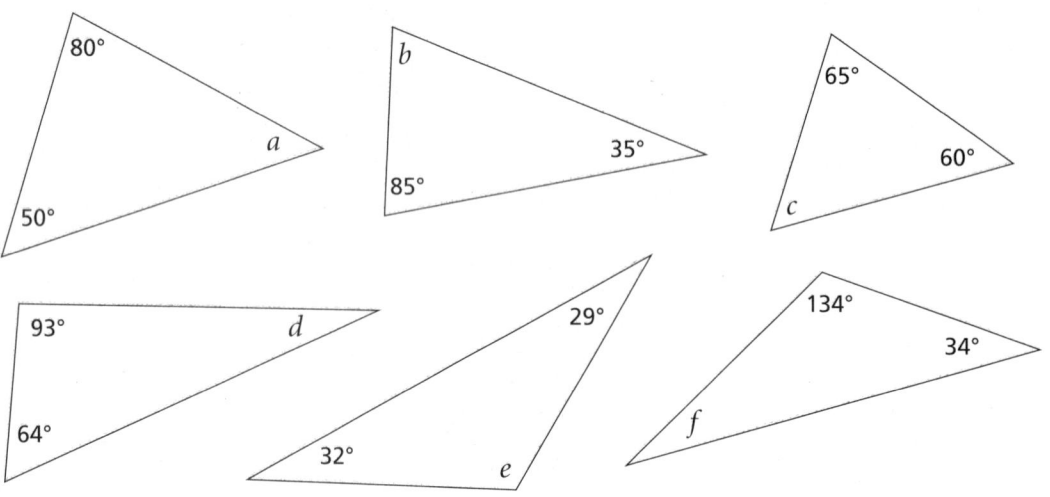

**F2** These are all right-angled triangles.
Work out the size of each angle marked with a letter.

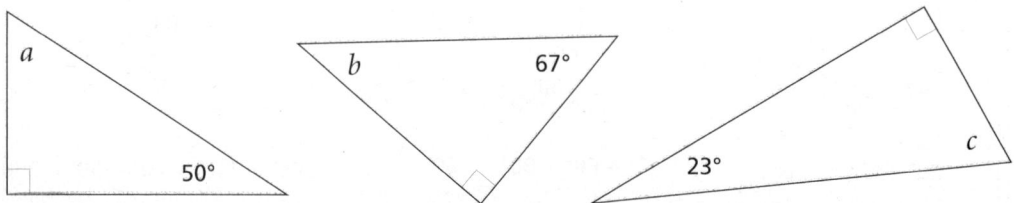

10 • 18 Patchwork

**F3** Part of the 'Palm leaf, Hosannah' block is shown.

(a) Calculate angles *a*, *b* and *c* in the shaded pieces.

(b) Each white piece is a right-angled triangle.

Calculate the marked angles in the white pieces.

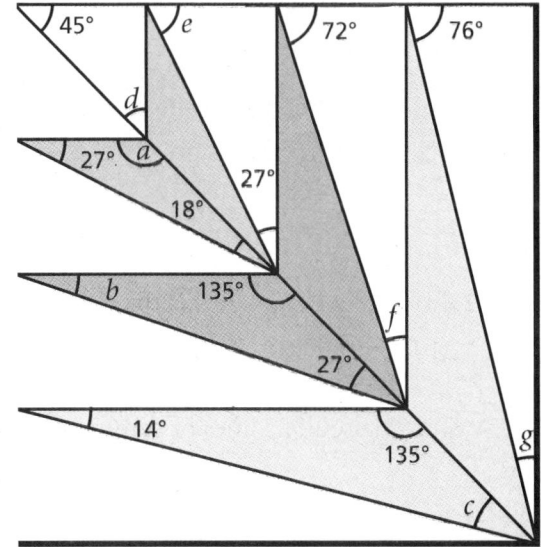

Palm leaf, Hosannah

***F4** Work out the size of the angles marked with letters.

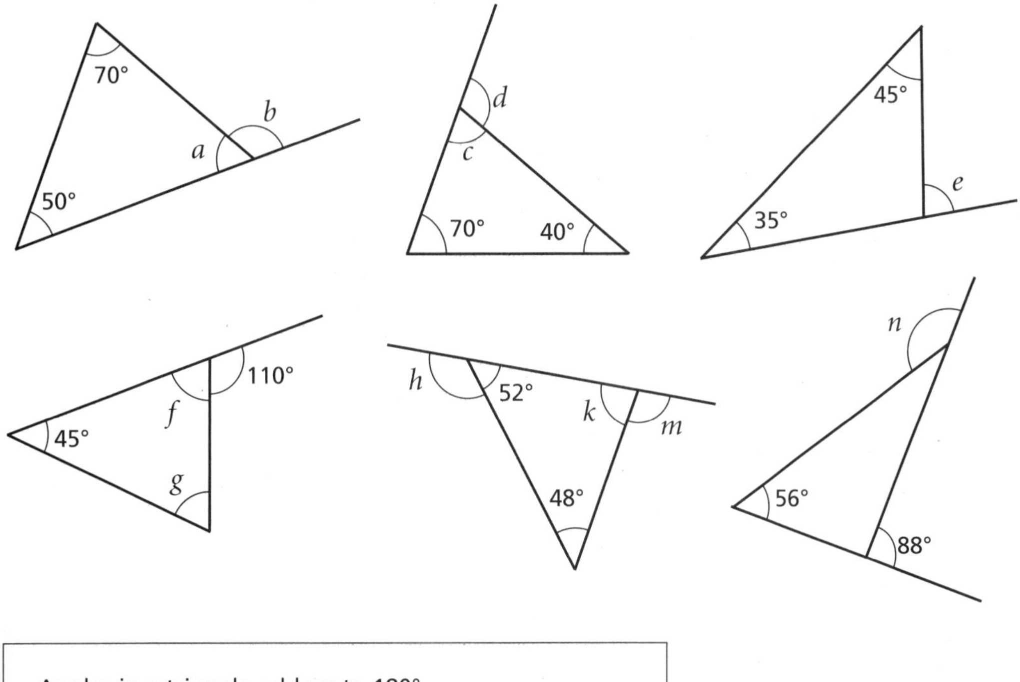

Angles in a triangle add up to 180°.

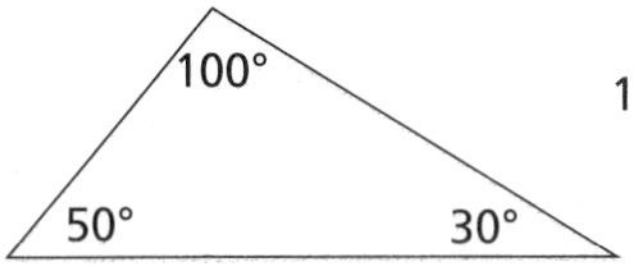

100° + 50° + 30° = 180°

## Test yourself with these questions

**T1** (a) Make a copy of this cushion cover design.
(b) What fraction of the cover is black?
(c) What fraction is grey?

**T2** (a) Make a copy of this diagram.
(b) Complete it so that it has rotation symmetry of order 4.
(c) Mark all its lines of symmetry.

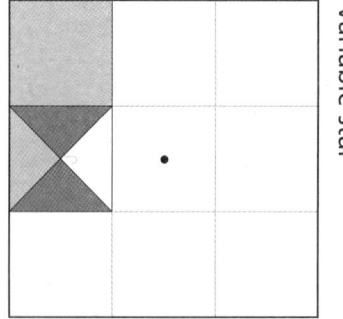

Variable star

**T3** Work out the size of the angles marked with letters.

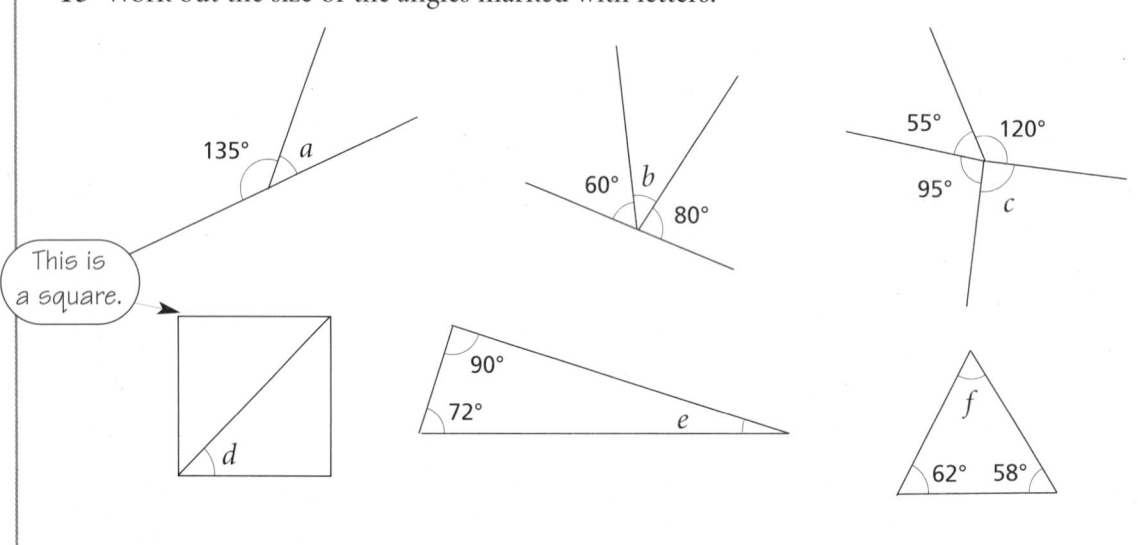

This is a square.

12 • 18 Patchwork

# 19 Cuboids

You will revise
- how to find the surface area of objects

You will learn
- how to find the volume of cuboids
- how to change between cm³ and m³

## A Volume

The net for this box has been drawn on centimetre squared paper.
The box measures 6 cm by 4 cm by 3 cm.

- How many 1 cm cubes would it take to make a layer to cover the bottom of this box?
- How many layers the same would you need to fill this box to the top?
- How many centimetre cubes would it take to fill the box to the top?

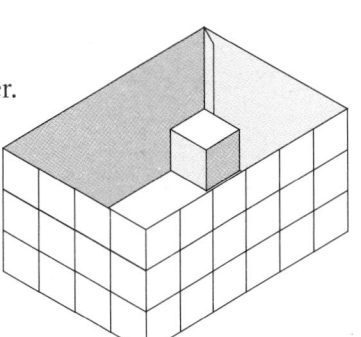

**A1** For each of these boxes work out how many 1 cm cubes it would take to

(i) make a layer to cover the bottom

(ii) completely fill it

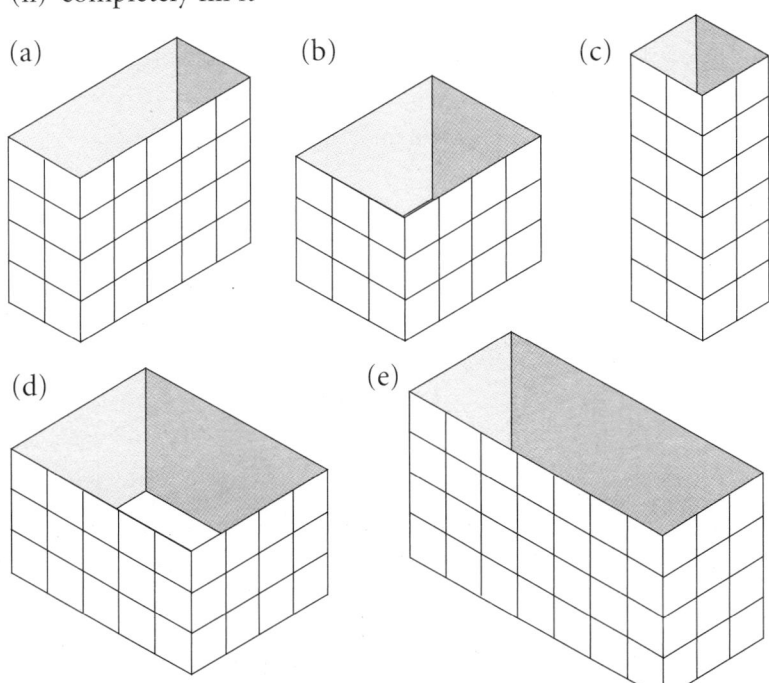

19 Cuboids • 13

Counting the number of 1 cm cubes that will fit inside a cuboid gives the **volume**.

The volume of a cuboid can be found by multiplying the height, length and width together.

Volume = $h \times l \times w$

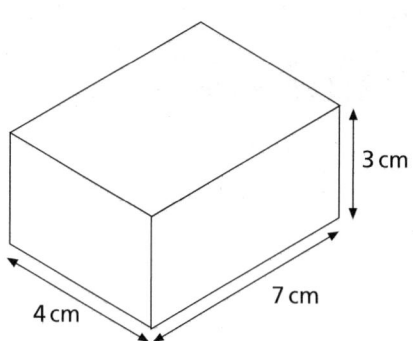

If the measurements are in centimetres then the volume is measured in $cm^3$.
The volume of the cuboid here is 3 cm × 7 cm × 4 cm = 84 $cm^3$.

**A2** Find the volume of these cuboids.

(a)


(b)


(c)


(d)


(e)


(f)


(g)


(h)


(i)

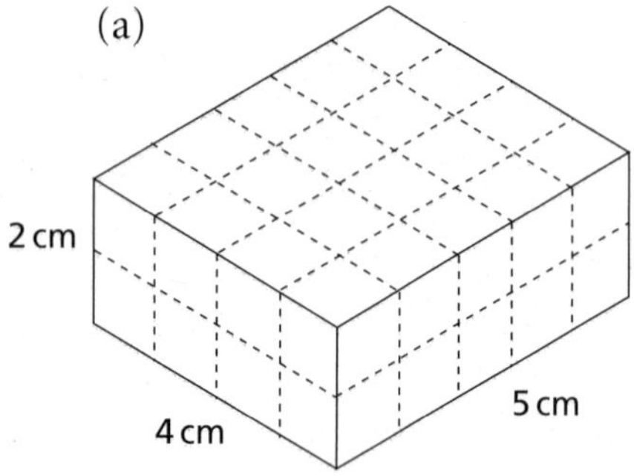

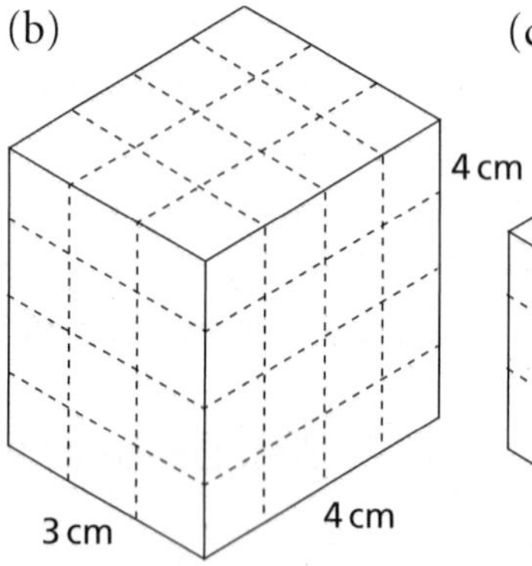

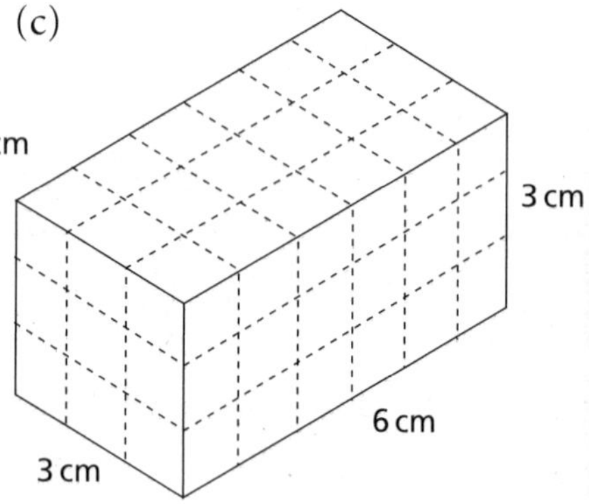

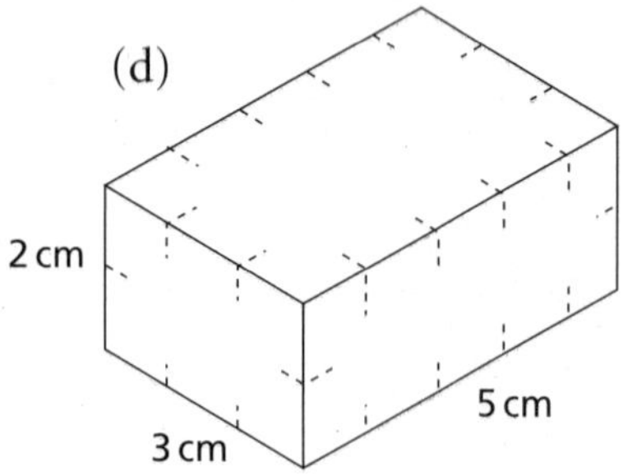

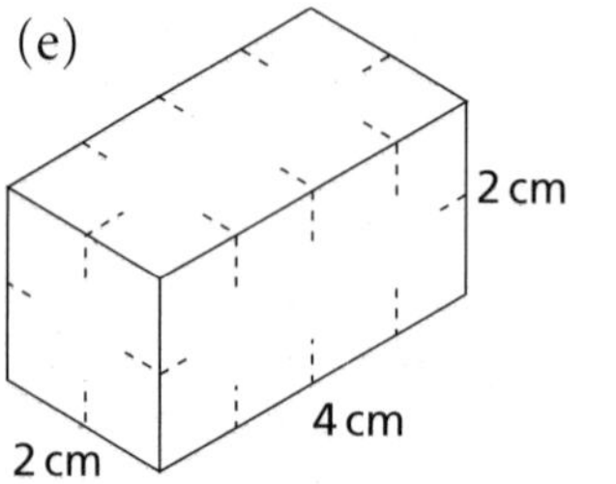

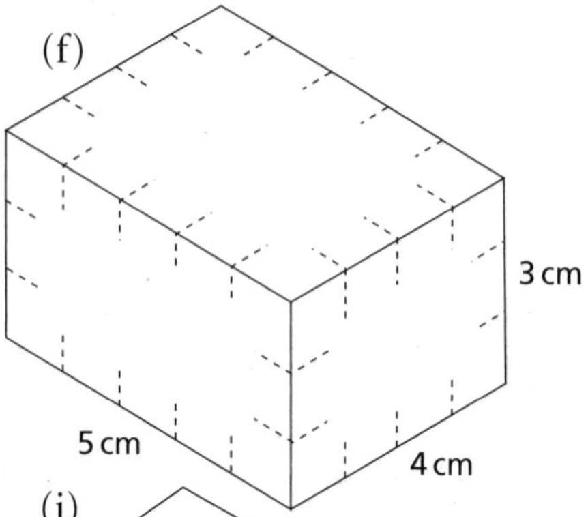

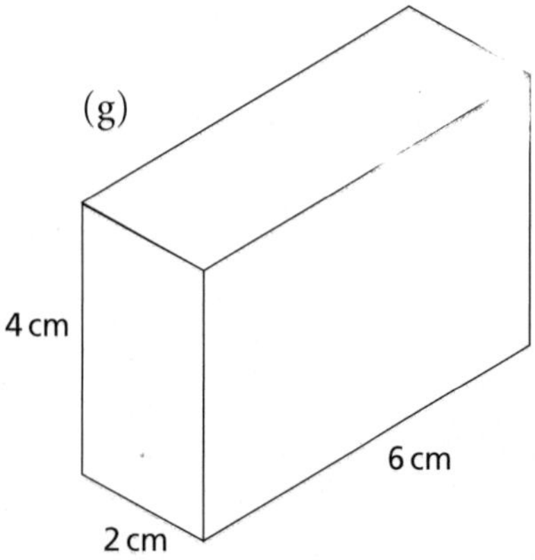

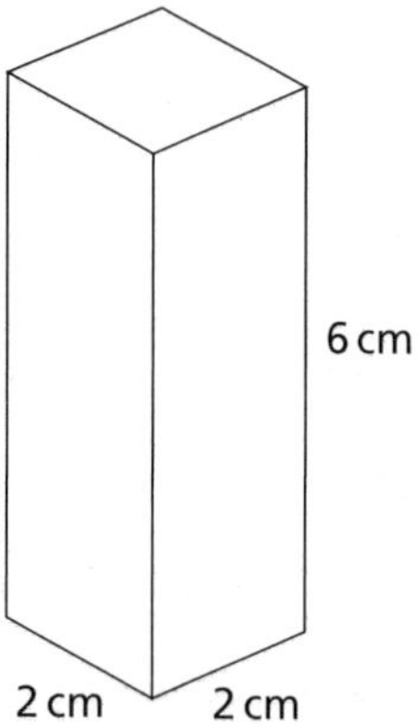

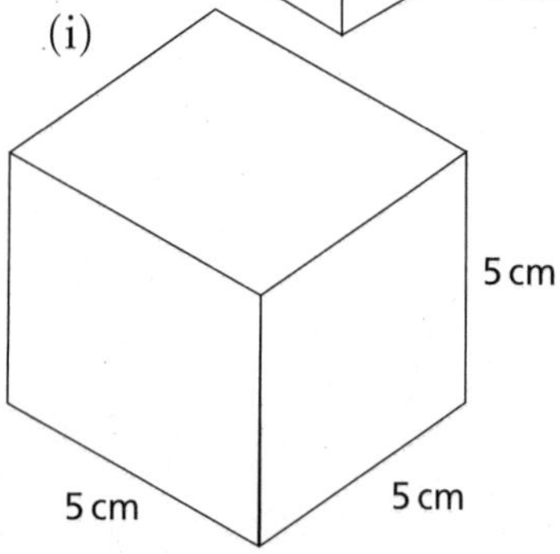

**A3** The height, length and width of four cuboids are given below. Find the volume of each cuboid. (You may sketch them)
   (a)  6 cm, 2 cm, 5 cm
   (b)  2 cm, 3 cm, 6 cm
   (c)  1 cm, 7 cm, 4 cm
   (d)  3 cm, 3 cm, 4 cm

**A4** Work out the volume of each of these cartons.

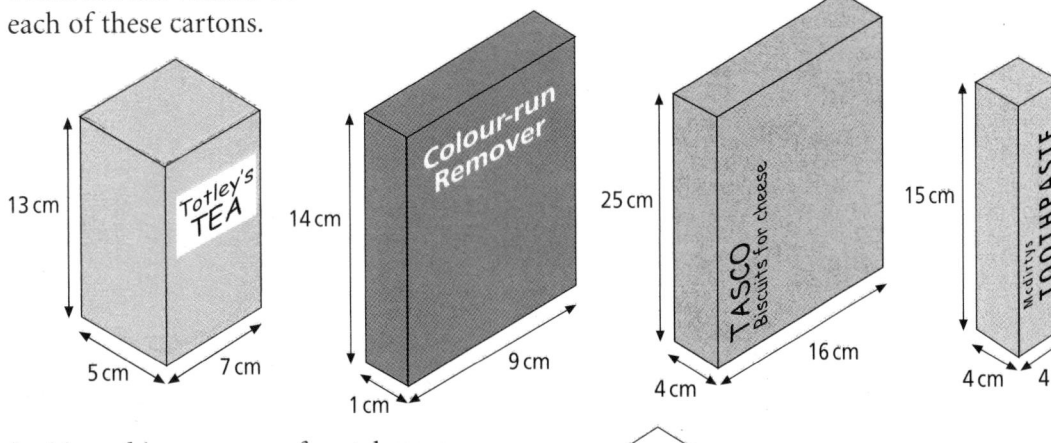

**A5** Jeni is making a range of metal vases.

One vase, in the shape of a cuboid has the measurements shown.

What volume of water can it hold? State the units of your answer.

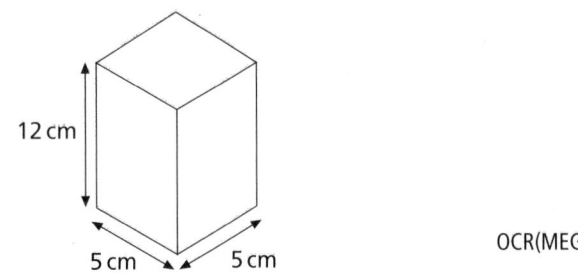

OCR(MEG)

**A6** The dimensions of a metal waste bin are 30 cm by 10 cm by 40 cm.

Calculate the volume of the bin, stating your units.

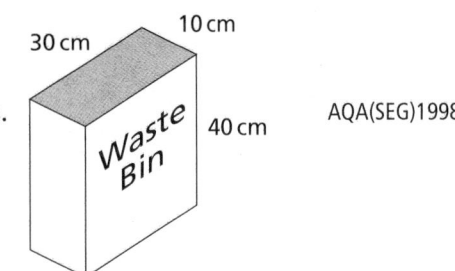

AQA(SEG)1998

**A7** Find the volume of these cuboids

(a)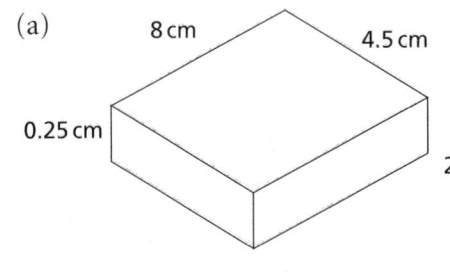

(b)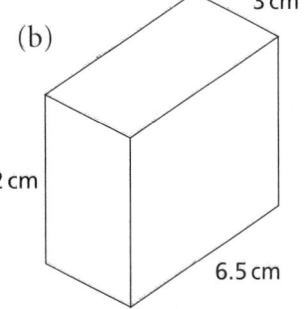

(c)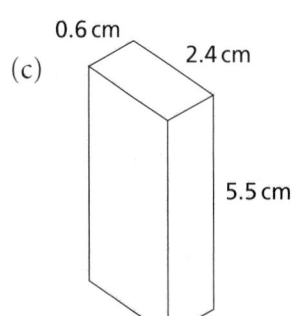

19 Cuboids • 15

**A8** These cuboids all have the same volume.
Find the missing measurements.
(The diagrams are not drawn to scale.)

***A9** A block of pastry has a volume 300 cm³.
How thick will it be if it is rolled out to form a rectangle
(a) 15 cm by 10 cm    (b) 25 cm by 24 cm

---

**Filling boxes**

You will need some empty packets which are cuboids, a ruler and a few centimetre cubes

For each of your boxes try to estimate how many centimetre cubes will fit inside.

Now measure the dimensions of each box to the nearest centimetre.
Use these to find the volume of each box.

How good were your estimates?

---

**Maximum volume**

Cut a rectangle 25 cm by 18 cm out of centimetre squared paper.
Cut a 1 cm square from each corner.
Fold the net to form a cuboid without a lid.

What is the volume of this cuboid?

If you cut a 2 cm square at each edge what would the volume of the cuboid you made be?

What size square cut from each corner gives the greatest volume?

B **Cubic metres**

**Living in a box!**

Large volumes are measured in **cubic metres** (m³).

A cube 1 m by 1 m by 1 m would have a volume of 1 m³.

How many pupils could you get in the metre cube shown in this picture?

What do you think the volume of these are roughly in m³?

- your classroom
- a swimming pool
- a home freezer
- a container on a lorry
- your school hall

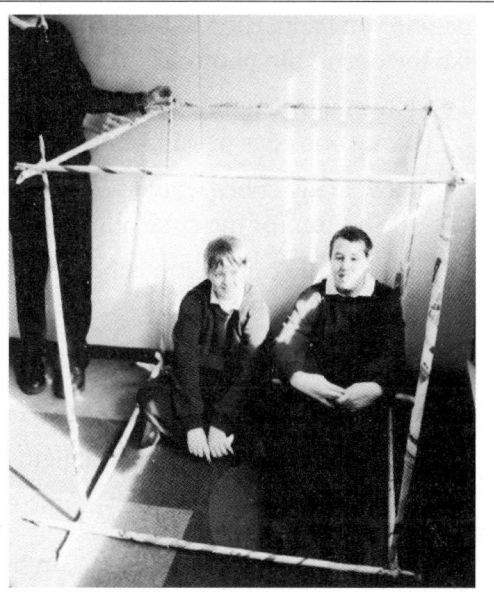

**B1** Find the volume of these cuboids in m³.

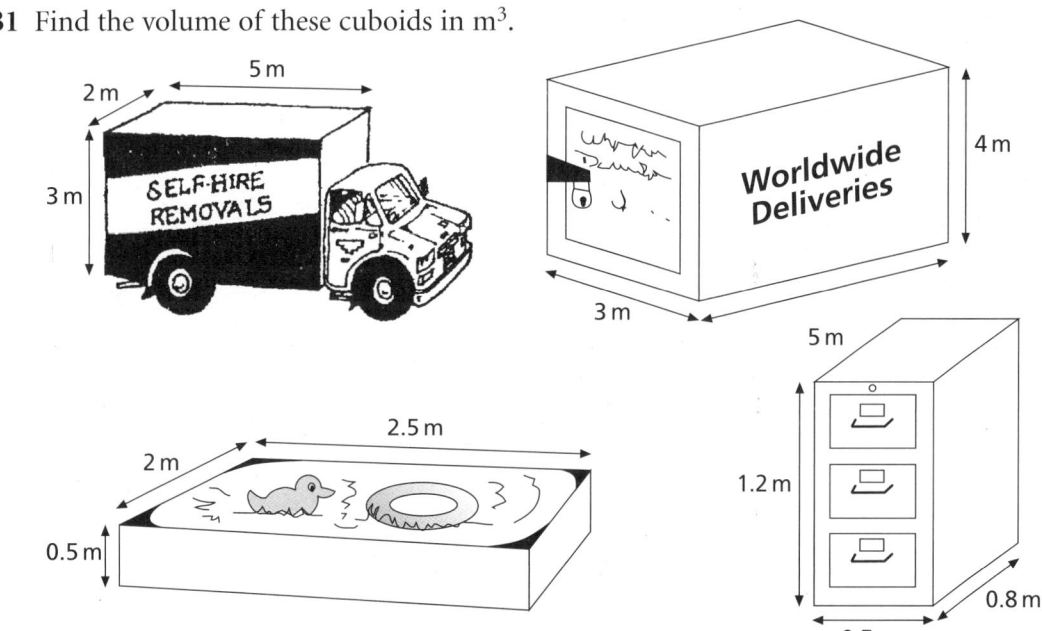

**B2** A swimming pool is 25 m long and 10 m wide.

(a) What is the volume of water in the swimming pool if the water is 1.5 m deep?

(b) How deep would the water be if the pool was filled with 200 m³ of water?

## C  Changing units

Imagine you had a cube with side lengths one metre (like the one in the photo in section B).

- How many centimetre cubes could you put along one edge of your metre cube?
- How many cubes would you need to cover the bottom of the cube one layer thick?
- How many centimetre cubes would it take to fill the metre cube?

**C1** The measurements of this cuboid are given in metres.
  (a) Calculate the volume of this cuboid in $m^3$.
  (b) Write down the height length and width in centimetres.
  (c) Use these to find the volume of the cuboid in $cm^3$.

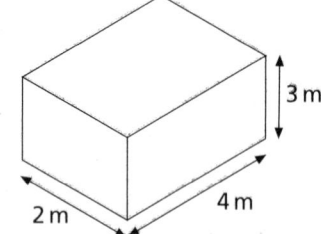

**C2** A cuboid measures 1.5 m by 2 m by 0.5 m.
  (a) Calculate the volume of this cuboid in $m^3$.
  (b) Write down the measurements in centimetres.
  (c) Use these to find the volume of the cuboid in $cm^3$.

**C3** The measurements of this cuboid are given in centimetres.
  (a) Calculate the volume of this cuboid in $cm^3$.
  (b) Write down the height, length and width in metres.
  (c) Use these to find the volume of the cuboid in $m^3$.

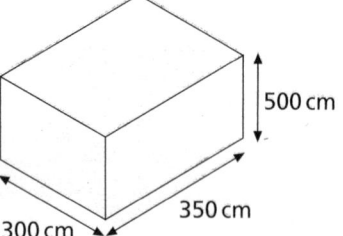

**C4** For each of these cuboids:
  (i) Find the volume in $m^3$
  (ii) Find the volume in $cm^3$

(a)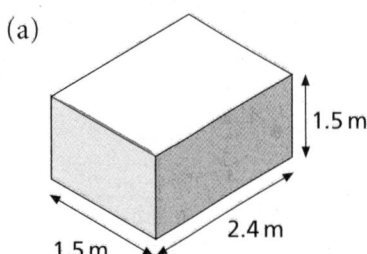

(b)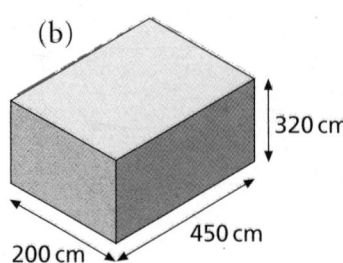

## D Surface area

The **surface area** of a shape is the total area of all of the outside faces.

It is useful to sketch the **net** of a shape and write down the area of each face.

### Example

Find the surface area of this cuboid.

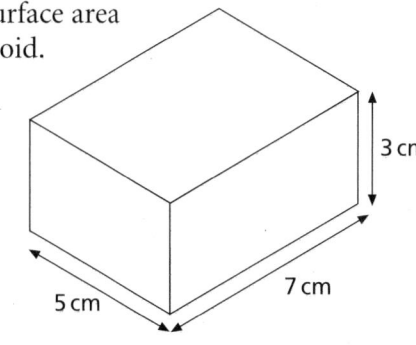

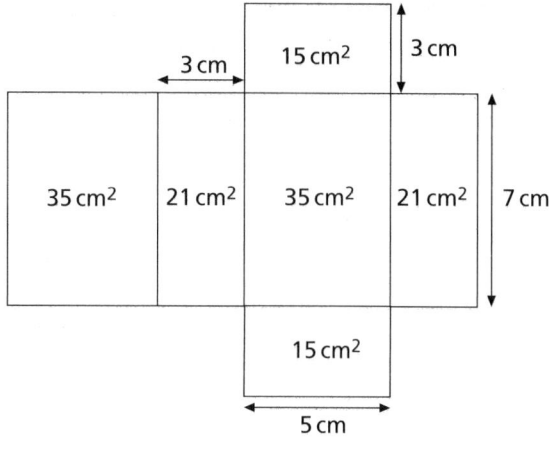

Total surface area = 142 cm²

**D1** Find the surface area of these cuboids:

(a)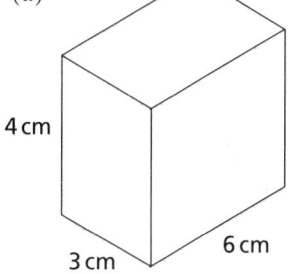

(b)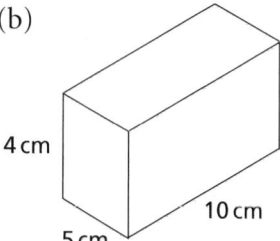

(c)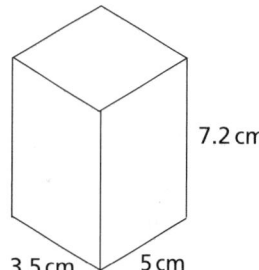

**D2** Find the surface area of these cartons.

(a)

(b)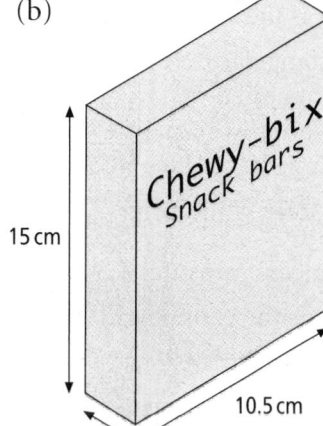

19 Cuboids • 19

**D3** A freight company uses containers which are cuboids measuring 3 m by 4 m by 8 m. What is the surface area of one of these containers?

**D4** This is a triangular prism.
(a) What special type of triangle is the end?
(b) Use a ruler and compasses to draw an accurate net for this prism.
(c) Work out the surface area of this prism. You will need to take some measurements from your net.

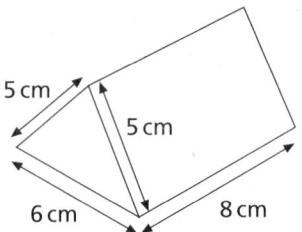

**\*D5** A prism has this trapezium as its cross section. The prism is 10 cm long.
(a) Find the area of this trapezium.
(b) Find the total surface area of the prism. (You may find sketching a net useful.)

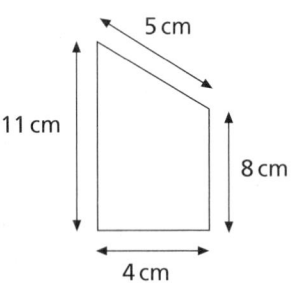

### Test yourself with these questions

**T1** This shows a cuboid which is 6 cm by 4 cm by 2 cm.
(a) Find the volume of this cuboid.
(b) Find the surface area of this cuboid.
State the units clearly in your answers.

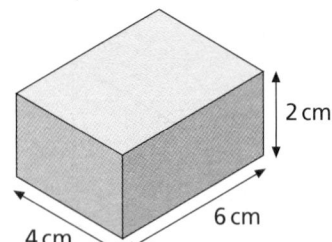

**T2** A garage has a rectangular base.
(a) The base is 8 metres long and 3.5 metres wide. The depth of the base is 0.25 metres.
What is the volume of the base?

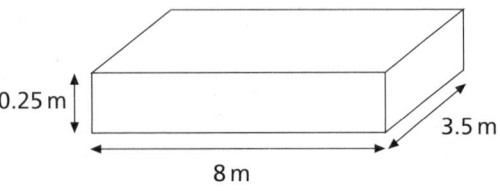

(b) A rectangular hole is dug for the base of a shed.
The volume of soil dug out is 1.2 m³.
The hole is 3 m long and 2 m wide.
How deep is the hole?

AQA(SEG)2000

**T3** A packing case measures 1.5 m by 4.2 m by 1.8 m.
(a) What is the volume of this box in m³?
(b) Write the dimensions of the box in centimetres.
(c) What is the volume of the box in cm³?

20 • *19 Cuboids*

# 20 Sequences

This will help you learn how to
- find the next term in a sequence
- describe a rule you use to find the next term
- find, and explain how you found, for example, the 20th term in a sequence

## A Next term

How do each of these sequences continue?

| | |
|---|---|
| 1, 3,… | Add two to the previous term. |
| 1, 3,… | Double the previous term and add one. |
| 1, 3,… | Multiply the last term by four and take off 1 |
| 1, 3,… | Add the previous two terms together |

**A1** Look at this sequence.

    1    4    7    10    13…

The rule to find the next term of this sequence is **Add 3 to the previous term**.
Write down the next three terms in this sequence.

**A2** For each of these sequences the first four terms and the rule are given.
Write down the next three terms of each sequence.

(a)  2  4  6  8…    Add 2 to the last term
(b)  2  4  6  10…    Add the previous two terms together
(c)  2  4  8  16…    Double the last term
(d)  2  4  10  28…    Multiply the last term by 3 and take off 2

**A3** Work out the next two terms in each of these sequences.
Write down the rule for finding the next term in your sequence.

(a)  5  7  9  11  13  15…
(b)  2  5  8  11  14  17…
(c)  2  6  10  14  18  22…
(d)  5  10  20  40  80  160…
(e)  1  2  3  5  8  13…

**A4** Work out the next two terms in each of these sequences.
Write down the rule for finding the next term.
(a)  6    4    2    0    -2    -4...
(b)  9    5    1    -3   -7    -11...
(c)  11   9    7    5    3     1...
(d)  6    $5\frac{1}{2}$    5    $4\frac{1}{2}$    4    $3\frac{1}{2}$...

**A5** (a) Write down the next two numbers in the number pattern.

  1,    4,    7,    10,    13,    ...,    ...

(b) Write down the rule that you used to find the next two numbers.

Edexcel

**A6** (a) Charles has this number pattern.

  1,    5,    9,    13,    _

Write down the next number in his pattern.
Explain how you worked out your answer.

(b) Mary has this number pattern.

  1,    2,    4,    8,    _

Explain how to work out the next number in Mary's pattern.

OCR

**A7** Write down the next two terms of the sequence

  21    15    9    _    _

OCR

**A8** (a) A sequence begins  3,  4,  6,  10,...

The rule for continuing the sequence is

> Double the last number and subtract 2

What is the next number in this sequence?

(b) A different sequence begins  -2,  -4,  -6,  -8,...

What is the next number in this sequence?

AQA 2003

**A9** In the sequence shown below, you add the last two numbers to get the next number.

  ...    5    8    13    21    ...    ...

(a) Write down the next two numbers of the sequence.
(b) Write down the number that came before 5.

AQA(SEG) 2000

22 • 20 Sequences

## B *Patterns*

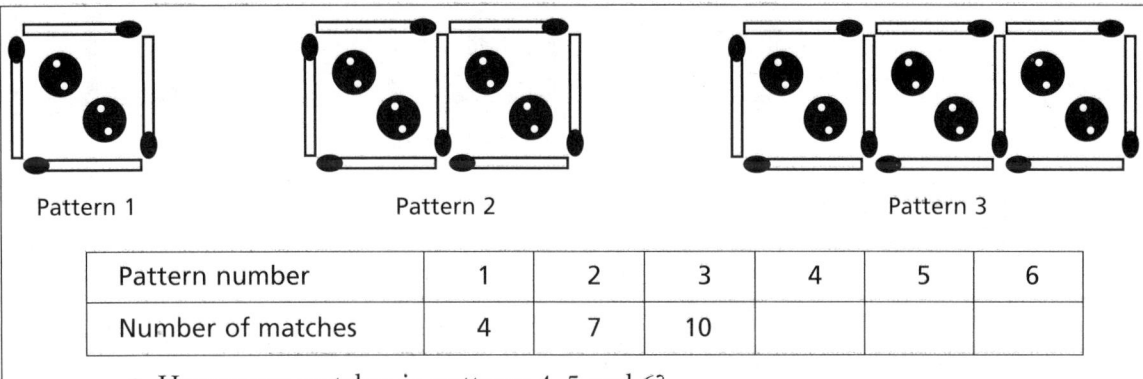

| Pattern number | 1 | 2 | 3 | 4 | 5 | 6 |
|---|---|---|---|---|---|---|
| Number of matches | 4 | 7 | 10 | | | |

- How many matches in patterns 4, 5 and 6?
- How many matches in pattern number 20?
- If you know the pattern number, how do work out the number of matches?
- One pattern has 100 matches in it. Which pattern is that?

**B1** Look at the number of buttons in the patterns above.

(a) How many buttons will there be in pattern 4?

(b) How many will there be in pattern 5?

(c) Copy and complete this table.

| Pattern number | 1 | 2 | 3 | 4 | 5 | 6 |
|---|---|---|---|---|---|---|
| Number of buttons | 2 | 4 | 6 | | | |

(d) How many buttons will there be in the 10th pattern?

(e) Explain how you can work out the number of buttons if you know the pattern number.

(f) One pattern has 42 buttons in it. Which pattern is it?

**B2** The diagram shows some patterns made with matches.

 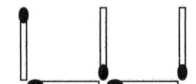 

(a) Copy and complete the table.

| Pattern | 1 | 2 | 3 | 4 | 5 |
|---|---|---|---|---|---|
| Number of matches | 3 | 5 | | | |

(b) Which pattern can be made with exactly 15 matches?

(c) Explain how you could work out the number of matches needed for Pattern 12 without doing any drawing.

OCR

**B3** Look at these matchstick shapes.

Shape 1

5 matchsticks

Shape 2, Shape 3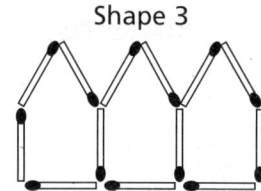

9 matchsticks

(a) Copy and complete this table.

| Shape number | 1 | 2 | 3 | 4 | 5 |
|---|---|---|---|---|---|
| Number of matchsticks | 5 | 9 | | | |

(b) How many matchsticks are there in shape 12?
Explain how you can work this out without drawing a diagram.

OCR

**B4** Here are some patterns of dots.

Pattern number 1      Pattern number 2      Pattern number 3

(a) Draw pattern number 4
(b) Copy and complete the table.

| Pattern number | 1 | 2 | 3 | 4 | 5 |
|---|---|---|---|---|---|
| Number of dots | 3 | 5 | 7 | | |

(c) (i) Write down the number of dots needed for pattern number 12.
   (ii) Explain how you found this answer.

Edexcel

**B5** Shape 1 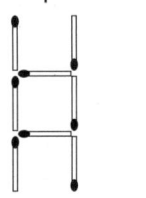  Shape 2 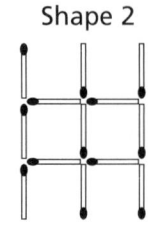  Shape 3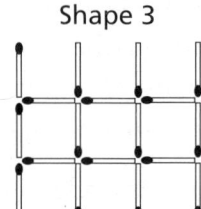

(a) Copy and complete this table for the shapes above.

| Shape | 1 | 2 | 3 | 4 | 5 |
|---|---|---|---|---|---|
| Number of matches | 8 | | | | |

(b) How many matches would there be in shape 20?
Explain carefully how you got your answer.

(c) One shape is made from 148 matches.
Which shape is this?

24 • 20 Sequences

**Test yourself with these questions**

**T1** Continue each of these patterns for another 3 terms.
Write down the rule for finding the next term in each pattern.

(a)  3   6   9   12   15…
(b)  4   7   11   15   19…
(c)  7   5   3   1   ⁻1…
(d)  64   32   16   8   4…
(e)  1   $1\frac{1}{2}$   2   $2\frac{1}{2}$   3…

**T2** Here is the rule for finding a term in a sequence.

> Multiply the previous term by 3 and add 2

The first three terms in the sequence are 2, 8 and 26.
Work out the next two terms.

*Edexcel*

**T3** A sequence begins 1, 2, 6, 16,…
This is the rule to continue the sequence.

> Add the previous two numbers together then multiply the answer by two

Deepak says the next term in the sequence is 22. Is he correct?
Explain your answer.

*AQA 2003*

**T4**   Pattern 1      Pattern 2      Pattern 3

(a) Copy and complete this table for the patterns above.

| Pattern number | 1 | 2 | 3 | 4 | 5 |
|---|---|---|---|---|---|
| Number of dots | 5 |   |   |   |   |

(b) How many dots would there be in shape 20?
Explain carefully how you got your answer.

(c) One pattern is made from 86 dots. Which pattern is this?

**T5** (a) These are the first four terms of a sequence   5   9   13   17
  (i) Write down the tenth term
  (ii) Explain how you worked out your answer.
(b) The rule for another sequence is 'multiply the previous term by 2 and add 1'
The first term of the sequence is 3.
  (i) Write down the second term
  (ii) Work out the sixth term.

*OCR*

20 Sequences • 25

# 21 More circle facts

You will revise
- how to find the circumference of a circle

You will learn how to find
- the areas of awkward shapes
- the area of a circle

## A Circumference

The perimeter or **circumference** (C) of a circle is just over three times the diameter (d).

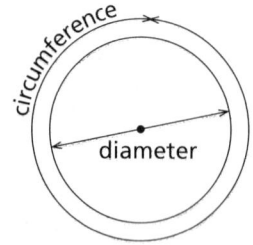

**A1** Find the rough circumference of each of these circles.

(a) 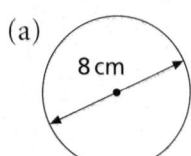  (b) 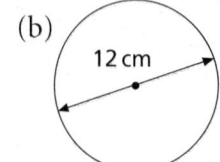  (c) 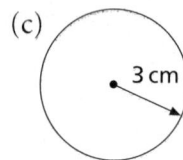  (d)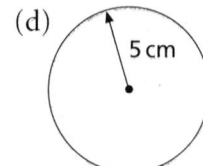

**A2** **Roughly** what are the diameters of these circles?

(a) 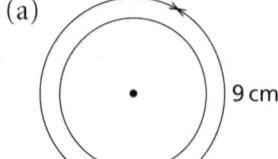  (b) 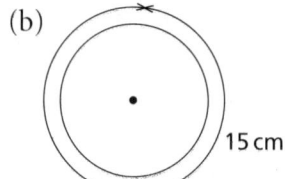  (c)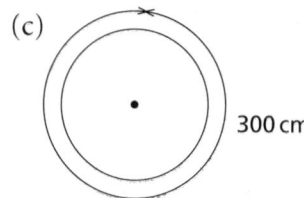

**A3** A circular tower has circumference 15 m.
(a) What is the diameter of the tower roughly?
(b) What is the radius of the tower roughly?

---
The circumference of a circle can be found more accurately by
$$C = \pi \times d$$
You can use the $\pi$ button on your calculator. $\pi$ is roughly 3.14.

---

**A4** A bicycle wheel measures 70 cm in diameter.
(a) What is the circumference of the wheel?
(b) How far will the wheel have gone if it is rolled 100 turns? Give your answer to the nearest metre.

## B Areas of awkward shapes

This diagram shows part of a map of the island of Scalpay in the north-west of Scotland.

Each grid square has an area of 1 km².

A full copy of this is on sheet P159.

What is the area of this island roughly?

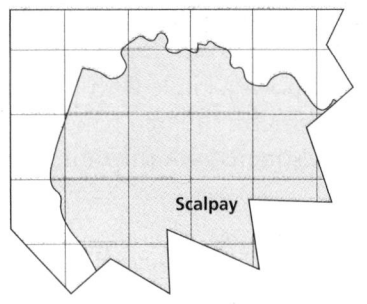

**B1** Sheet P160 has some more maps of Scottish Islands drawn on a 1 km square grid. Find the areas of these islands.

**B2** These shapes are drawn on centimetre squared paper. Use the centimetre square grid to find their areas.

(a)

(b)

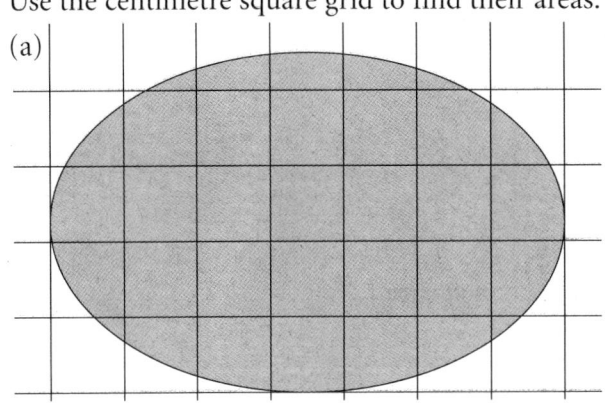

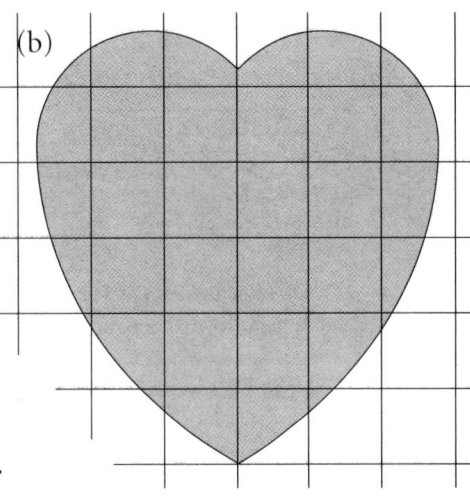

**B3** These are drawn on a scale where 1 cm represents 1 m. Use a centimetre squared grid to find their true areas.

(a) tunnel entrance

(b) wing of a plane

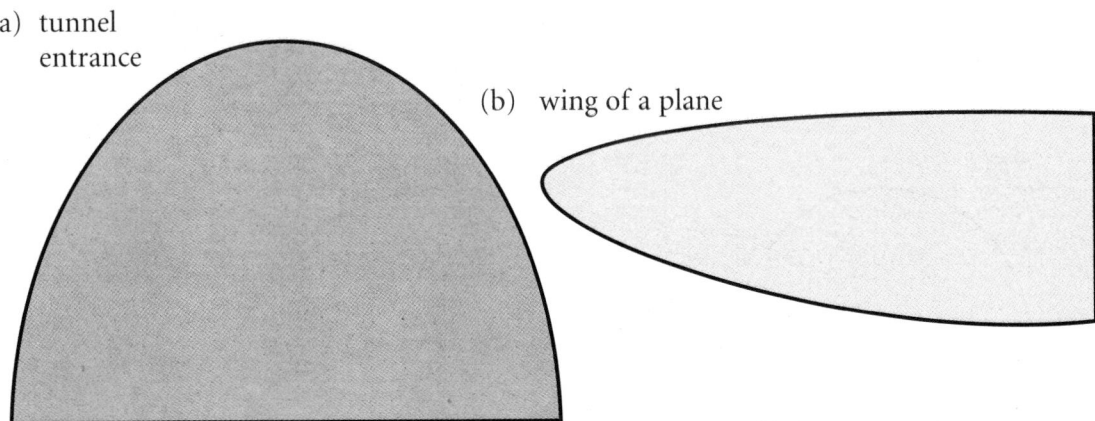

**Forests and lakes**

An Ordnance Survey map with a scale of 2 cm represents 1 km has kilometre squares marked on it.
Find the area of a forest, lake or town near you.

21 More circle facts • 27

## C Areas of circles

This diagram shows a circle with radius 3 cm drawn on centimetre squared paper.
There is also a square with the same side length as the radius.

- What is the area of the square?
- Copy this diagram onto centimetre squared paper and find the area of the circle by counting squares.

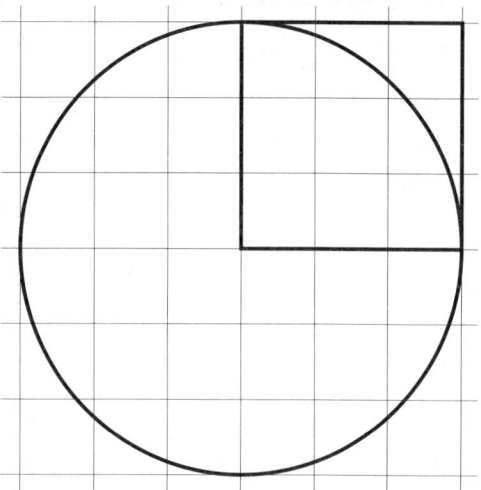

On centimetre squared paper draw circles with radiuses 4 cm, 5 cm, 8 cm and 10 cm.
For each circle draw the square with side length equal to the radius.

Copy and complete this table:

| Radius | Area of square | Area of circle |
|---|---|---|
| 3 cm | | |
| 4 cm | | |
| 5 cm | | |

- What rule connects the area of a circle and a square with side length equal to its radius?

**C1** Use the rule you found above to find the approximate areas of these circles

(a) 2 cm   (b) 6 cm   (c) 14 cm   (d) 20 cm

**C2** Use your rule to work out the approximate areas of these shapes.

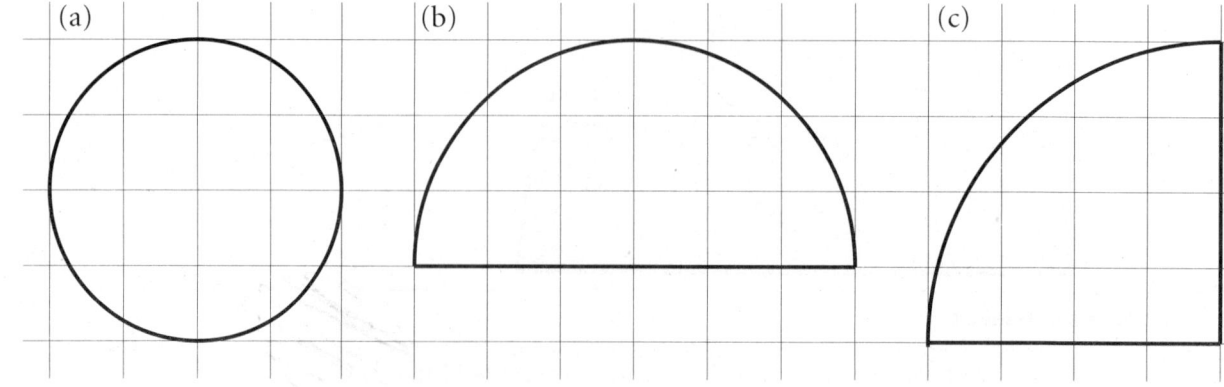

Check your answers by counting the squares.

28 • 21 More circle facts

**The area of a circle**

Multiplying the area of a square drawn on the radius by π gives an even better value for the area of a circle.

So the area (A) of a circle can be found from the radius (r) by

$A = π \times (r \times r)$  or  $A = π \times r^2$

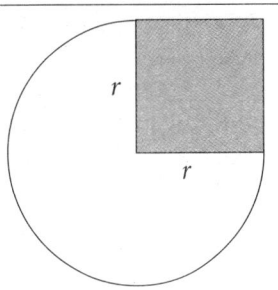

In these questions use the π button on your calculator, otherwise use 3.14.
Round all your answers to 1 decimal place.

**C3** Find the areas of these circles:

(a) 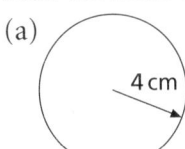  (b) 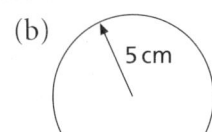  (c) 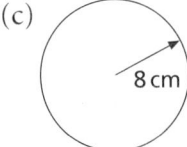  (d)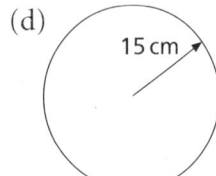

**C4** For each of these circles  (i) find the radius
(ii) find the area

(a) 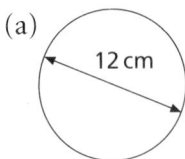  (b) 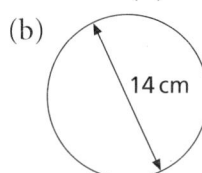  (c) 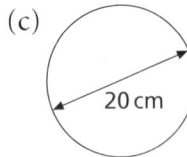  (d)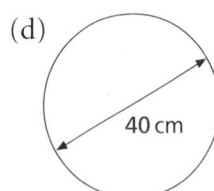

**C5** Find the areas of circles with radius

(a) 2.5 cm  (b) 7.5 cm  (c) 6.4 cm  (d) 3.6 cm

**C6** For circles with these diameters  (i) find the radius
(ii) find the area

(a) 13 cm  (b) 25 cm  (c) 8.4 m  (d) 24.6 m

**C7** Here are pictures of some Euro coins
- measure the diameter of these coins to the nearest 0.1 cm
- work out the radius of each coin
- calculate the area of one side of each coin

  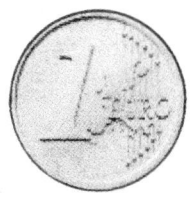  

(a) 10 Euro cent  (b) 1 Euro  (c) 2 Euro

**C8** A landing pad on an aircraft carrier is a white circle radius 4.5 m. What is the area of this landing pad?

**C9** Find the areas of these shapes

(a)

(b)

(c)

(d)

(e)

(f)

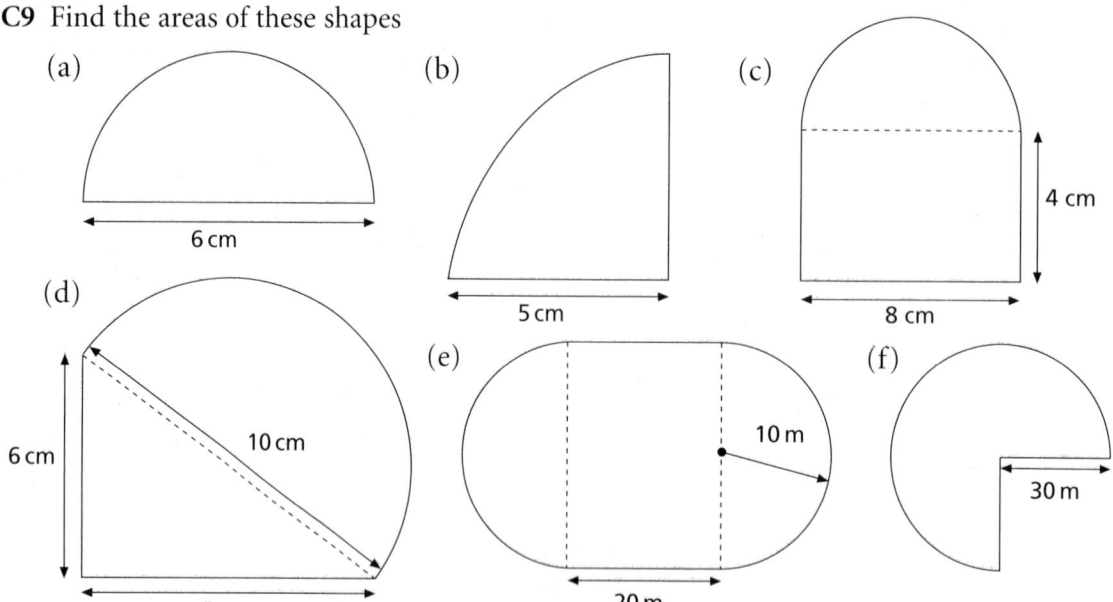

**Which looks bigger?**

Which of these shapes looks to have the biggest area?
Calculate the area of each shape and check.

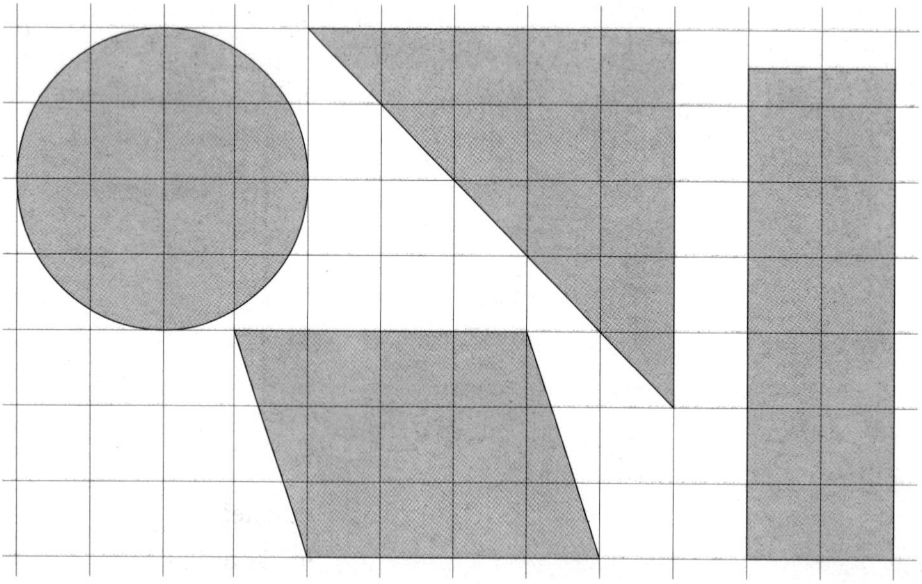

**C10** This diagram shows two circles with the same centre.
  (a) Find the area of the smaller circle.
  (b) Find the area of the larger circle.
  (c) Hence find the shaded area.

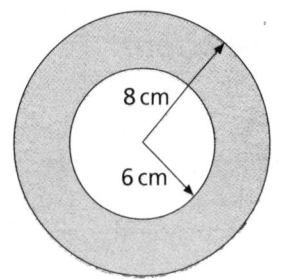

**C11** Circular bottle tops are punched from a rectangular sheet of silver foil. Each of the bottle tops has diameter 4 cm.
  (a) How big is the piece of foil?
  (b) What is the total area of the silver foil?
  (c) What is the area of one bottle top?
  (d) What area of silver foil is wasted?

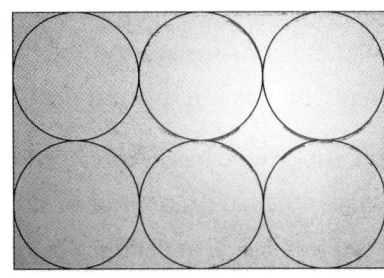

**C12** Paulo's Pizzas come in two sizes:  Large with diameter 40 cm
                                          Small with diameter 20 cm

Which has the largest surface area, one large pizza or two small ones?

**\*C13** This shows the Circus Maximus in Rome. The Romans used a measurement called a 'stadium' which is about 180 m.
  (a) Sketch the diagram giving the measurements in metres.
  (b) Find the area in $m^2$ of the Circus Maximus.
  (c) How far is it to run once around the edge of the Circus Maximus?

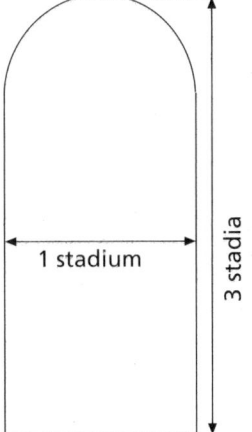

---

**In the groove!**

Put a CD on centimetre square paper and trace around it.

Estimate the area of the CD by counting squares.

Measure the diameter of a CD. What is its radius?
Calculate the area of the CD accurately. How good was your estimate?

Ask your parents or a record collector if they have any 'vinyl' singles or LPs. Calculate the area of these.

What is the actual 'playing area' of each type of disc?

# D Around about

**D1** A farmer finds a crop circle in his field.
He measures the diameter as 15 metres.

What is the area of the crop circle?
(Give your answer to one decimal place.)

**D2** The dome on Florence Cathedral has
a diameter of 44 m.
A circular gallery runs around the base.

How many metres is it around the gallery?

**D3** A roll of sticky tape has diameter 8 cm.

(a) What is the circumference of the roll to the nearest centimetre?

(b) If the roll has 50 m of tape on it, roughly how many times does the tape go around the roll?

**D4** A model railway track is made up of these pieces.

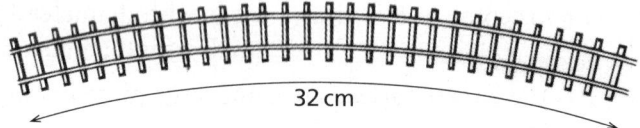

12 of the pieces make a complete circle.
What is the diameter of this circle to 1 decimal place?

**D5** An odometer is an instrument used by surveyors
for measuring the distances along roads.
The wheel goes round once for every metre
the odometer is pushed.

Calculate the radius of the wheel.

**D6** A farmer has 48 m of wire fencing.

(a) If he made a square pen with the wire, how long would the sides be?
(b) What would be the area of this square pen?
(c) If he made a circular pen, what would be the diameter of this pen?
(d) What would the area of this circular pen be to the nearest m$^2$?
(e) Which shape of pen contains the largest area?

**Largest area**

Investigate what other shapes you can make with 48 m of wire.
What shape contains the largest area?

## Test yourself with these questions

**T1** A leaf is drawn here, full size on a 1 cm grid.

Estimate the area of the leaf, stating the units of your answer.

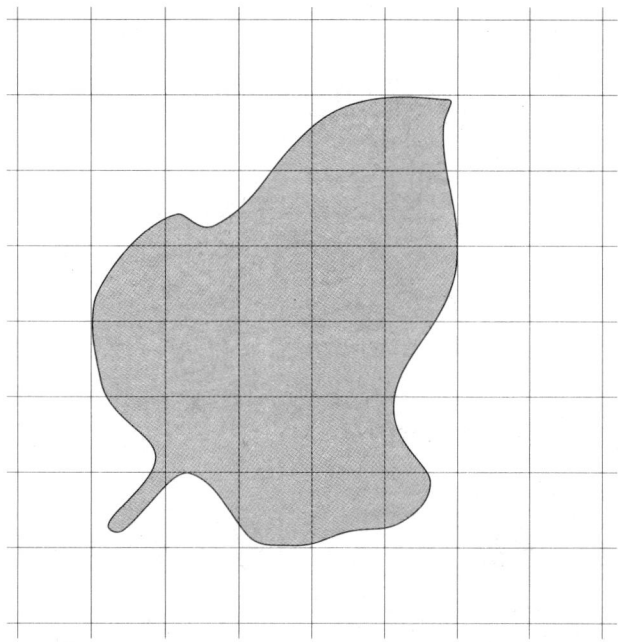

OCR

**T2** Calculate the area of a circle with

(a) radius 5 cm  (b) radius 2.5 cm  (c) diameter 8 m.

**T3** Calculate the area of a semi-circle, radius 20 cm.

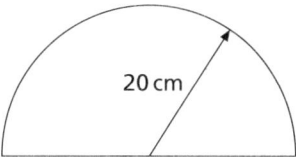

AQA(SEG) 1998

**T4** The clock on the Royal Liver building is the largest in Britain.
Each clock face is a circle with radius 3.81 m.

(a) Each minute hand reaches to the perimeter of its face.

How far does the tip of a minute hand travel in an hour?

(b) What is the area of one of the clock faces?

OCR

*21 More circle facts* • 33

# 22 Travel

You will revise
- how to read times using a 24-hour clock
- how to read timetables

You will learn
- how to make and use distance tables
- how to read distance/time graphs
- how to carry out calculations involving speed

## A Clocking on

**A** 18:15

**B** 8:45 AM/PM

**C** 20:15

**D** 17 45

**E** 6.15 pm — Consternation St. Mabel finally gets her come uppance and Charlie and Pat manage to see the baby. Hani thinks about getting hi...

**F** I was so tired last night I went to bed at a quarter to eight.

**G** FLIGHT DEPARTURES
FLIGHT    DESTINATION    TIME
KU341     MARRAKESH      1945

**H** (clock showing Morning)

**J** (clock showing Evening)

**I** **Notice to all staff**
Please note that morning registration does not finish until a quarter to nine. Do not let your pupils out early.

I. M. Strict (Headmaster)

**K** TELEPHONE NUMBER 0876634265 CALLED TODAY AT SIX FIFTEEN HOURS

Some of the pieces above refer to the same time. Match up the pieces.

**A1** Change these times into 24-hour clock times.

(a) 3.40 p.m.
(b) half past midnight
(c) twenty to two in the morning
(d) 9.15 p.m.
(e) 8.40 a.m.
(f) 10 minutes before midday

**A2** Put these times in order, earliest first.

23:15     7.45 a.m.     2.00 p.m.     03:05     17:35     7.15 p.m.

**A3** The flight to Marrakesh leaves at 19:45.
You must check in two and a half hours earlier.

What time must you check in?

**A4** Consternation St. starts at a quarter past six. It is now 5.55 p.m.
How long is it till Consternation St. starts?

**A5** Morning break at Hardgraft High School starts at 10:40 and ends at 11:05.
How long is the break?

**A6** (a) Copy and complete this diagram

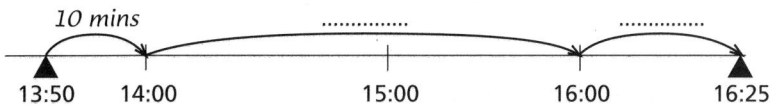

(b) How long is it from 13:50 to 16.25?

**A7** How long is it from
   (a) 8.15 a.m. to 11.30 a.m.
   (b) 10.45 a.m. to 1.15 p.m.
   (c) 06:15 to 10:45
   (d) 11:30 to 13:15
   (e) 14:40 to 16:25
   (f) 20:40 to 23:35

**A8** Here are the listings for some of the main TV channels one afternoon.

| BBC1 | BBC2 | ITV1 | CH4 |
|---|---|---|---|
| 1.45 Neighbours | 1.10 The Barefoot Contessa | 1.40 House of Horrors | 1.25 The Good Die Young |
| 2.10 Doctors |  | 2.10 Crossroads | 3.15 Watercolour Challenge |
| 2.40 Diagnosis Murder | 3.20 BBC News | 2.40 Wheel of Fortune | 3.45 Fifteen to One |
| 3.25 CBBC | 3.30 Esther | 3.05 News | 4.15 Countdown |
| 5.35 Neighbours | 4.30 Ready Steady Cook | 3.20 CITV | 5.00 Location, Location, .... |
| 6.00 BBC News | 5.15 The Weakest Link | 5.05 The People Versus | 5.25 Home from Home |
|  | 6.00 The Simpsons | 5.30 Crossroads | 6.00 Friends |

(a) How long are each of these programmes?
   (i) Neighbours (BBC1)
   (ii) News on ITV1
   (iii) The Barefoot Contessa
   (iv) Diagnosis Murder (BBC1)

(b) How long is it between the start of the first showing of Neighbours and the second?

(c) Which programmes last longer than two hours?

(d) What is the longest programme listed here for ITV1?

(e) The ITV1 News was extended by 15 minutes.
Write down at what time the next three programmes actually started.

## B Timetables

Here is the timetable for early morning trains from Norwich to London.

| Mondays to Fridays | ✗ | R ■ | ✗ | R ✗ | ■ | R ■ |  | ■ ✗ |
|---|---|---|---|---|---|---|---|---|
| Norwich    | 0600 | 0630 | 0655 | 0710 | 0724 | 0751 | 0800 | 0830 |
| Diss       | 0618 | 0647 | 0713 | 0727 | 0741 |      | 0817 | 0847 |
| Stowmarket | 0631 | 0659 | 0725 | 0740 | 0753 |      | 0829 | 0859 |
| Ipswich    | 0642 | 0710 | 0737 | 0752 | 0807 | 0830 | 0842 | 0912 |
| Manningtree| 0651 | 0721 |      | 0801 | 0816 |      | 0852 | 0921 |
| Colchester | 0703 | 0732 |      | 0812 | 0827 |      | 0902 | 0931 |
| London     | 0756 | 0828 | 0848 | 0905 | 0926 | 0937 | 0955 | 1020 |

✗ – Restaurant      ■ – Buffet/Trolley      R – reservations recommended

**B1** How many of the trains shown have a buffet/trolley service?

**B2** How many of the trains shown stop at Colchester?

**B3** What time does the 0724 train from Norwich arrive in London?

**B4** How long does the 0600 train from Norwich take to get to London?

**B5** (a) How long does the 0751 train from Norwich take to get to London?
    (b) How much quicker is this than the 0600 train?

**B6** Sarah wants to arrive in London by ten in the morning.
    What is the latest train she can get from Diss station?

**B7** Jim wants to be in Colchester by 9am.
    What is the latest train he can catch from Ipswich?

**B8** Mervyn misses the 0655 train from Norwich and waits for the next train.
    How much later will he arrive in London than he should have done?

---

**Railroaded**

You will need sheets P162, P163 and a dice for this game.

Wick is the most northerly station in the UK with a regular train service. Can you get from Wick to the port of Dover in one day by rail?

Sheet P162 has the timetables that will take you from Wick to Dover.

All trains leave on time.
However the train's arrival might be delayed.

For each train you travel on roll a dice:    Score 6 and the train arrives 10 minutes early,
Score 5 and the train arrives on time.
Score 1 and the train arrives 10 minutes late,
Score 2 and the train arrives 20 minutes late ....

Record your journey on sheet P163

## C Distance tables

This map shows the main towns in the Republic of Ireland.

The distances shown are the shortest distances by road between the places.

- What is the shortest distance between Longford and Limerick?
- What is the shortest distance between Dublin and Limerick?

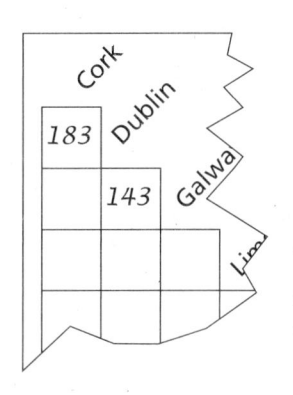

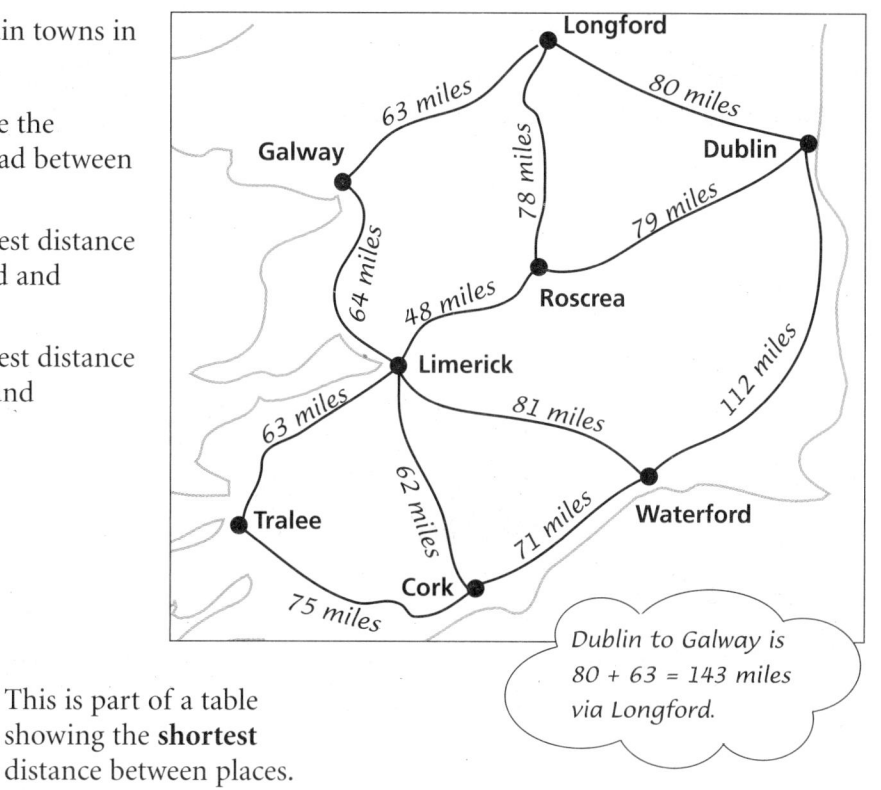

*Dublin to Galway is 80 + 63 = 143 miles via Longford.*

This is part of a table showing the **shortest** distance between places.

**C1** Use sheet P164 to complete the distance table above.

This table shows the rough distances between some of the main UK airports in miles.

**C2** (a) How far is it between East Midlands and Heathrow?

(b) Which two airports in this list are the furthest apart?

**C3** Roger flies from Gatwick to Glasgow and back.
On the way there he flies direct.
On the way back he flies via Manchester.

(a) How far did he fly going to Glasgow?

(b) How far did he fly coming back in total?

(c) How much further was the journey coming back?

## D Average speed

These boys are running away from Fang the dog after teasing him.

The distances show how far they have run in 10 seconds.

- Who is fastest?
- What are their average speeds?

**Average speed**

A speedboat travels 24 metres in 4 seconds.

What was its average speed?

If the boat travels at constant speed, then it travels 24 m in 4 seconds or 6 m in 1 second.

The speed is 6 metres per second or 6 m/s.

**D1** A cyclist takes 6 seconds to travel 48 metres.
What is her average speed in metres per second (m/s)?

**D2** Find the average speed, in metres per second of
  (a) a horse running 200 m in 20 seconds
  (b) a boy walking 50 m in 10 seconds
  (c) a hedgehog walking 24 m in 8 seconds
  (d) a car travelling 150 m in 5 seconds
  (e) a train travelling 600 m in 15 seconds

**D3** Work out the average speed of these in km/h
  (a) a train that goes 140 km in 2 hours
  (b) a ship that takes 5 hours to sail 75 km
  (c) a plane that flies 630 km in 3 hours
  (d) a space shuttle that travels 54 000 miles in 3 hours

**D4** Four pigeons are released together. These are the distances they flew and the times taken.

| Pigeon | Flatford Flyer | Walter | Bolton Queen | Caeredwen |
|---|---|---|---|---|
| Distance flown (km) | 100 | 90 | 174 | 144 |
| Time taken (hours) | 4 | 3 | 6 | 6 |

(a) Calculate the average speed in kilometres per hour (km/h) of each pigeon.

(b) Which pigeon flew  (i) the fastest?  (ii) the slowest?

**D5** Calculate the average speed of these.
State the units clearly in your answer.

(a) a man who runs 150 m in 15 seconds

(b) an aircraft that takes 3 hours to fly 840 miles

(c) a coach that travels 160 km in 4 hours

(d) a car that goes 75 miles in 2 hours

**D6** A car travels 12 kilometres in 15 minutes.

(a) At the same average speed, how far would it travel in one hour?

(b) What is the speed of the car in km/h?

**D7** For each of these find
- the distance it would travel in one hour
- the speed in km/h

(a) a plane that travels 150 km in half an hour

(b) a horse that travels 5 km in 15 minutes

(c) a ship that travels 8 km in 20 minutes

---

**Using a calculator**

A plane travels 400 km in $2\frac{1}{2}$ hours. What is its average speed?

$2\frac{1}{2}$ hours = 2.5 hours so on a calculator  $400 \div 2.5 = 160$

---

**D8** How would you enter these into a calculator?

(a) $1\frac{1}{2}$ hours

(b) three and a quarter hours

(c) 5 hours and 30 minutes

(d) 1 hour and 45 minutes

**D9** Work out the average speeds of these

(a) A coach takes $3\frac{1}{2}$ hours to travel from Hull to Birmingham.
This was a distance of 140 miles.

(b) Catherine flies from Manchester to Glasgow, a distance of 225 miles.
The journey takes 1 hour 15 minutes.

(c) A non-stop flight of 5625 miles which takes twelve and a half hours.

# E Distance/time graphs

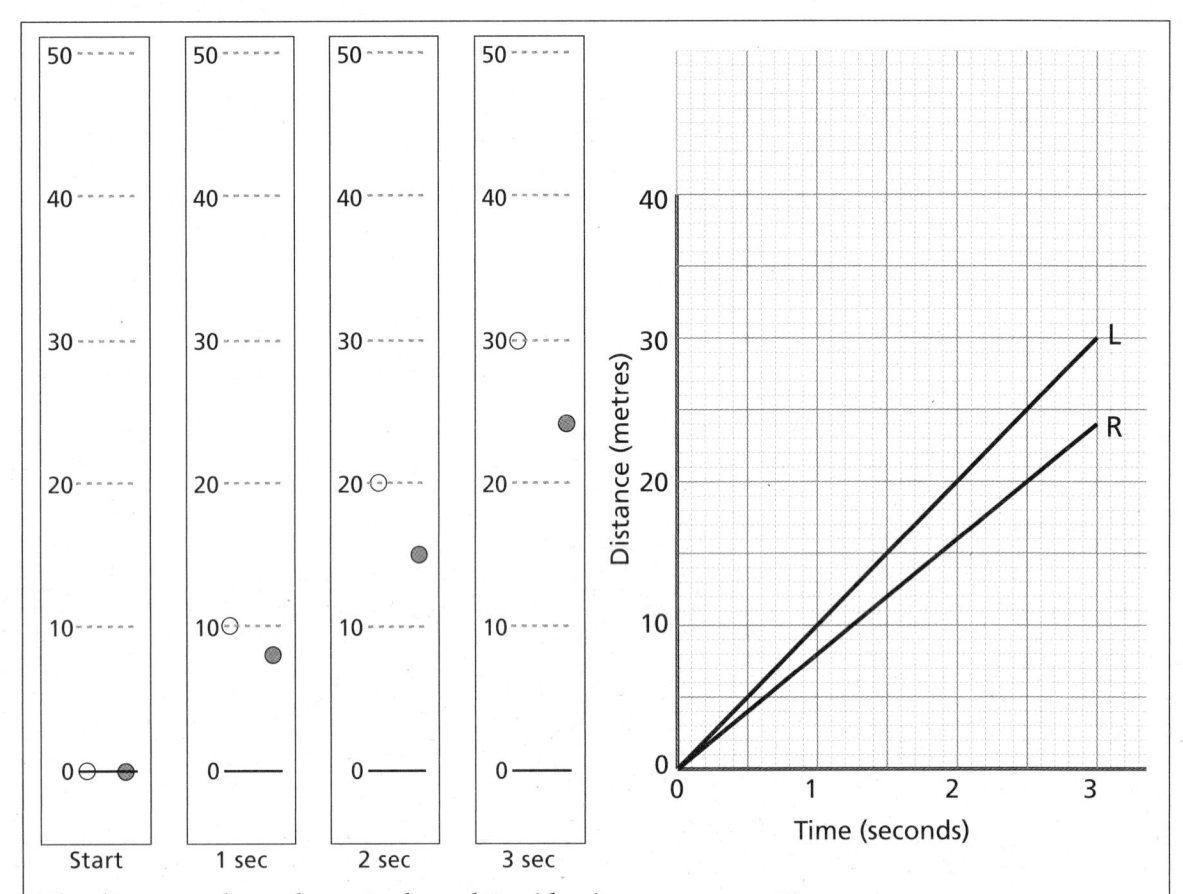

The diagrams above shows Lazlo and Rani having a race over 50 metres..

- How fast is Lazlo going?
- How fast is Rani going?
- How far apart are they after 3 seconds?
- If their speeds do not change, where will each of them be after 4 seconds?

This graph shows the journey of some friends who go out walking one day.

- How fast were they walking for the first two hours?
- What did they do after they had been walking for two hours?
- Describe what is happening in each part of the journey.

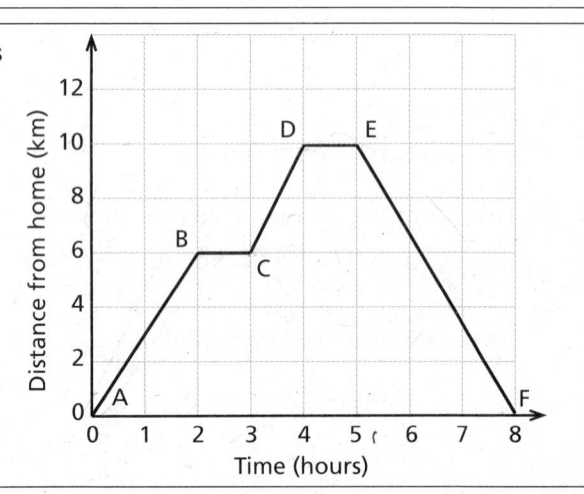

40 • 22 Travel

**E1** This graph shows people going along a path in a park.

(a) How far did person A go in 1 second?

(b) Who was going faster, B or D?

(c) Work out the speed in m/s of each person.

(d) One of the people was a man on a bike. Which of these is this most likely to be?

(e) One of these was an old lady with a stick. Which of these is this most likely to be?

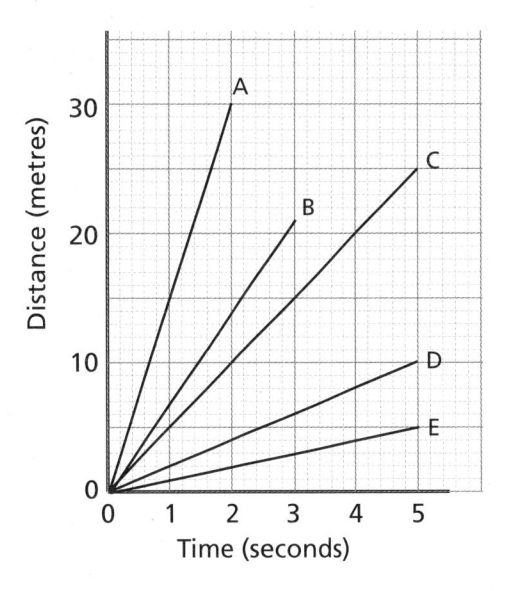

**E2** Here are three graphs which represent journeys.

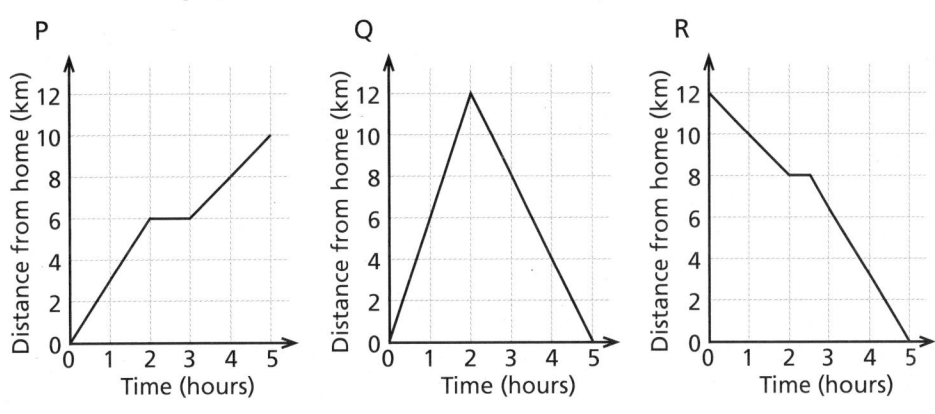

Match each of these statements to one of the graphs above

(a) *We stopped for a break for an hour.*

(b) *We headed for home and it took five hours to get there.*

(c) *We only stopped for a half an hour break.*

(d) *It took two hours to get there but three hours to get back.*

(e) *For the first two hours we went at 6 km/h.*

(f) *Coming home we went at 4 km/h.*

**E3** (a) In journey Q did they go faster going away from home or coming back?

(b) What was the average speed for the first two hours of journey P?

(c) What was the average speed for the first two hours of journey R?

**E4** Barry goes on a hike with his Duke of Edinburgh group.
This graph shows their journey.

(a) What was their average speed for the first two hours?

(b) What was their average speed between 12 p.m. and 2 p.m.?

(c) What happened between 2 p.m. and 3 p.m.?

(d) How far did they walk between 3 p.m. and 5 p.m.?

(e) What was their average speed between 3 p.m. and 5 p.m.?

(f) What was their average speed between 5 p.m. and 7 p.m.?

(g) Between which times were they walking fastest?

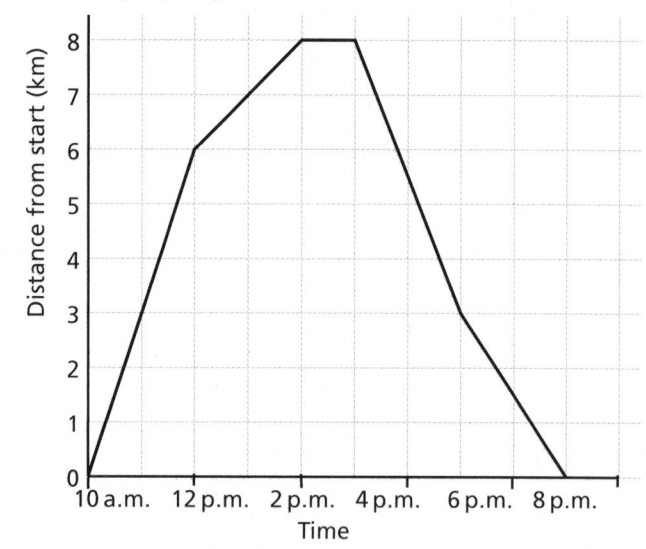

**E5** Draw a set of axes on squared paper the same size as E4.

(a) Draw the graph to show this journey
- We left home at 10 a.m. and for the first 3 hours we had an average speed of 3 km/h
- After that we stopped for lunch for an hour
- After lunch we started to head back and went for 2 hours at 2 km/h
- Then we found this brilliant stream and messed about there for a whole hour
- Although we were very tired we managed to get back home after another 2 hours

(b) What was the average speed for the last part of the walk?

**E6** Elaine went for a walk.
Her walk is represented by the graph below.

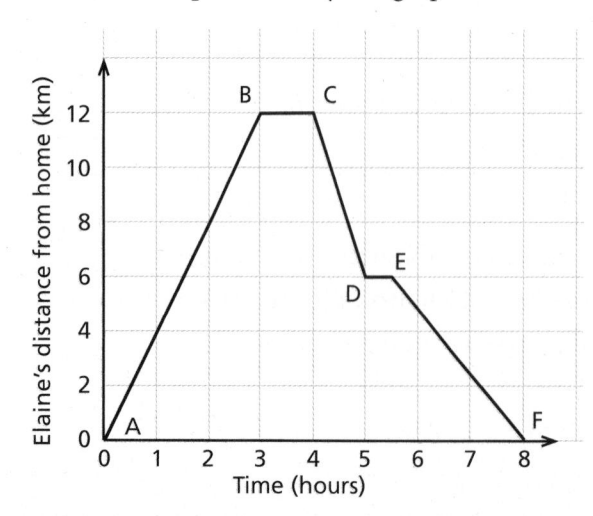

(a) Describe the part of her walk represented by the sections CD, DE and EF.

(b) On which section of her walk did she walk fastest?

(c) What was her average speed for the first 2 hours?

OCR

# F Distance and time calculations

A greyhound runs at a speed of roughly 16 m/s.
How far will it run in 5 seconds?

In 1 second it goes 16 m     16 metres →

In 5 seconds it goes
5 × 16 m = 80 m     16 metres → 16 metres → 16 metres → 16 metres → 16 metres →

**F1** How far will these animals travel in 5 seconds
  (a) a chicken at 4 m/s
  (b) a black mamba snake at 9 m/s
  (c) a warthog at 13 m/s
  (d) a wildebeest at 25 m/s

**F2** How far will these animals go
  (a) a pig going at 5 m/s for 10 seconds
  (b) an elephant going at 10 m/s for 8 seconds
  (c) a grizzly bear going at 13 m/s for 20 seconds
  (d) a horse going at 20 m/s for 15 seconds

**F3** How far are these journeys
  (a) a car travelling at 50 m.p.h. for 3 hours
  (b) a plane travelling at 600 km/h for 4 hours
  (c) a train travelling at 120 km/h in two hours
  (d) a ship going at 40 km/h for 12 hours
  (e) a cyclist going at 25 km/h for 5 hours.

**F4** A car driver estimates he drives long distances at an average speed of 60 m.p.h. How far should he have travelled after
  (a) half an hour
  (b) $3\frac{1}{2}$ hours
  (c) $2\frac{1}{4}$ hours
  (d) $6\frac{1}{4}$ hours

**\*F5** A three-toed sloth travels at a speed of about 0.1 m/s. How far will it travel in 20 seconds?

### A tricky problem

You are in a game reserve and 100 m away from your safe truck. A wildebeest 100 m in the other direction starts to chase you.

A human being can run at 8 m/s, a wildebeest at 25 m/s.

Will you make it back to the truck before he catches you?

A lion can run at 22 m/s – would it catch you in the same situation?

Find out the speeds of some other animals. Would they catch you?

Truck
↑
100 m
↓
○ You
↑
100 m
↓
○ Wildebeest

> A car can travel long distances at an average speed of 50 m.p.h.
> How long will it take to go 250 miles?
>
> 250 miles
>
> $\dfrac{50 \text{ miles}}{1 \text{ hour}}$ → so find out how many 50 miles are in 250 miles
>
> 250 ÷ 50 = 5    so it takes 5 hours

**F6**  Pam walks at a steady speed of 4 km/h. How long does she take to walk 12 km?

**F7**  Alvin's speedboat travels at 20 m.p.h. How long does it take to travel 80 miles?

**F8**  Yves cycles at a steady speed of 25 km/h. How long does it take him to cycle 150 km?

**F9**  How long would each of these animals take to cover 120 metres?
   (a) an elk running at 20 m/s
   (b) an elephant running at 12 m/s
   (c) a cat running at 15 m/s
   (d) a cheetah running at 30 m/s

**F10**  In a tall office block the difference between the top and bottom floors is 90 m.
The lift in the block goes up at an average speed of 5 m/s.
How long does it take to go from the bottom to the top floor?

**F11**  A boat travels at a speed of 8 km/h. How long will it take to travel 20 km?

**F12**  A car travels at a steady speed of 50 m.p.h. How long does it take to travel 175 miles?

## G  Mixed examples

**G1**  A French high speed train can travel at 180 m.p.h.
   (a) How far can it travel at this speed in 3 hours?
   (b) Marseilles to Paris is about 450 miles.
       How long would it take at 180 m.p.h.?

**G2**  Mr Nagra left home in his van at 07 30.
He arrived at the motorway at 08 10.
   (a) How long did this part of the journey take him?
He then drove along the motorway at a steady speed of 60 miles per hour.
   (b) How far did he travel along the motorway in $1\tfrac{1}{2}$ hours?     OCR

**G3**  These are the readings on the mileometer of a car before and after a journey.

Before  [ 7 8 3 4 5 ]    After  [ 7 8 5 7 0 ]

   (a) How long was the journey in miles?
   (b) The journey took 5 hours.
       What was the average speed for the journey?

## Test yourself with these questions

**T1**

| World Service Radio | |
|---|---|
| 8.00 a.m. | From our own correspondent |
| 8.20 | Off the Shelf |
| 8.35 | The Works |
| 8.55 | World News |
| 9.10 | Network |
| 9.20 | Britain Today |
| 9.50 | Sports Round-up till 10.00 a.m. |

(a) How many minutes long was 'The Works'?

(b) Which was the longest programme of those listed?

(c) Which programmes were 15 minutes long?

OCR

**T2** Here is part of a timetable

| Wigan – Atherton – Eccles – Manchester | | | | | |
|---|---|---|---|---|---|
| **Wigan**, Bus station | 0530 | 0555 | 0620 | | 0640 |
| Castle Hill | 0545 | 0610 | 0635 | | 0655 |
| Hindley Green | 0552 | 0617 | 0642 | | 0702 |
| **Atherton** | 0558 | 0623 | 0648 | 0700 | 0710 |
| Tyldesley | 0604 | 0629 | 0654 | 0706 | 0716 |
| Monton Green | 0625 | 0650 | 0715 | 0729 | 0739 |
| **Eccles** | 0631 | 0656 | 0722 | 0736 | 0746 |
| Weaste | 0633 | 0658 | 0725 | 0739 | 0747 |
| Trafford Road | 0636 | 0701 | 0730 | 0744 | 0754 |
| **Manchester** Bus station | 0650 | 0717 | 0746 | 0800 | 0810 |

(a) At what time should the 0620 from Wigan arrive at Monton Green?

(b) How long should it take the 0629 bus from Tyldesley to travel to Trafford Road?

Susan catches a bus in Atherton.
She needs to be in Eccles by 0700.

(c) What is the time of the latest bus she could catch from Atherton?

Edexcel

**T3** (a) Brian travels 225 miles by train.
His journey takes $2\frac{1}{2}$ hours.

What is the average speed of the train?

(b) Val drives 225 miles at an average speed of 50 mph.
How long does her journey take?

AQA(NEAB) 2000

**T4** The table shows the distances, in miles, between some cities.
For example, the distance from Sheffield to Leeds is 36 miles.
A delivery driver makes journeys between these cities.

(a) One journey is between Manchester and Sheffield. How long is this journey?

(b) (i) The driver makes a trip from York to Leeds then to Nottingham and finally back to York.
How far did he travel?

(ii) The driver left York at 14:30.
Write this time as a 12 hour clock time.

(iii) When the driver arrived back in York, the time was 21:05.
How long did the journey take?

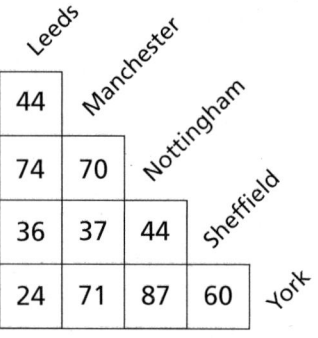

*OCR*

|  | Leeds | Manchester | Nottingham | Sheffield | York |
|---|---|---|---|---|---|
|  | 44 |  |  |  |  |
|  | 74 | 70 |  |  |  |
|  | 36 | 37 | 44 |  |  |
|  | 24 | 71 | 87 | 60 |  |

**T5** Elizabeth went for a cycle ride.
The distance-time graph shows her ride.

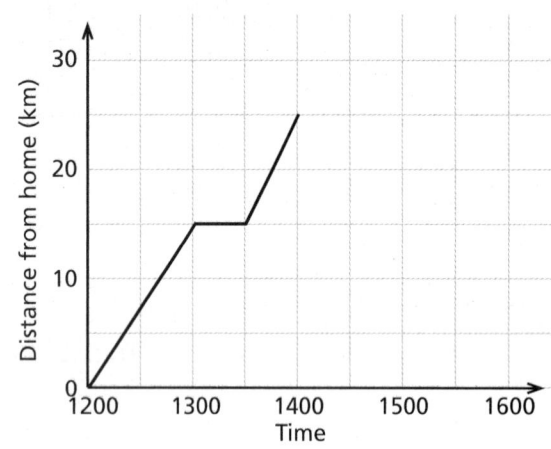

She set off from home at 1200 and had a flat tyre at 1400.
During her ride she stopped for a rest.

(a) (i) At what time did she stop for a rest?

(ii) At what speed did she travel after her rest?

It took Elizabeth 15 minutes to repair the flat tyre.

She then cycled home at 25 kilometres per hour.

(b) Copy the graph onto squared paper.
Complete the distance time graph to show this information.

*Edexcel*

# 23 Looking at data 2

You will revise
- how to find the mean, median, mode and range for simple sets of data
- how to group data using a stem and leaf diagram or frequency table

You will learn
- how to group continuous data and draw bar charts for continuous data

## A Just a few

### Mean streak

Sheet P165 has a game board and rules for Mean streak.
You will need dice and counters to play this game.
Is it possible to use the hexagon with 0 on it?

### On the cards

Sheet P166 has a set of cards with the numbers 3, 3, 4, 5, 6, 6, 7 and 8 on them.
- Find 3 cards whose mean is 4.
- Find 4 cards whose mean is 5.
- Find 5 cards with median 6 and range 4.
- Find 4 cards with median 5 and range 5.
- Find 6 cards with the same mean and median.

Make up some puzzles of your own. Try them out on a partner.

### Families

Can you solve these problems?

> In my family the three kids are 6, 10 and 16.
> The mean age of the whole family is 24, the range is 41.
> How old are my Mum and Dad?

> There are 5 children in my family.
> The youngest is 8 and I am 15.
> The median child's age is 13.
> The range of children's ages is 17.
> The mean of our ages is 14.
> How old are we?

**A1** Tim counts the number of jumpers owned by each of seven friends.
His results are   9,   3,   2,   9,   2,   8,   2

(a) Work out the median.

(b) Calculate the mean.

(c) Work out the range.

AQA 2003

**A2** A group of five friends took part in a sponsored swim.
Here are the number of completed lengths each person swam.
  13,   10,   19,   20,   18

For these numbers find

(a) the mean          (b) the median          (c) the range          OCR

**A3** The boys in a class measure their handspan to the nearest centimetre.
Their results are:   13,  14,  14,  15,  14,  14,  15,  17,  16,  14,  16,  12

(a) Find the range of their handspans.

(b) Calculate the mean handspan.

The mean handspan for the girls in this class was 13.2 cm and they had a range of 7 cm.

(c) Make two statements about the differences between
    the boys' and girls' handspans in this class.

**A4** A greengrocer sold bags of apples from different countries.
A bag contained 9 French apples.

The weight of each apple is given below, in grams.
101,  107,  98,  109,  115,  103,  96,  112,  104

(a) Calculate the mean weight of a French apple.

(b) Find the range of the weights of the French apples.

Another bag contained 9 South African apples.
Their mean weight was 107 g and their range was 19 g.

(c) Make two comments on the weights of the apples in the two bags.          OCR

**A5** A group of children were asked how many hours they spent on the Internet last week.
The results were

**Girls:** 9, 12, 4, 3, 7          **Boys:** 12, 16, 5, 5, 6, 2, 6, 16

(a) Find the mean numbers of hours for the girls in the survey.

(b) Find the mean number of hours for the boys.

(c) Who do the means suggest spent more time on the Internet, girls or boys?

(d) Find the median number of hours for     (i) girls     (ii) boys.

(e) Find the range of the number of hours for   (i) girls   (ii) boys.

(f) What do the median and range tell you about the amount of time
    spent by these girls and boys on the Internet?

## B Frequency tables

Question A3 gave the handspans of a group of boys in centimetres as:

13, 14, 14, 15, 14, 14, 15, 17, 16, 14, 16, 12

When the data is repeated it can be listed in ....

..... a frequency table and .....  ..... displayed in a frequency diagram

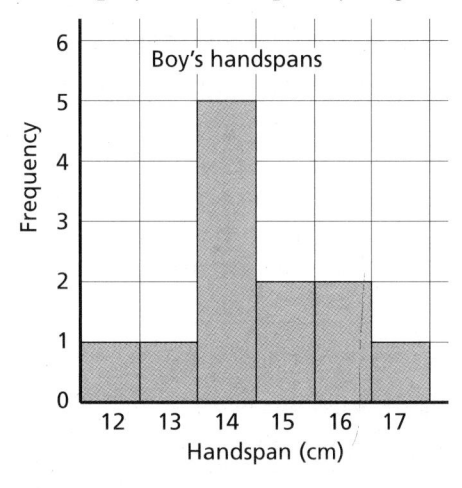

| Handspan (cm) | Frequency |
|---|---|
| 12 | 1 |
| 13 | 1 |
| 14 | 5 |
| 15 | 2 |
| 16 | 2 |
| 17 | 1 |
| Total | 12 |

- What is the modal handspan for these boys?
- What is the median handspan? How can the table help you?

**B1** Saira is trying to estimate how many words she has written in an essay. She records the number of words she wrote on each line on one page.

| Words on a line | Frequency |
|---|---|
| 10 | 1 |
| 11 | 3 |
| 12 | 6 |
| 13 | 9 |
| 14 | 7 |
| 15 | 4 |

(a) How many lines in total were there on the page?
(b) How many lines had 14 words on them?
(c) What is the range of the number of words on a line?
(d) What is the modal number of words on a line?
(e) Find the median number of words per line.
(f) What is the total number of words on this page?
(g) Draw a frequency diagram of these results.

## C  Grouping data

With larger sets of data the data needs to be grouped.
Here are the pulse rates of class 10M taken at the beginning of a lesson:

*Pulse rates (beats per minute)*   77, 74, 85, 76, 72, 73, 55, 60, 91, 85, 80, 83, 68, 71, 60, 77, 77, 86, 97, 47, 71, 72, 63, 68, 84, 87, 77, 61

A useful way to record this data is a stem and leaf table with the data written in order.

Pulse rates (beats per minute)

*Do a rough copy first and then put the numbers in order.*

```
4 | 7
5 | 5
6 | 0 0 1 3 8 8
7 | 1 1 2 2 3 ④ 6 ⑦ 7 7 7
8 | 0 3 4 5 5 6 7
9 | 1 7
```
Stem = 10 beats

As the data is listed in order it is easy to find the median from a stem and leaf diagram.

The median pulse rate is between 74 and 76 so is 75 b.p.m.

We can also see that the largest group of people have pulse rates between 70 and 79 b.p.m..

A grouped frequency table shows the number of people in each range of pulse rates.

| Pulse rate | Frequency |
|---|---|
| 40–49 | 1 |
| 50–59 | 1 |
| 60–69 | 6 |
| 70–79 | 11 |
| 80–89 | 7 |
| 90–99 | 2 |
| Total | 28 |

The frequency table clearly shows the **modal group** of this data is a pulse rate of 70–79 b.p.m.

The table can also be used to draw a **frequency diagram**.

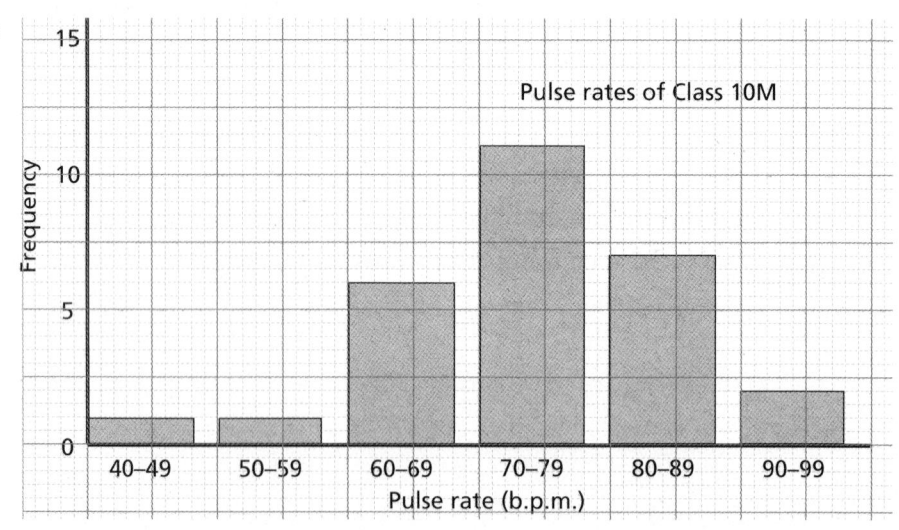

50 • 23 Looking at data 2

**C1** The data below shows the ages of the male teachers in a school.

| 33 | 45 | 24 | 58 | 32 | 47 | 48 | 36 | 28 | 41 |
| 26 | 48 | 44 | 55 | 38 | 40 | 33 | 46 | 37 | 52 |
| 34 | 58 | 42 | 57 | 38 | 46 | 51 |    |    |    |

(a) Put this data into a stem and leaf table with this stem.

**Male age (years)**
2 |
3 |
4 |
5 |
Stem = 10 years

(b) Find the median and range of the male age.

This is the data for female teachers in the same school.

**Female age (years)**
2 | 2 4 5 8 8
3 | 0 1 1 2 3 5 7 8 9
4 | 2 4 6 9
5 | 0 2 6 8
6 | 0
Stem = 10 years

(c) Find the median and range of the age of female teachers.

(d) Write two statements about the differences in the ages of male and female teachers at the school.

**C2** (a) Using the data in question C1 make a frequency table for the ages of the male teachers. Use groups 20–29, 30–39 etc.

(b) What is the modal age group for the male teachers?

(c) What will the modal age group of the female teachers be?

(d) Draw a frequency diagram to show the ages of the male teachers.

**C3** There are 30 people in a class. They are asked how many pets they have. Here are the results.

| 1 | 4 | 7 | 3 | 1 | 0 | 0 | 1 | 3 | 8 | 3 | 3 | 5 | 1 | 0 | 2 |
| 8 | 1 | 4 | 2 | 1 | 1 | 7 | 5 | 1 | 0 | 2 | 4 | 1 | 6 | 3 | 5 |

(a) Copy and complete this frequency table for this data.

| Number of pets | Tally | Frequency |
|---|---|---|
| 0–1 | | |
| 2–3 | | |
| 4–5 | | |
| 6–7 | | |
| 8–9 | | |

(b) Draw the frequency diagram to show this data on sheet P167.

AQA(NEAB) 1997

## D Continuous data

Some students are playing 'Target'.
A large piece of paper has a target and circles with radiuses 10 cm, 20 cm, 30 cm, 40 cm and 50 cm around the target.

Players try to throw a coin onto the target. A mark is placed on the edge of the coin nearest to the target.

Each player has 30 throws.

The picture shows Aled's throws.

To record these throws a frequency table could be used

| Distance from target (cm) | Frequency |
|---|---|
| 0–10 | |
| 11–20 | |
| 21–30 | |

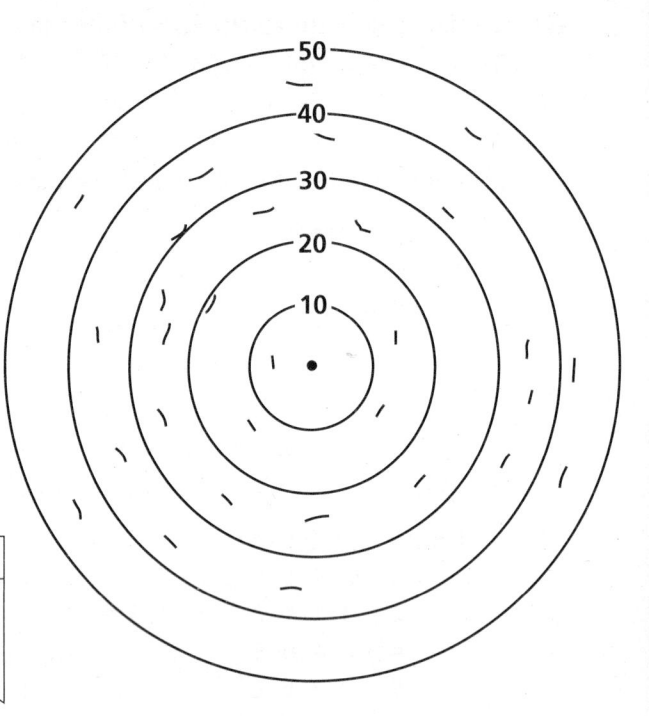

However if there was a mark between 20 and 21 cm it would be difficult to know which group to put it into.
Groups can be labelled to make this clearer.

| Distance from target (cm) | Frequency |
|---|---|
| Less than or equal to 10 | 1 |
| More than 10 but less than or equal to 20 | 4 |
| More than 20 but less than or equal to 30 | 9 |
| More than 30 but less than or equal to 40 | 10 |
| More than 40 but less than or equal to 50 | 6 |
| Total | 30 |

or

| Distance from target $x$ (cm) | Frequency |
|---|---|
| $0 < x \leq 10$ | 1 |
| $10 < x \leq 20$ | 4 |
| $20 < x \leq 30$ | 9 |
| $30 < x \leq 40$ | 10 |
| $40 < x \leq 50$ | 4 |
| TOTAL | 30 |

- What group would a distance of exactly 20 cm go in?
- What group would a distance of exactly 19 cm go in?
- What group would a distance of 19.5 cm go in?

The **modal group** for Aled's throws is 'more than 30 but less than or equal to 40' or '$30 < x \leq 40$'.

This type of data is called **continuous** because it does not have to be a whole number value.

52 • 23 Looking at data 2

**D1** Aled's friend Britney writes down the distances of her coins from the target.

*Distances from target (cm)*

| 13.5 | 33.2 | 41.8 | 27.2 | 33.1 | 47.4 | 21.5 | 19.3 | 34.6 | 31.2 |
| 30.6 | 43.7 | 16.2 | 8.9  | 25.5 | 40.8 | 39.4 | 27.6 | 33.1 | 5.4  |
| 44.8 | 19.4 | 37.6 | 33.1 | 7.5  | 34.6 | 47.7 | 26.4 | 18.9 | 25.5 |

(a) Make a frequency table for Britney's scores using the same groups as Aled.

(b) What is the modal group for Britney's throws?

**D2** The maximum daily temperature for the month of October was recorded at a Sussex weather station as follows:

Max. Temp. (°C) 16.7 13.9 15.4 14.6 14.1 14.2 12.5 14.6 12.2 12.9 12.2 13.1 14.7
12.7 13.9 12.7 13.9 14.4 13.9 14.5 14.7 14.1 14.7 12.9 14.4 13.1
13.6 14.6 12.8 13.3 12.4

(a) Copy and complete this grouped frequency table to record the temperatures.

| Max. Temp. (°C) | Frequency |
|---|---|
| $12.0 \leq t < 13.0$ | |
| $13.0 \leq t < 14.0$ | |
| $14.0 \leq t < 15.0$ | |
| $15.0 \leq t < 16.0$ | |
| $16.0 \leq t < 17.0$ | |
| Total | |

(b) What is the modal group of temperatures at Sussex during October?

(c) On how many days in October did the temperature not reach 14°C?

**D3** (a) Measure accurately the length of these two lines.

(i) _____

(ii) _____

(b) The lengths, in centimetres, of eleven other lines are shown.

7.2   12.0   5.2   6.9   9.2   15.4   4.0   18.4   4.3   10.4   3.9

Copy and complete the frequency table for **all** thirteen lines

| Length of line (x centimetres) | Tally | Frequency |
|---|---|---|
| $0 \leq x < 4$ | | |
| $4 \leq x < 8$ | | |
| $8 \leq x < 12$ | | |
| $12 \leq x < 16$ | | |
| $16 \leq x < 20$ | | |

(c) What is the modal group?

AQA(SEG)1998

### Frequency graphs

A frequency diagram can be drawn for Aled's data on page 52.

As the data is continuous a normal scale is drawn on the *y*-axis.

No gaps are left between the bars.

To see the pattern of data better a line can be drawn from the middle of the top of each bar.

This is called a **frequency polygon**. It can be drawn on its own without the bar graph.

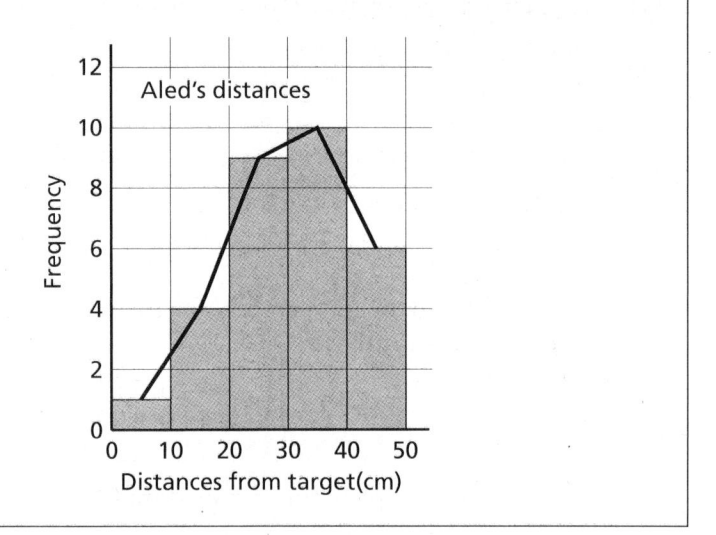

**D4** Use your answer to D1(a) to draw a frequency graph for Britney's results. Draw a frequency polygon on your graph.

**D5** A class recorded their weights in kilograms as follows:

Weight (kg)  46  45  52  61  57  47  61  52  47  47  42  59  51  35  48
             62  62  47  52  39  72  69  57  43  50  38  61  47  54  40

The teacher asks the students to record this data in a grouped frequency table with these groupings.

(a) Which group will the weight 50 kg go into?

(b) Which group will the weight 40 kg go into?

(c) Copy and complete a table showing these students' weights using these groupings

(d) Write down the modal group of weights.

(e) Use your table to copy and complete this frequency diagram for the weights of students.

(f) Draw a frequency polygon on your graph.

| Weight *w*(kg) | Frequency |
|---|---|
| 30 < w ≤ 40 | |
| 40 < w ≤ 50 | |
| 50 < w ≤ 60 | |
| 60 < w ≤ 70 | |
| 70 < w ≤ 80 | |
| Total | |

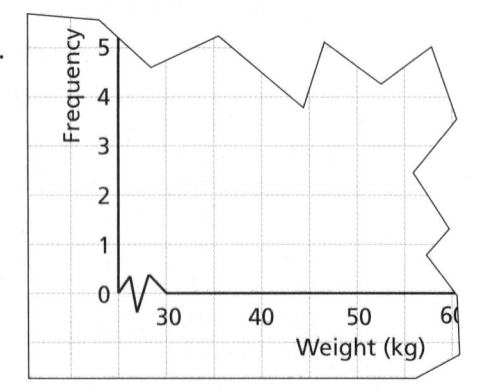

## Test yourself with these questions

**T1** Nicky recorded the numbers of people getting off her bus at 10 stops. Here are her results.

    2    4    3    6    3    6    3    7    11    8

For these 10 numbers, work out

(a) the mean    (b) the median    (c) the range    *Edexcel*

**T2** Twelve boys ran a 100 metres.
Their times, in seconds, are shown.

    11.0  11.5  11.5  12.3  12.9  13.1
    13.6  14.2  14.8  15.6  16.4  17.1

(a) (i) What is the range of running times of these boys?

    (ii) Calculate the mean running time.

(b) Twelve girls run a 100 metres and their times are recorded.
The range in running times for the girls is 5.6 seconds and the mean is 14.3 seconds.

Comment on the differences in running times for boys and girls.    *AQA 1998*

**T3** A school tuck shop records the number of packets of crisps sold on all the school days in June.
These are the results:

26  40  25  44  51  45  54  28  42  35  38  25  33
38  43  35  36  35  33  26  30  25  46  50  43  34

(a) Copy and complete this stem and leaf table for these results

Packets of crisps sold

**2**
**3**
**4**
**5**

Stem = 10 packets

(b) Use your table to find    (i) the median number of packets sold
    (ii) the range of the number of packets sold

**T4** In a competition 20 children each had one minute to put coffee beans into a jar using chopsticks.
The results were

15  12  8  3  10  16  2  7  11  3
5  9  4  7  12  1  6  8  13  14

Copy and complete the tally and frequency columns in this table.

| Number of beans | Tally | Frequency |
|---|---|---|
| 1–5 | | |
| 6–10 | | |
| 11–15 | | |
| 16–20 | | |

AQA 2000

**T5** Use your table in T4 to draw a frequency diagram to show the number of coffee beans picked up.

**T6** A set of 25 times in seconds is recorded.

12.9  10.0  4.2  16.0  5.6  18.1  8.3  14.0  11.5  21.7
22.2  6.0  13.6  3.1  11.5  10.8  15.7  3.7  9.4  8.0
6.4  17.0  7.3  12.8  13.5

(a) Copy and complete the frequency table below using intervals of 5 seconds.

| Time ($t$) seconds | Tally | Frequency |
|---|---|---|
| $0 \leq t < 5$ | | |
| | | |
| | | |
| | | |
| | | |

(b) Write down the modal class interval.

Edexcel

**T7** The table shows the weight of the luggage for passengers on one plane.

| Weight ($w$ kg) | Number of passengers |
|---|---|
| $0 < w \leq 5$ | 14 |
| $5 < w \leq 10$ | 28 |
| $10 < w \leq 15$ | 12 |
| $15 < w \leq 20$ | 9 |
| $20 < w \leq 25$ | 2 |

(a) What was the modal class?
(b) On graph paper draw a frequency diagram for this distribution.

OCR

# 24 Enlargement

You will revise
- how to enlarge a shape using squared paper

You will learn
- how to enlarge a shape using a centre of enlargement
- how the perimeter and angles of a shape are affected by enlargement

## A Using squares

**A1** Use centimetre squared paper to make enlargements of these with scale factor 2.

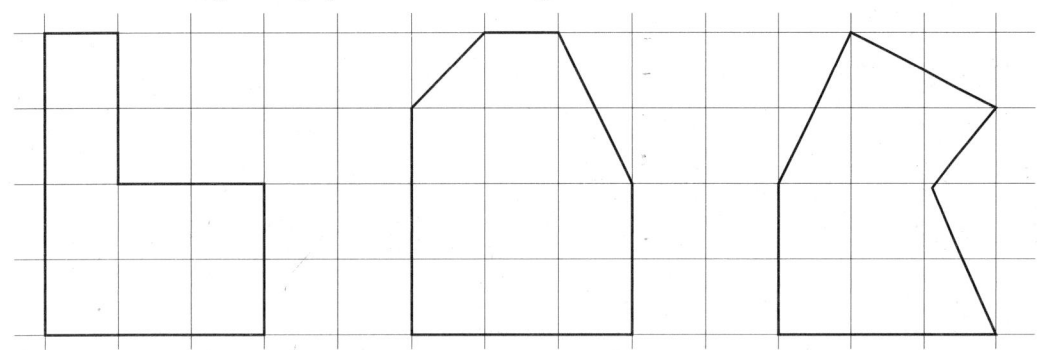

**A2** Which of these are correct enlargements of shape A?
What scale factor has been used?

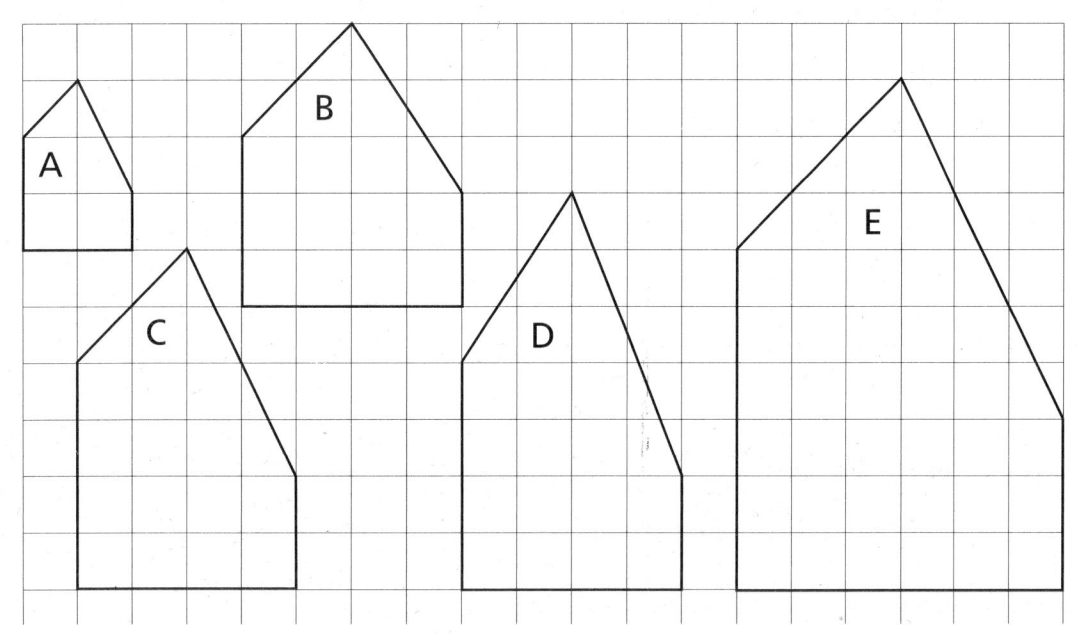

24 Enlargement • 57

## B Using a centre

Sheet P168 shows the start of a scale factor 2 enlargement of shape ABCDE.
A′ is where point A goes to after the enlargement.

- Complete the enlargement
- Label the points B′, C′, D′ and E′.
- Draw a line from A′ through A to the edge of the paper.
  Do the same for the other four pairs of points.
  All the lines should cross at one point. Call this X.
- Measure the length XA.
  Measure the length XA′.
  Repeat for all the other points.
  What do you notice?

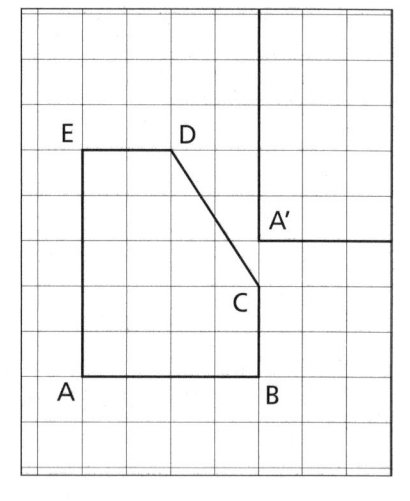

**B1** Sheet P169 shows shape ABCDEF and a scale factor 2 enlargement of it.
  (a) Label points A′, B′, C′, D′, E′, F′ on the enlargement.
  (b) Draw extended lines between matching points on the shapes.
      Mark the point where they cross with an X.
  (c) Measure the distance from X to each of the points on the two shapes.
      Complete a table like this:

  | Point | Distance X to original (D1) | Distance X to enlargement (D2) |
  |-------|-----------------------------|--------------------------------|
  | A     |                             |                                |

  (d) Check that each distance D2 is twice distance D1.

**B2** Sheet P170 shows triangle JKL and a scale factor 3 enlargement of it.
  (a) Draw lines between the matching points on the shapes to find
      the centre of enlargement O.
  (b) Measure the distance from O to each of the points on the original.
      Measure the distance from O to each of the points on the enlarged shape.
      Copy and complete this table:

  | Point | Distance Y to original (D1) | Distance Y to enlargement (D2) | D2 ÷ D1 |
  |-------|-----------------------------|--------------------------------|---------|
  | J     |                             |                                |         |

  (c) What do you notice about D2 ÷ D1 each time?

**B3** This question is on sheet P171.

58 • 24 Enlargement

**Using a grid**

Making an accurate enlargement can be hard.

The squares on a grid can be used to help.

Count the squares across and up or down from the centre.

Double these distances for a scale factor 2 enlargement.

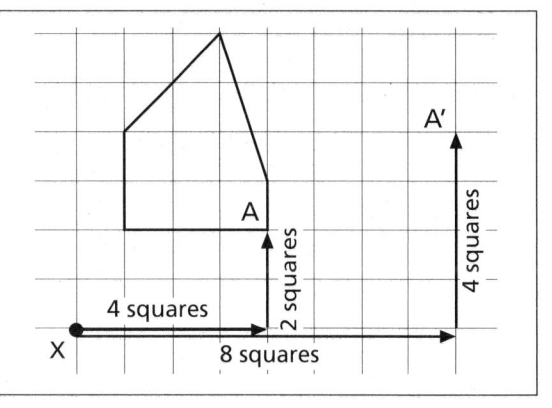

**B4** Copy the shape and point X in the diagram above.
Complete the enlargement scale factor 2 using centre X.

**B5** A pentagon is shown.
Copy the pentagon and point X onto centimetre squared paper.

Draw an enlargement of the pentagon, scale factor 2, centre X.

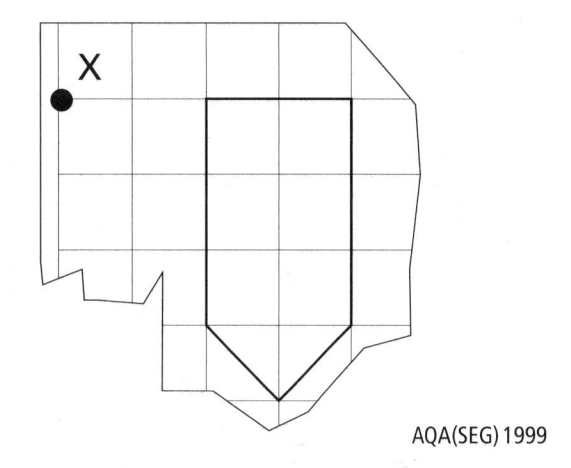

AQA(SEG) 1999

**B6** Copy this shape and point P onto the middle of a sheet of centimetre squared paper.

Draw an enlargement of the shape, scale factor 3 using P as the centre.

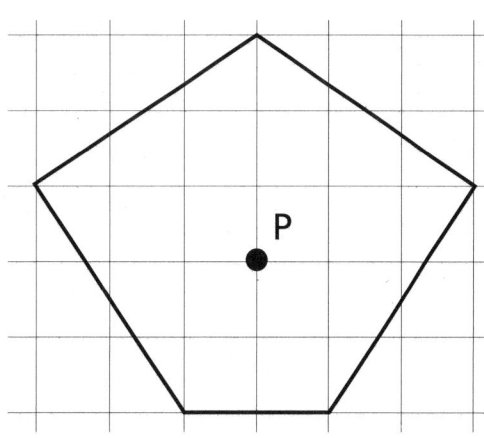

**Enlarge a design**

Make up your own shape or simple design on centimetre squared paper.

Use a centre to enlarge your drawing.

24 Enlargement • 59

## C  Effects of enlargement

This diagram shows shape ABCDE and an enlargement of it using scale factor 2.

- Find the perimeter of the original shape.
  Find the perimeter of the enlargement.
  (You will need to measure some lengths.)
  What do you notice?

- Measure angle ABC in the original.
  Measure angle A'B'C' in the enlargement.
  What do you find?
  Is this the same for other angles?

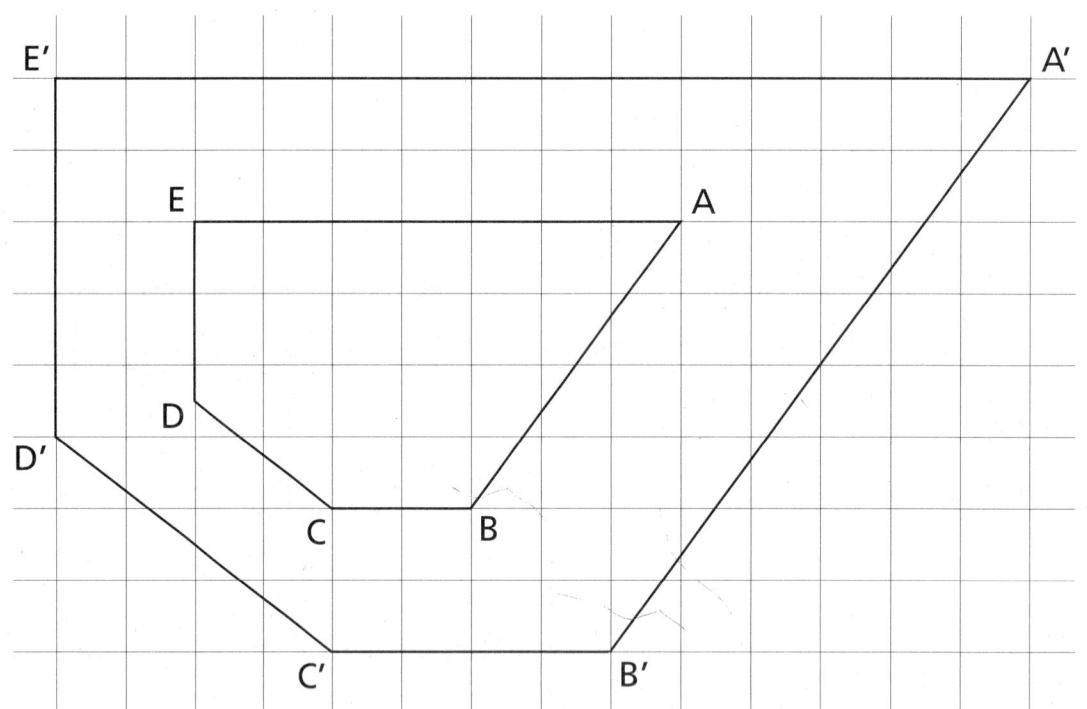

**C1** (a) Find the perimeter of this triangle ABC.

(b) If the triangle was enlarged by scale factor 2, what would the perimeter of the enlarged triangle be?

(c) If the triangle was enlarged by scale factor 4, what would the perimeter of the enlarged triangle be?

(d) Angle CAB is 37°.
What would this angle be in a scale factor 3 enlargement?

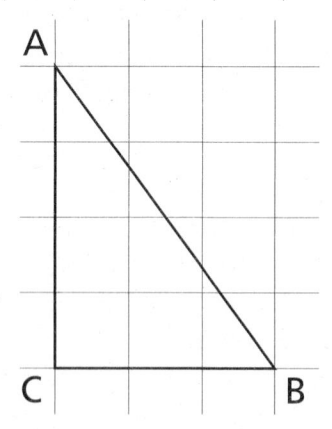

**C2** A triangle is enlarged by scale factor 3.
The perimeter of the enlarged triangle is 24 cm.
The angles in the enlarged triangle are 36°, 68° and 76°.

(a) What is the perimeter of the original shape?

(b) What are the angles in the original shape?

60 • 24 Enlargement

**C3** (a) Squares B and C are enlargements of square A.
Find the scale factor of enlargement for B and C.

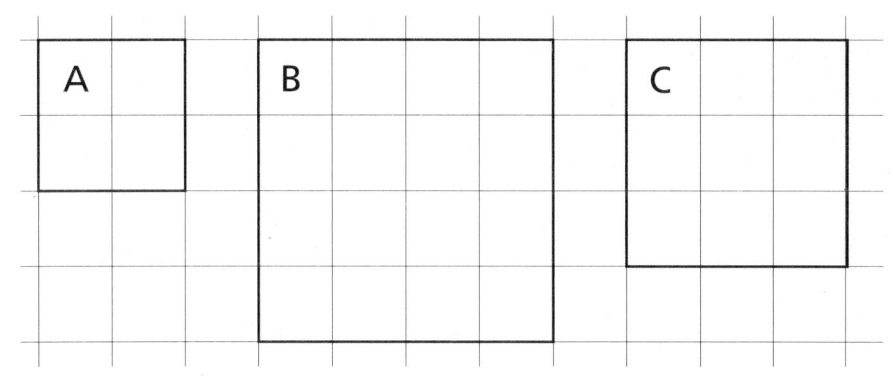

(b) Is it possible to draw a square which is not an exact enlargement of A?

**C4** (a) Draw a circle with radius 2 cm.
Can you draw another circle which is not an enlargement of this one?

(b) Draw a rectangle 5 cm by 3 cm.
Is it possible to draw a rectangle which is not an enlargement of this one?

---

### Test yourself with these questions

**T1** Copy this shape onto centimetre squared paper.
Draw an enlargement of the shape.
Use a scale factor of 2.

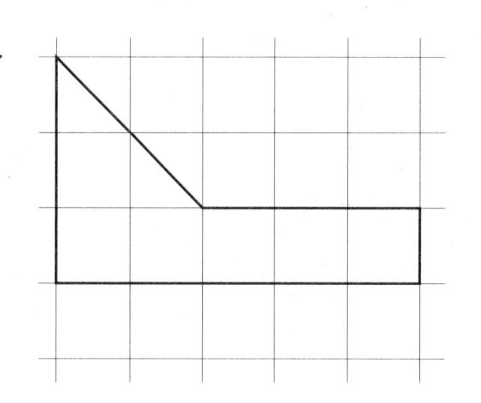

OCR

**T2** Copy this shape in the middle of a sheet of centimetre squared paper.

Enlarge the shape by a scale factor of 2, centre X.

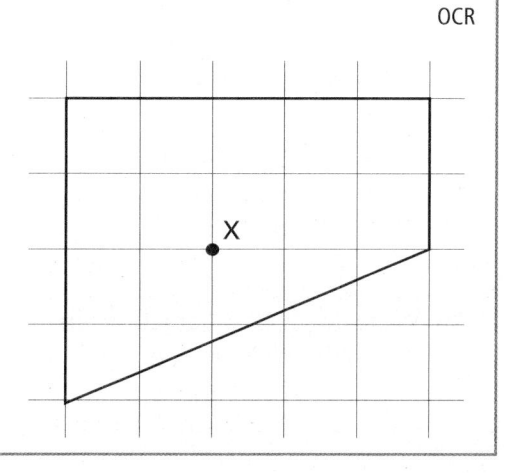

# 25 Calculating with fractions 1

You should know
- about equivalent fractions
- how to simplify fractions

You will learn how to
- put fractions in order of size
- work with mixed numbers
- add and subtract fractions
- multiply a fraction by an integer

## A Review

**A1** Find five matching pairs of fractions.

A $\frac{1}{3}$   B $\frac{3}{4}$   P four ninths   Q three quarters   R three fifths

C $\frac{3}{5}$   D $\frac{5}{6}$   E $\frac{4}{9}$   S one third   T five sixths

**A2** Copy and complete each statement.
(a) $\frac{1}{2} = \frac{\blacksquare}{10}$   (b) $\frac{1}{4} = \frac{3}{\blacksquare}$   (c) $\frac{2}{3} = \frac{4}{\blacksquare}$   (d) $\frac{2}{5} = \frac{\blacksquare}{20}$

**A3** What fraction of the circle is shaded?
Write this fraction is its simplest form.

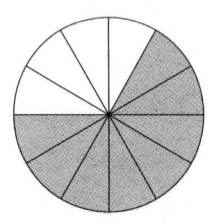

**A4** Write these fractions in their simplest form.
(a) $\frac{4}{8}$   (b) $\frac{3}{15}$   (c) $\frac{2}{12}$   (d) $\frac{8}{10}$   (e) $\frac{9}{12}$

**A5** What fraction of the cakes have candles?
Write this fraction in its simplest form.

**A6** Write down all the fractions in the bubble that are equivalent to
(a) $\frac{1}{2}$   (b) $\frac{1}{4}$   (c) $\frac{3}{5}$

$\frac{2}{8}$  $\frac{6}{10}$  $\frac{4}{16}$  $\frac{2}{6}$  $\frac{6}{12}$  $\frac{9}{15}$  $\frac{6}{8}$  $\frac{3}{6}$  $\frac{10}{20}$

## B  Mixed numbers

- $\frac{3}{4}$ is a **proper** fraction (the top number is smaller than the bottom number)
- $\frac{4}{3}$ is an **improper** fraction (the top number is larger than the bottom number)
- $3\frac{1}{4}$ is a **mixed number** (it has a whole number part and a fraction part)

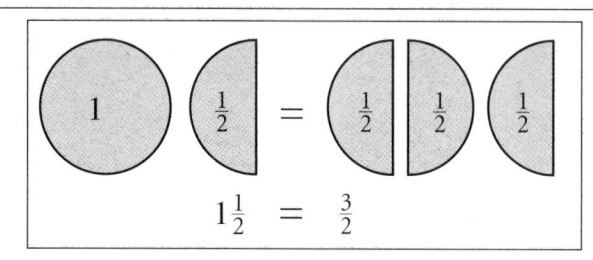

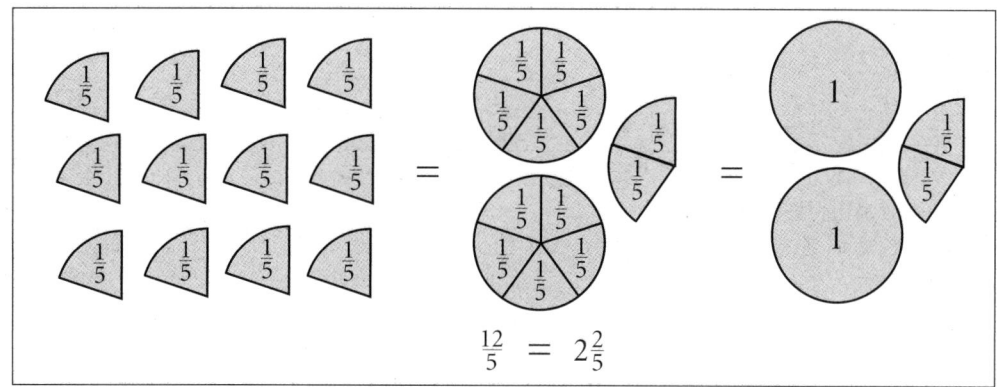

$1\frac{1}{2} = \frac{3}{2}$

$\frac{12}{5} = 2\frac{2}{5}$

**B1** Change these mixed numbers into improper fractions.
(a) $2\frac{1}{2}$  (b) $1\frac{1}{4}$  (c) $1\frac{1}{5}$  (d) $1\frac{1}{3}$  (e) $2\frac{1}{4}$
(f) $1\frac{2}{3}$  (g) $1\frac{3}{10}$  (h) $3\frac{1}{2}$  (i) $2\frac{3}{5}$  (j) $4\frac{2}{5}$

**B2** Change these improper fractions into mixed (or whole) numbers.
(a) $\frac{7}{5}$  (b) $\frac{7}{4}$  (c) $\frac{11}{10}$  (d) $\frac{7}{6}$  (e) $\frac{9}{2}$
(f) $\frac{11}{4}$  (g) $\frac{11}{5}$  (h) $\frac{20}{10}$  (i) $\frac{13}{4}$  (j) $\frac{7}{3}$

**B3** Which of these fractions is the largest: $\frac{9}{2}$, $\frac{13}{10}$, $\frac{17}{4}$, $\frac{18}{5}$

**B4** Arrange these fractions in order of size, smallest first.
$\frac{11}{4}$  $\frac{15}{5}$  $\frac{17}{10}$  $\frac{10}{3}$  $\frac{8}{7}$

**B5** Jane is a teacher and has $9\frac{1}{2}$ bars of chocolate.
She gives $\frac{1}{2}$ of a bar to each of her pupils and has no chocolate left for herself.
How many pupils are in her class?

**B6** John has two cakes.
He cuts them into eighths.
How many pieces of cake does he have in total?

## C Calculating 1

Adding and subtracting are straightforward when the fractions have the same denominators (bottom numbers).

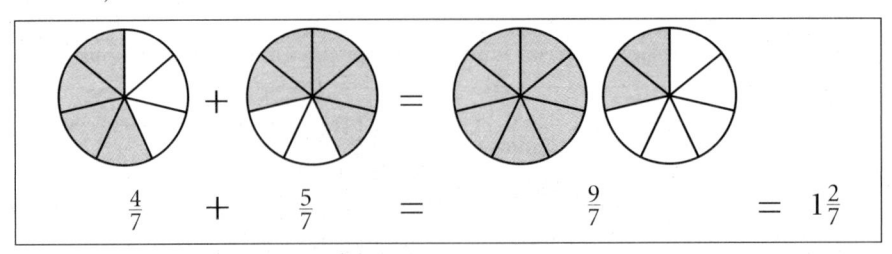

$$\frac{4}{7} + \frac{5}{7} = \frac{9}{7} = 1\frac{2}{7}$$

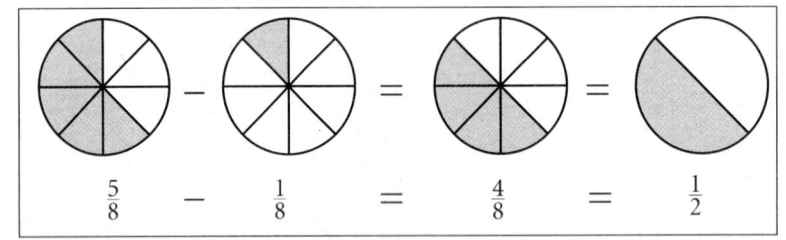

$$\frac{5}{8} - \frac{1}{8} = \frac{4}{8} = \frac{1}{2}$$

**C1** Simon and Allison buy a cake.
Simon eats $\frac{1}{5}$ of the cake and Allison eats $\frac{2}{5}$ of the cake.
What fraction of the cake have they eaten altogether?

**C2** Work these out.
(a) $\frac{1}{3} + \frac{1}{3}$  (b) $\frac{1}{5} + \frac{3}{5}$  (c) $\frac{4}{7} + \frac{1}{7}$  (d) $\frac{2}{5} + \frac{2}{5}$  (e) $\frac{3}{10} + \frac{4}{10}$
(f) $\frac{3}{7} - \frac{1}{7}$  (g) $\frac{4}{5} - \frac{3}{5}$  (h) $\frac{7}{8} - \frac{2}{8}$  (i) $\frac{7}{9} - \frac{5}{9}$  (j) $\frac{5}{6} - \frac{4}{6}$

**C3** Steve drinks $\frac{3}{4}$ of a can of lemonade.
What fraction of the drink is left?

**C4** Work these out.
Give your answers as mixed (or whole) numbers.
(a) $\frac{3}{5} + \frac{4}{5}$  (b) $\frac{2}{3} + \frac{2}{3}$  (c) $\frac{3}{4} + \frac{1}{4}$  (d) $\frac{3}{7} + \frac{5}{7}$  (e) $\frac{5}{9} + \frac{8}{9}$

**C5** Match each calculation with its result.

| A $\frac{3}{4} - \frac{1}{4}$ | B $\frac{2}{9} + \frac{1}{9}$ | C $\frac{3}{4} + \frac{3}{4}$ | P $\frac{1}{3}$ | Q $\frac{2}{5}$ | R $\frac{1}{2}$ |
| D $\frac{3}{10} + \frac{1}{10}$ | E $\frac{7}{8} - \frac{1}{8}$ | F $\frac{5}{6} - \frac{1}{6}$ | S $1\frac{1}{2}$ | T $\frac{2}{3}$ | U $\frac{3}{4}$ |

**C6** Work these out.
Simplify each answer.
(a) $\frac{1}{4} + \frac{1}{4}$  (b) $\frac{3}{8} + \frac{1}{8}$  (c) $\frac{5}{9} + \frac{1}{9}$  (d) $\frac{7}{8} - \frac{5}{8}$  (e) $\frac{7}{10} - \frac{1}{10}$

**C7** Solve the cover up puzzle on sheet P172.

**Multiplying**

$\frac{1}{2} \times 5 = \frac{1}{2} + \frac{1}{2} + \frac{1}{2} + \frac{1}{2} + \frac{1}{2}$
$= \frac{5}{2}$
$= 2\frac{1}{2}$

$\frac{1}{4} \times 6 = \frac{1}{4} + \frac{1}{4} + \frac{1}{4} + \frac{1}{4} + \frac{1}{4} + \frac{1}{4}$
$= \frac{6}{4}$
$= 1\frac{2}{4}$
$= 1\frac{1}{2}$

$\frac{2}{5} \times 3 = \frac{2}{5} + \frac{2}{5} + \frac{2}{5}$
$= \frac{6}{5}$
$= 1\frac{1}{5}$

**C8** Snowy the cat eats $\frac{1}{2}$ a tin of cat food each day.
  (a) How many tins of cat food does Snowy eat in a week?
  (b) How many days food is 5 tins of cat food for Snowy?

**C9** Morag uses $\frac{1}{4}$ of a pint of milk each day to make her porridge.
How much milk will she need for her porridge for a 12 day holiday?

**C10** Work these out and give your answers as mixed (or whole) numbers.
  (a) $\frac{1}{2} \times 3$  (b) $\frac{1}{4} \times 5$  (c) $\frac{1}{2} \times 4$  (d) $\frac{1}{3} \times 5$  (e) $\frac{1}{3} \times 7$
  (f) $\frac{3}{4} \times 3$  (g) $\frac{2}{5} \times 4$  (h) $\frac{1}{6} \times 8$  (i) $\frac{3}{8} \times 4$  (j) $\frac{2}{9} \times 6$

**C11** Pluto eats $\frac{2}{3}$ of a tin of dog food each day.
How many tins of dog food will Pluto eat in 12 days?

**Calculating with mixed numbers**

$1\frac{1}{9} + 1\frac{4}{9} = 1 + 1 + \frac{1}{9} + \frac{4}{9}$
$= 2\frac{5}{9}$

$1\frac{1}{5} - \frac{4}{5} = \frac{6}{5} - \frac{4}{5}$
$= \frac{2}{5}$

$1\frac{3}{10} + \frac{9}{10} = 1 + \frac{3}{10} + \frac{9}{10}$
$= 1 + \frac{12}{10}$
$= 1 + 1\frac{2}{10}$
$= 2\frac{2}{10}$
$= 2\frac{1}{5}$

$3\frac{2}{3} \times 2 = 3\frac{2}{3} + 3\frac{2}{3}$
$= 3 + 3 + \frac{2}{3} + \frac{2}{3}$
$= 6 + \frac{4}{3}$
$= 6 + 1\frac{1}{3}$
$= 7\frac{1}{3}$

In questions C12 to C14, simplify your answers where possible.

**C12** Work these out.
  (a) $1\frac{1}{2} + 3\frac{1}{2}$  (b) $1\frac{2}{5} + \frac{4}{5}$  (c) $2\frac{1}{4} + 1\frac{1}{4}$  (d) $1\frac{7}{10} + 3\frac{1}{10}$  (e) $1\frac{3}{8} + 1\frac{7}{8}$

**C13** Work these out.
  (a) $2\frac{1}{2} \times 2$  (b) $1\frac{1}{4} \times 3$  (c) $2\frac{1}{6} \times 3$  (d) $1\frac{1}{3} \times 5$  (e) $1\frac{4}{9} \times 3$

**C14** Work these out.
  (a) $1\frac{4}{5} - \frac{1}{5}$  (b) $2\frac{5}{8} - \frac{3}{8}$  (c) $3\frac{4}{9} - 1\frac{1}{9}$  (d) $2\frac{1}{4} - \frac{3}{4}$  (e) $1\frac{1}{10} - \frac{3}{10}$

**C15** Prakash's family drink about $1\frac{1}{2}$ pints of milk each day.
How much milk does the family drink in a week?

## D Comparing fractions 1

• Which fraction is the larger in each pair?

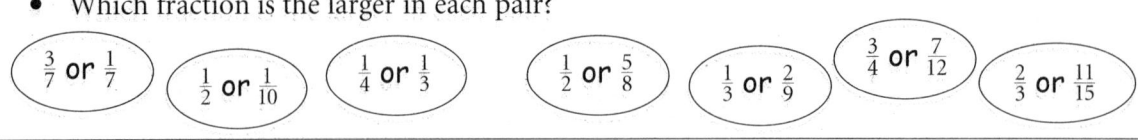

$\frac{3}{7}$ or $\frac{1}{7}$   $\frac{1}{2}$ or $\frac{1}{10}$   $\frac{1}{4}$ or $\frac{1}{3}$   $\frac{1}{2}$ or $\frac{5}{8}$   $\frac{1}{3}$ or $\frac{2}{9}$   $\frac{3}{4}$ or $\frac{7}{12}$   $\frac{2}{3}$ or $\frac{11}{15}$

**D1** Write down the larger fraction in each pair.
(a) $\frac{1}{3}$ and $\frac{2}{3}$ (b) $\frac{1}{2}$ and $\frac{1}{4}$ (c) $\frac{1}{3}$ and $\frac{1}{5}$ (d) $\frac{2}{3}$ and $\frac{2}{6}$

**D2** Brooke and Greg are each given a chocolate bar.
Brooke eats $\frac{1}{2}$ of her bar.
Greg eats $\frac{3}{8}$ of his bar.
Who has eaten the most chocolate?

**D3** For each pair of fractions, write down the smaller fraction and the letter that goes with it. What word do you make?

| $\frac{5}{6}$ | $\frac{1}{2}$ |
|---|---|
| M | P |

| $\frac{3}{12}$ | $\frac{1}{3}$ |
|---|---|
| A | O |

| $\frac{7}{20}$ | $\frac{1}{4}$ |
|---|---|
| S | R |

| $\frac{2}{15}$ | $\frac{1}{5}$ |
|---|---|
| K | T |

**D4** Write down two different fractions that lie between $\frac{1}{8}$ and $\frac{3}{4}$.

**D5** Twins Poppy and Daniel each have identical birthday cakes.
Poppy and her friends eat $\frac{2}{3}$ of her cake.
Daniel and his friends eat $\frac{7}{12}$ of his cake.
Which group has eaten more cake?

**D6** For each pair or fractions, write down the larger fraction and the letter that goes with it. What word do you make?

| $\frac{7}{9}$ | $\frac{2}{3}$ |
|---|---|
| C | B |

| $\frac{2}{5}$ | $\frac{3}{10}$ |
|---|---|
| R | L |

| $\frac{3}{4}$ | $\frac{7}{8}$ |
|---|---|
| I | A |

| $\frac{5}{16}$ | $\frac{3}{8}$ |
|---|---|
| S | M |

| $\frac{5}{7}$ | $\frac{9}{14}$ |
|---|---|
| P | S |

**D7** Write down a fraction that lies between $\frac{3}{4}$ and $\frac{14}{16}$.

**D8** Write each set of fractions in order of size, starting with the smallest.
(a) $\frac{1}{2}$  $\frac{1}{5}$  $\frac{1}{4}$ (b) $\frac{2}{5}$  $\frac{1}{10}$  $\frac{1}{5}$ (c) $\frac{1}{3}$  $\frac{4}{9}$  $\frac{1}{6}$

**D9** Write the fractions $\frac{4}{5}$, $\frac{11}{20}$, $\frac{1}{4}$, $\frac{9}{10}$ in ascending order.

**D10** (a) Copy and complete: (i) $\frac{5}{6} = \frac{\blacksquare}{30}$ (ii) $\frac{7}{10} = \frac{\blacksquare}{30}$

(b) Use the results of part (a) to decide which fraction is larger, $\frac{5}{6}$ or $\frac{7}{10}$?

66 • 25 Calculating with fractions 1

## E Calculating 2

- Can you work these out?

  $\frac{3}{7} + \frac{1}{7}$     $\frac{1}{2} + \frac{1}{8}$     $\frac{1}{3} - \frac{2}{9}$     $\frac{3}{4} - \frac{1}{12}$     $\frac{2}{3} + \frac{5}{6}$

**E1** Work these out.
(a) $\frac{1}{2} + \frac{1}{4}$   (b) $\frac{1}{2} - \frac{1}{4}$   (c) $\frac{1}{4} + \frac{1}{8}$   (d) $\frac{1}{2} - \frac{1}{8}$   (e) $\frac{1}{5} + \frac{1}{10}$

**E2** Work these out.
Give your answers as mixed numbers.
(a) $\frac{1}{2} + \frac{3}{4}$   (b) $\frac{1}{2} + \frac{5}{8}$   (c) $1\frac{1}{2} + \frac{1}{4}$   (d) $2\frac{3}{4} - \frac{1}{2}$   (e) $1\frac{1}{4} - \frac{1}{8}$

**E3** Work these out.
Simplify your answers.
(a) $\frac{1}{2} + \frac{1}{10}$   (b) $\frac{1}{5} + \frac{3}{10}$   (c) $\frac{1}{2} + \frac{1}{6}$   (d) $\frac{1}{2} - \frac{1}{6}$   (e) $\frac{1}{2} - \frac{3}{10}$

**E4** David and Sue share a bar of chocolate.

David eats $\frac{2}{5}$ of the bar.
Sue eats $\frac{1}{10}$ of the bar.

What fraction of the bar have they eaten altogether?

**E5** Work these out.
Simplify your answers where possible.
(a) $\frac{2}{3} + \frac{1}{6}$   (b) $\frac{3}{4} - \frac{1}{8}$   (c) $\frac{1}{4} + \frac{1}{12}$   (d) $\frac{2}{3} - \frac{5}{12}$   (e) $\frac{3}{5} - \frac{1}{10}$

**E6** Work these out.
Give your answers as mixed numbers and simplify them where possible.
(a) $\frac{11}{14} + \frac{2}{7}$   (b) $\frac{1}{2} + \frac{5}{6}$   (c) $\frac{2}{3} + \frac{5}{6}$   (d) $\frac{1}{3} + \frac{7}{9}$   (e) $1\frac{3}{4} - \frac{3}{8}$

**\*E7** The sketch below shows the positions of three villages along a country road.

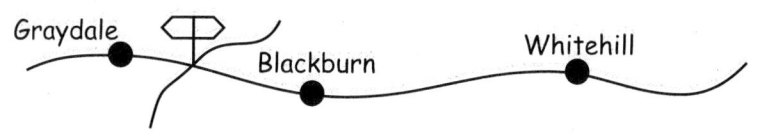

Graydale    Blackburn    Whitehill

This signpost is at the crossroads between Graydale and Blackburn.
It shows some distances in miles.

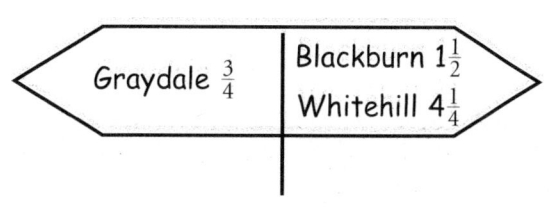

Graydale $\frac{3}{4}$ | Blackburn $1\frac{1}{2}$ | Whitehill $4\frac{1}{4}$

What is the distance along the road
(a) from Graydale to Blackburn   (b) from Graydale to Whitehill
(c) from Blackburn to Whitehill

## F Comparing fractions 2

Dean wants to compare $\frac{2}{3}$ and $\frac{4}{7}$.

He writes out a set of equivalent fractions for both of them.

$\frac{2}{3} = \frac{4}{6} = \frac{6}{9} = \frac{8}{12} = \frac{10}{15} = \frac{12}{18} = \boxed{\frac{14}{21}} = \frac{16}{24} =$

$\frac{4}{7} = \frac{8}{14} = \boxed{\frac{12}{21}} = \frac{16}{28} = \frac{20}{35} =$

He circles the first pair of fractions with the same denominator.

So $\frac{4}{7}$ is smaller than $\frac{2}{3}$.

$\frac{12}{21}$ is smaller than $\frac{14}{21}$ so $\frac{4}{7}$ is smaller than $\frac{2}{3}$.

**F1** Dean has written down sets of equivalent fractions for $\frac{4}{5}$ and $\frac{3}{4}$.

$\frac{4}{5} = \frac{8}{10} = \frac{12}{15} = \frac{16}{20} = \frac{20}{25} =$

$\frac{3}{4} = \frac{6}{8} = \frac{9}{12} = \frac{12}{16} = \frac{15}{20} =$

Which fraction is smaller, $\frac{4}{5}$ or $\frac{3}{4}$? Explain how you decided.

**F2** For each pair or fractions, write down the larger fraction and the letter that goes with it. What word do you make?

| $\frac{1}{3}$ | $\frac{2}{5}$ |
|---|---|
| T | M |

| $\frac{3}{4}$ | $\frac{2}{3}$ |
|---|---|
| I | A |

| $\frac{7}{10}$ | $\frac{3}{4}$ |
|---|---|
| S | L |

| $\frac{2}{5}$ | $\frac{3}{7}$ |
|---|---|
| K | L |

**F3** Work out which of the fractions $\frac{3}{5}$ or $\frac{2}{3}$ is larger. Show all your working.

**F4** Arrange these fractions in ascending order.

$\frac{5}{8}$  $\frac{2}{3}$  $\frac{1}{2}$

**F5** Arrange these fractions in ascending order.

$\frac{2}{3}$  $\frac{2}{5}$  $\frac{1}{3}$  $\frac{3}{5}$

**F6** Arrange these fractions in ascending order.

$\frac{1}{2}$  $\frac{1}{4}$  $\frac{2}{5}$  $\frac{1}{10}$  $\frac{3}{5}$

*__F7__ Find a fraction that lies between $\frac{3}{5}$ and $\frac{5}{9}$.

*__F8__ Find two different fractions that lie between $\frac{1}{3}$ and $\frac{1}{5}$.

## G Calculating 3

Dean wants to work out $\frac{2}{5} + \frac{1}{4}$.

He writes out a set of equivalent fractions for both of them.

$$\frac{2}{5} = \frac{4}{10} = \frac{6}{15} = \boxed{\frac{8}{20}} = \frac{10}{25} = \ldots$$

$$\frac{1}{4} = \frac{2}{8} = \frac{3}{12} = \frac{4}{16} = \boxed{\frac{5}{20}} = \frac{6}{24} = \ldots$$

He circles the first pair of fractions with the same denominator.

So $\frac{2}{5} + \frac{1}{4} = \frac{8}{20} + \frac{5}{20}$

$= \frac{13}{20}$

Now he can add them.

Diagrams for $\frac{2}{5} + \frac{1}{4}$.

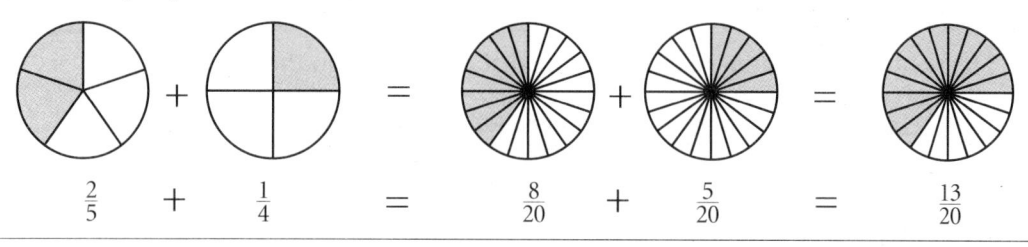

$\frac{2}{5} + \frac{1}{4} = \frac{8}{20} + \frac{5}{20} = \frac{13}{20}$

**G1** Dean has written down sets of equivalent fractions for $\frac{2}{3}$ and $\frac{1}{5}$.

$$\frac{2}{3} = \frac{4}{6} = \frac{6}{9} = \frac{8}{12} = \frac{10}{15} = \frac{12}{18} = \frac{14}{21} = \frac{16}{24} = \ldots$$

$$\frac{1}{5} = \frac{2}{10} = \frac{3}{15} = \frac{4}{20} = \frac{5}{25} = \ldots$$

(a) Write down two fractions, one from each set, that have the same denominator.
(b) Work out $\frac{2}{3} + \frac{1}{5}$.

**G2** (a) Copy and complete to give a set of four equivalent fractions for $\frac{1}{2}$.

$$\frac{1}{2} = \frac{2}{4} = ? = ?$$

(b) Copy and complete to give a set of four equivalent fractions for $\frac{1}{3}$.

$$\frac{1}{3} = ? = ? = ?$$

(c) Work out $\frac{1}{2} + \frac{1}{3}$.

**G3** Work these out.
(a) $\frac{1}{4} + \frac{1}{3}$
(b) $\frac{1}{3} + \frac{2}{5}$
(c) $\frac{1}{4} - \frac{1}{10}$
(d) $\frac{1}{2} - \frac{2}{7}$
(e) $\frac{3}{4} + \frac{2}{3}$

## Test yourself with these questions

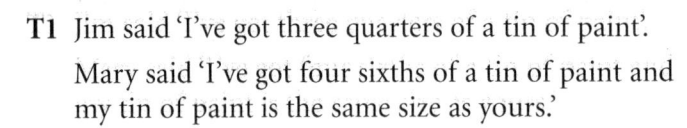

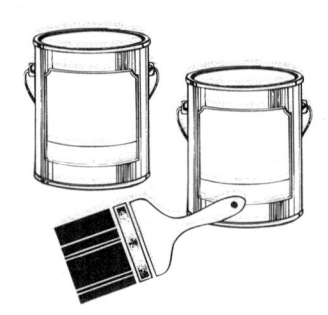

**T1** Jim said 'I've got three quarters of a tin of paint'.

Mary said 'I've got four sixths of a tin of paint and my tin of paint is the same size as yours.'

Who has got the most paint, Mary or Jim?
Explain your answer.

*Edexcel*

**T2** Write the fractions $\frac{5}{8}$, $\frac{3}{4}$, $\frac{17}{24}$, $\frac{7}{12}$ in ascending order.

*Edexcel*

**T3** Arrange these fractions in ascending order.

$\frac{1}{2}$, $\frac{3}{4}$, $\frac{1}{3}$, $\frac{2}{3}$, $\frac{1}{4}$

*Edexcel*

**T4** Write $\frac{17}{5}$ as a mixed number.

**T5** The sketch shows three villages and the distances between them.

Wyford — $3\frac{3}{4}$ miles — Greenhaugh — $1\frac{3}{4}$ miles — Byfield

Work out the total distance along the road between Wyford and Byfield.

**T6** Write down two different fractions that lie between $\frac{1}{2}$ and $\frac{1}{4}$.

*Edexcel*

**T7** A sheet of plastic $\frac{1}{2}$ inch thick is stuck to a wooden framework $\frac{3}{4}$ inch thick to make a working surface.

Find the total thickness of the working surface.

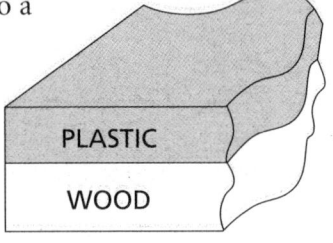

*OCR*

**T8** Alec's cat eats $\frac{2}{3}$ of a tin of Korky each day.
What is the least number of tins Alec needs to buy to feed his cat for 7 days?

*AQA(NEAB) 1998*

**T9** Work these out.

(a) $\frac{1}{4} \times 8$  (b) $2 - \frac{7}{8}$  (c) $\frac{1}{3} - \frac{1}{5}$  (d) $\frac{2}{3} + \frac{1}{12}$

# 26 Substitution

You will revise
- substituting numbers into formulas and expressions
- using formulas and expressions with brackets

This work will help you to learn
- how to substitute decimals, fractions and negative numbers into formulas
- how to form expressions and formulas

## A Review

**A1** Work out each of these. Do them in your head if you can.
(a) $2 + 3 \times 4$
(b) $2 \times (3 + 4)$
(c) $2 \times 3 + 4$
(d) $(2 + 3) \times 4$

**A2** Find the four pairs that give the same answers here.

| A | B | C | D | E | F | G | H |
|---|---|---|---|---|---|---|---|
| $6 + 4 \times 5$ | $6 \times (2 + 7)$ | $8 \times 3 + 5$ | $(6 + 4) \times 5$ | $6 \times 4 + 5$ | $6 + 2 \times 10$ | $(8 + 2) \times 5$ | $6 \times (4 + 5)$ |

**A3** Work out the value of the expressions below, when $a = 2$ and $b = 3$.
(a) $2a + b$
(b) $2(a + b)$
(c) $a + 2b$
(d) $a + b^2$

**A4** When $p = 4$ and $q = 5$,
(a) Which is smaller, $p + 999$ or $q + 999$?
(b) Which is bigger, $p^2$ or $3q$?

**A5** Do these in your head.
(a) $10 - 0.1$
(b) $10 - 2 \times 0.2$
(c) $10 - 10 \times 0.2$
(d) $10 \times (0.2 + 0.3)$

**A6** Work out
(a) $2 \times {}^-3$
(b) $5 - 10$
(c) $10 - 5 \times 6$
(d) $4 \times (3 - 5)$

**\*A7**

| T | W | A | F | R | U | G | E | L | A |
|---|---|---|---|---|---|---|---|---|---|
| ⁻6 | 1 | ⁻10 | 12 | 8 | 2.4 | 3.7 | 9.4 | 10 | 2 |

Work out each of the expressions below when $r = 4$, $s = 0.3$, $t = {}^-2$ and $u = 10$. Then use the code above to write a word.

$r - s$   $t + u$   $u - 2s$   $5t$   $t - r$

## B What an expression!

$a = 2, b = 3, c = 6$

| $a + bc$ | $a(b + c)$ | $5a^3$ | $\dfrac{bc}{3a}$ |
|---|---|---|---|
| $= a + b \times c$ | $= a \times (b + c)$ | $= 5 \times a \times a \times a$ | $= \dfrac{b \times c}{3 \times a}$ |
| $= 2 + 3 \times 6$ | $= 2 \times (3 + 6)$ | $= 5 \times 2 \times 2 \times 2$ | $= \dfrac{3 \times 6}{3 \times 2}$ |
| $= 2 + 18$ | $= 2 \times 9$ | $= 5 \times 8$ | $= \dfrac{18}{6} = 3$ |
| $= 20$ | $= 18$ | $= 40$ | |

**B1** Work out these expressions when $a = 2$, $b = 3$ and $c = 5$.
(a) $ab$  (b) $c + ab$  (c) $a(b + c)$  (d) $\frac{1}{2}ca$  (e) $a^2 + b^2$

**B2** Work out when $u = 4$, $v = 8$ and $w = 12$.
(a) $\dfrac{uv}{2}$  (b) $\dfrac{v + w}{u}$  (c) $\dfrac{2w}{v}$  (d) $\dfrac{vw}{u}$  (e) $\dfrac{v^2}{u}$

**B3**

| A | B | C | H | I | K | L | O | R | W |
|---|---|---|---|---|---|---|---|---|---|
| 1 | 30 | 4 | 3 | 24 | 18 | 27 | 13 | 36 | 2 |

Work out each of these expressions when $p = 2$, $q = 3$ and $r = 6$.
Find the letter in the box above.
Unjumble the letters in each part to make the name of a tree.

(a) $p(q+r)$    $p^2 + q^2$    $\dfrac{pq}{r}$

(b) $pqr$    $\dfrac{pq}{2}$    $r(p+q)$    $3p^3$    $\dfrac{4pq}{r}$

(c) $3q^2$    $1 + pr$    $\dfrac{r^2}{2} + q^2$    $q^3 - q$    $\dfrac{r}{q}$    $\dfrac{2r}{pq}$

**B4** Work out these expressions when $d = {-}2$, $e = 3$ and $f = {-}6$.
(a) $de$  (b) $e + f$  (c) $\dfrac{ef}{2}$  (d) $e(d + f)$  (e) $d^2 + f^2$

**B5** When $m = {-}1$, $n = {-}2$ and $p = 8$, there are four matching pairs here. Can you find them?

| A | B | C | D | E | F | G | H |
|---|---|---|---|---|---|---|---|
| $mp$ | $mp - n$ | $2mn - p$ | $n + p$ | $\dfrac{p}{n}$ | $4n$ | $\dfrac{p}{m} - n$ | $-3n$ |

**B6** $R = 3x + 4y$. Work out $R$ when $x = 4$ and $y = {-}2$.

**B7** The expression $n^2 + n + 17$ generates prime numbers for some values of $n$.
Substitute these numbers into this expression.
(a) $n = 4$  (b) $n = {-}3$

OCR

**B8** (a) Find the value of $5x - 2y$ when $x = 3$ and $y = 7$.

(b) Find the value of $xy$ when $x = 13$ and $y = {}^-7$.

AQA 2003 Specimen

**B9** Given that $a = 5$, $b = 8$ and $c = 19$, find the value of

(a) $3a$     (b) $b + 2c$     (c) $b^3$     (d) $\dfrac{c}{a}$     (e) $2(a + b)$

AQA(NEAB) 2000 Specimen

**B10** $x = 2$, $y = {}^-3$ and $z = 4$.

Work out the values of   (a) $5x - y$     (b) $5z^2$.

OCR

**B11** To work out the approximate area of a semi-circle you can use the formula
$$A = \frac{3 \times r \times r}{2}$$
$A$ is the area in cm$^2$, $r$ is the radius in cm.

Work out the approximate area of a semi-circle with a radius of 24 cm.

OCR

**B12** It can be dangerous to give a child an adult's dose of medicine.
There are several formulas which help doctors to give a safe children's dose.

Here is one. It is called Cowling's rule.
$$C = \frac{(A + 1)D}{24}$$
$C$ is the safe dose for a child aged $A$ years. $D$ is the adult dose.

(a) The adult dose for a certain medicine is 30 mg.
Use Cowling's rule to find the safe dose for an eleven year old.

(b) For the same medicine, what dose would Cowling's rule give for a one year old baby?

(c) Why would it be dangerous to use Cowling's rule for someone over 25?
Support your answer with some figures.

OCR

**B13** John uses this rule to change a temperature from °C into °F.

> Multiply the temperature in °C by two and add 30 to the answer.

Use his rule to change

(a) 19°C into °F          (b) ${}^-3$°C into °F

OCR(MEG)

## C Brackets and fractions

$a = 2, b = 3, c = 6$

$c - (a + b)$
$= 6 - (2 + 3)$
$= 6 - 5$
$= 1$

Work out the brackets first

$20 - (4b - a)$
$= 20 - (4 \times 3 - 2)$
$= 20 - (12 - 2)$
$= 20 - 10$
$= 10$

$10 - \dfrac{bc}{a}$
$= 10 - \dfrac{3 \times 6}{2}$
$= 10 - \dfrac{18}{2}$
$= 10 - 9$
$= 1$

**C1** When $r = 4$, $s = 3$ and $t = 5$ which is bigger, $20 - (r + s)$ or $10 + (s + t)$?

**C2** When $a = 1$, $b = 2$ and $c = 4$, work out which is the bigger in each of these pairs.
   (a) $100 - (2b + c)$ or $80 + (5c - b)$
   (b) $20 - (bc + 10)$ or $a + (c - b)$

**C3** Work out each of these when $u = {}^-2$, $v = 2$ and $w = {}^-4$.
   (a) $10 - \dfrac{v}{2}$
   (b) $10 - \dfrac{u+v}{2}$
   (c) $10 - \dfrac{uv}{w}$

**C4** The letters in a formula sometimes stand for fractions.
   (a) Copy and complete this working for when $a = \frac{1}{2}$ and $b = \frac{1}{4}$ in the formula $T = 2 - (a + b)$.
   (b) Work out the value of $T$ when $a = \frac{1}{4}$ and $b = \frac{3}{4}$.

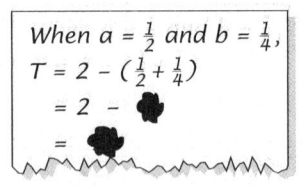

When $a = \frac{1}{2}$ and $b = \frac{1}{4}$,
$T = 2 - (\frac{1}{2} + \frac{1}{4})$
$= 2 - \blacklozenge$
$= \blacklozenge$

**C5** Work out the value of each of these when $r = 2$, $s = 4$, $t = \frac{1}{2}$ and $u = \frac{1}{4}$.
   (a) $10 - \frac{1}{2}(r + s)$
   (b) $10 - (t - u)$
   (c) $5 - 4t$
   (d) $5 - 2(r + t)$

**C6** This candle was lit at 2 o'clock.
Its height, $h$, in cm after $t$ hours is given by the formula $h = 20 - 4t$.
   (a) Find the value of $h$ when $t = 0$.
   (b) How high will the candle be after 1 hour?
   (c) How high will it be at 4 o'clock?
   (d) How high was it after $\frac{1}{2}$ hour?
   (e) What is its height at a quarter past 2?
   (f) At what time will the candle burn out?

**C7** The top speed, $S$, in m.p.h. of David's veteran car is $S = 60 - (3n + 2m)$.
$n$ is the number of adult passengers and $m$ the number of children.
What is its top speed when carrying
   (a) 3 adults and 1 child
   (b) 5 adults
   (c) 4 adults and 2 children

## D Decimals

**D1** Natasha uses this formula to work out her total pay.

*Total pay = Rate per hour × Number of hours + Bonus*

Her rate per hour is £3.50. She works for 35 hours. She has a bonus of £5.50.
Work out her total pay.

Edexcel

**D2** Work out the value of $P$ in each of the following formulas
when $a = 1.6$ and $b = 2.5$

(a) $P = 2a + 4b$     (b) $P = 5(a + b)$     (c) $P = \dfrac{a}{2} + 5b$

**D3** Work out each of these expressions when $l = 2.4$, $m = 3.6$ and $n = 4.5$

(a) $4mn$   (b) $n(l + m)$   (c) $\dfrac{lm}{n}$   (d) $\dfrac{l+m}{5}$   (e) $l(5m + 4n)$

**D4** A formula to estimate the number of rolls of wallpaper, $R$, for a room is

$$R = \dfrac{ph}{5}$$ where $p$ is the perimeter of the room in metres and $h$ is the height of the room in metres.

The perimeter of Carol's bedroom is 15.5 m and it is 2.25 m high.

How many rolls of wallpaper will she have to buy?

AQA 1999

**D5** An exact formula to convert between °C and °F is $C = \dfrac{5(F - 32)}{9}$

where $C$ is the temperature in °C and $F$ the temperature in °F.

Use the formula to convert these temperatures into Centigrade.
Give your answers to the nearest degree.

(a) 80°F     (b) 150°F     (c) ⁻35°F     (d) 19.5°F

**D6** Answer this question on sheet P173.

**D7** The area, $A$, of a trapezium is given by the formula
$$A = \dfrac{h(a+b)}{2}$$

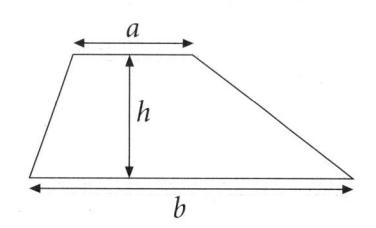

Calculate the area of a trapezium for which
$a = 1.5$ metres, $b = 2$ metres and $h = 1.2$ metres.

Include the units in your answer.

**D8** Work out the areas of these trapeziums.
You may not need to use all the measurements.

(a) 0.6 m, 0.5 m, 2.5 m

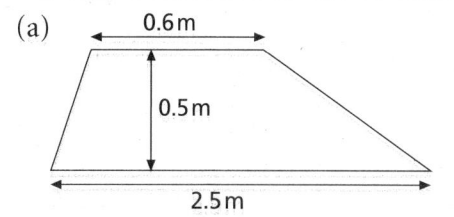

(b) 5 cm, 7 cm, 6 cm, 10 cm

26 Substitution • 75

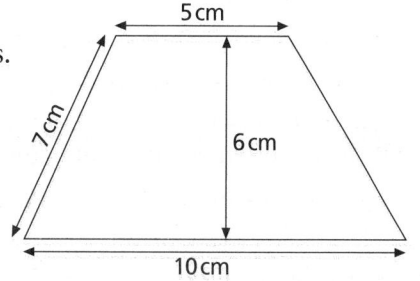

## E Forming and solving equations

The triangle ABC is isosceles, and CA is $x$ cm long.
The base, BC, is 6 cm less than CA.

- Write down an expression for the length of BC.
- Write an expression for the perimeter of triangle ABC.
- If the perimeter is 21 cm, work out the length of each side of the triangle.

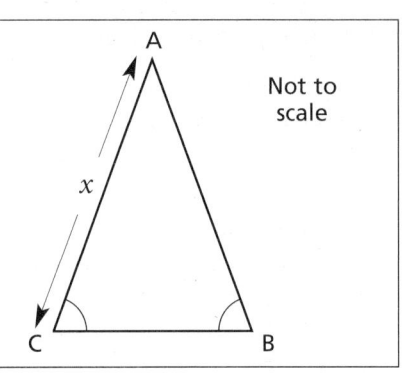

Not to scale

**E1** For the formula $y = 3x + 5$, find
  (a) $y$ when $x = 8$
  (b) $y$ when $x = {}^-8$
  (c) $x$ when $y = 32$

**E2** For the formula $l = 5r - 8$, find
  (a) $l$ when $r = 6$
  (b) $l$ when $r = 1.8$
  (c) $r$ when $l = 27$

**E3** Sue is an author. The formula for her weekly wage, £$W$, is $W = 2.5P + 50$ where $P$ is the number of pages she writes.
  (a) One week she writes 50 pages. What is her wage?
  (b) She gets paid £170 one week. How many pages did she write?

**E4** $$C = 180R + 2000$$
The formula gives the capacity, $C$ litres, of a tank needed to supply water to $R$ hotel rooms.
  (a) $R = 5$. Work out the value of $C$.
  (b) $C = 3440$. Work out the value of $R$.
  (c) A water tank has a capacity of 3200 litres. Work out the greatest number of hotel rooms it could supply.
  
  Edexcel

**E5** The width of this rectangle is $a$ centimetres. The rectangle is twice as long as it is wide.
  (a) Write down an expression for the length of the rectangle.
  (b) Write down an expression for the perimeter. Simplify your expression as far as you can.
  (c) The perimeter of the rectangle is 30 cm. Write down an equation in $a$ and solve it.
  What are the dimensions of the rectangle?

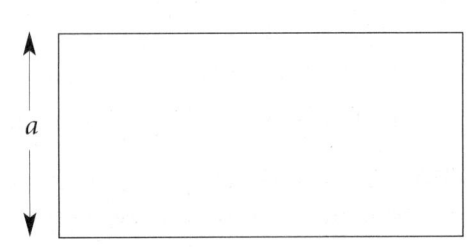

**E6** Use the formula $s = 2t + 32$ to work out the following.
  (a) Find $s$ when $t = {}^-7$.
  (b) Find $t$ when $s = 40$.
  (c) Show how to use approximation to estimate the value of $s$ when $t = 18.9$
      
      AQA(SEG) 1998 Specimen

**E7** The length of a rectangle is $y$ cm.
The width of the rectangle is 3 cm less than the length. 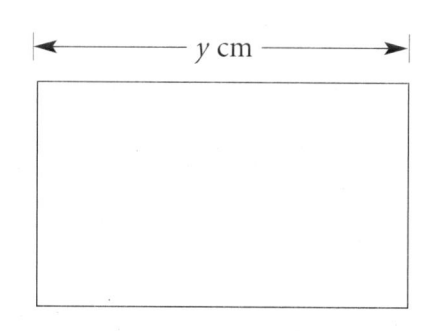
  (a) Write an expression, in terms of $y$, for the width of the rectangle.
  (b) Write the perimeter in terms of $y$. Give your answer in its simplest form.
  (c) The perimeter of the rectangle is 15 cm. Find the value of $y$.
  
  AQA(SEG) 1998

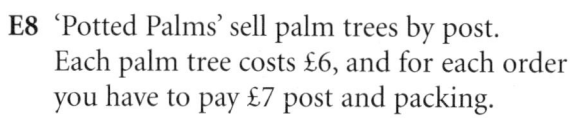

**E8** 'Potted Palms' sell palm trees by post. Each palm tree costs £6, and for each order you have to pay £7 post and packing. 
  (a) What is the total cost of buying 10 palm trees (including post and packing)?
  (b) Write down an expression for the total cost of buying $n$ palm trees.
  (c) Chelsea buys some palm trees. The total bill is £85.
  
  Use your expression from part (b) to write down an equation in $n$ showing this. Solve your equation to find how many palm trees Chelsea bought.

**E9** A shop sells two types of lollipops.
The shop sells Big lollipops at 80p each and Small lollipops at 60p each.

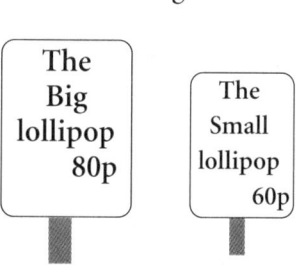

Henry buys $x$ Big lollipops.
  (a) Write down an expression, in terms of $x$, for the cost of Henry's lollipops.
  
  Lucy buys $r$ Big lollipops and $t$ Small lollipops.
  (b) Write down an expression, in terms of $r$ and $t$, for the total cost of Lucy's lollipops.
  
  The cost of $g$ Big lollipops and 2 Small lollipops is £10.80.
  (c) Write this as an equation in terms of $g$.
  (d) Use your equation to find the value of $g$.
  
  Edexcel

26 Substitution

**Test yourself with these questions**

**T1** Work out these when $a = 3$, $b = 4$ and $c = 6$.
 (a) $bc$
 (b) $5c - ab$
 (c) $a(c - b)$
 (d) $\dfrac{b + c}{2}$
 (e) $\dfrac{bc}{a}$

**T2** Work out these when $p = {}^-1$, $q = 2$ and $r = {}^-3$.
 (a) $p + q$
 (b) $qr$
 (c) $\dfrac{pq}{2}$
 (d) $q(p + r)$
 (e) $p^2 + q^2$

**T3** Work out the value of each of these when $e = 2$, $f = 4$, $g = \frac{1}{8}$ and $h = \frac{1}{4}$.
 (a) $4 - 4h$
 (b) $14 - (e + f)$
 (c) $e(h - g)$
 (d) $1 - (g + h)$

**T4** A formula for the area, $A$, of a rhombus is
$$A = \dfrac{ab}{2}$$
where $a$ and $b$ are the lengths of the two diagonals.

 (a) What is the area of a rhombus whose diagonals measure 12 cm and 6 cm?

Work out the areas of these rhombuses (you may not need all the measurements).

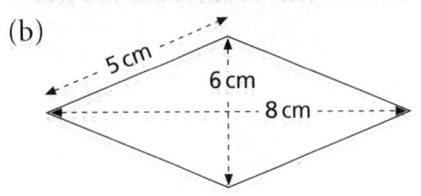

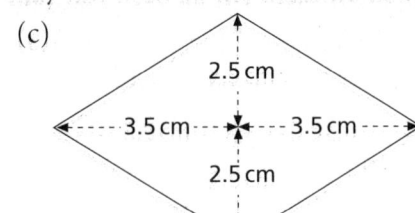

 (b) 5 cm, 6 cm, 8 cm

 (c) 2.5 cm, 3.5 cm, 3.5 cm, 2.5 cm

**T5** For the formula $p = 4q + 5$, find
 (a) $p$ when $q = 5$
 (b) $p$ when $q = 1.5$
 (c) $q$ when $p = 33$

**T6** Jan breeds fish. The amount she charges for a fish, £$P$, is $P = 2l + 6$ where $l$ is the length of the fish in inches.
 (a) How much will she charge for a 12 inch fish?
 (b) For one fish she charged £22. How long was the fish?

**T7** The side AB of this triangle is $x$ cm long.
BC is 3 cm longer than AB, and CA is 1 cm shorter.
 (a) Write down an expression for the length of BC.
 (b) Write down an expression for the length of CA.
 (c) Write down and simplify an expression for the perimeter of triangle ABC.
 (d) The perimeter of the triangle is 44 cm. Use your answer to part (c) to write down an equation in $x$.
 (e) Solve your equation and write down the lengths of the three sides.

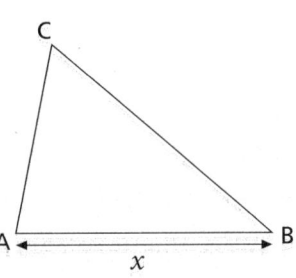

# Review 3

1  For each of these patterns write down
   (i) the order of rotation symmetry
   (ii) the fraction of the shape that is shaded

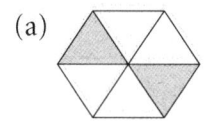

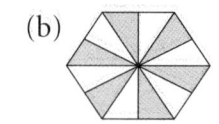

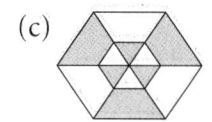

   (a)   (b)   (c)

2  A fish tank is 60 cm long and 40 cm wide.
   It is filled with water to a depth of 30 cm.

   Calculate the volume of water in the tank in m$^3$.

3  This diagram shows some patterns made from tiles.

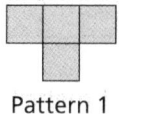

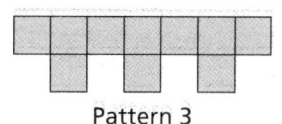

   Pattern 1    Pattern 2    Pattern 3

   (a) Copy and complete the table.

   | Pattern number | 1 | 2 | 3 | 4 | 5 | 6 |
   |---|---|---|---|---|---|---|
   | Number of tiles | 4 | 7 | 10 | | | |

   (b) Which pattern can be made with exactly 25 tiles?
   (c) How many tiles are there in pattern 10?
       Explain how you can work this out without drawing a diagram.

4  A CD has a diameter of 12 cm.
   (a) Calculate the circumference of the CD.
   (b) Calculate the area of the CD.

   Give your answers to 1 decimal place.

5  Darren left home at 8:30 a.m. to drive to a meeting.
   He arrived at the meeting at 10:15 a.m.
   He had travelled a distance of 98 miles.

   Calculate the average speed for his journey.

6  Write these fractions in order of size, starting with the smallest.

   $\frac{1}{2}$   $\frac{3}{10}$   $\frac{2}{5}$   $\frac{7}{20}$

7 There are 25 students in a class.
The data below shows their scores in a Geography exam.

|  |  |  |  |  |  |  |  |  |  |
|--|--|--|--|--|--|--|--|--|--|
| 42 | 47 | 51 | 65 | 73 | 31 | 46 | 50 | 58 | 35 |
| 48 | 63 | 68 | 70 | 52 | 66 | 78 | 46 | 51 | 74 |
| 58 | 44 | 57 | 64 | 69 |  |  |  |  |  |

(a) Copy and complete this stem and leaf table for these results.

Geography score

3 |
4 |
5 |
6 |
7 |

Stem = 10 marks

(b) Find the median and range of Geography scores.

8 Here is the rule for finding a term in a sequence.

> Multiply the previous term by 2 and subtract 3

The first three terms in the sequence are 6, 9 and 15.
Work out the next two terms.

9 Copy this shape and point X onto centimetre squared paper.
Draw an enlargement of the shape, scale factor 3, centre X.

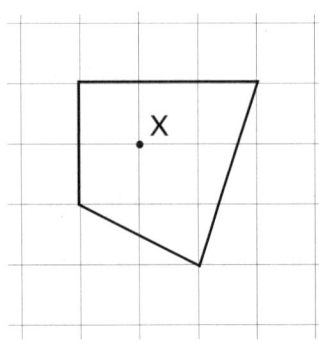

10 Each day he is at school, Luke drinks $\frac{1}{3}$ of a pint of milk.
How much milk does he drink in a week, from Monday to Friday?

11 Work out the value of these when $r = 2$, $s = {^-}3$ and $t = {^-}4$.

(a) $rs$ 
(b) $\frac{st}{2}$ 
(c) $r(s - t)$ 
(d) $4r - t^2$

12 Paula uses this formula to work out how much to charge for a repair job
$$C = 25h + 20$$
where $C$ is the charge in pounds and $h$ is the number of hours she works.

(a) How much would Paula charge for a job which takes 3 hours?
(b) How much would she charge if the job takes $2\frac{1}{2}$ hours?

# 27 Probability

You will revise
- how to find the probability in simple situations
- how to use lists and grids to record possible outcomes

You will learn
- how to find probabilities from an experiment
- how to calculate probabilities using decimals

## A Simply chance

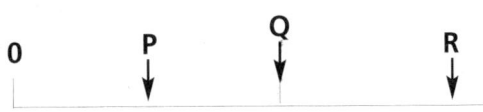

**A1** Here is a probability scale.

Which of the arrows above could represent the probability of

(a) getting a head when a coin is flipped

(b) choosing a heart from a pack of cards with the same number of hearts, clubs, spades and diamonds

(c) choosing a red sweet from a bag with 16 red sweets and 4 yellow ones

**A2** A set of cards has the numbers 1, 3, 4, 6, 8, 10 on them.
A card is chosen at random.

What is the probability of choosing

(a) the number 10      (b) an even number

(c) a number less than 7      (d) the number 9

**A3** When you spin the arrow on this spinner it can stop on black, grey or white.

What is the probability it stops on

(a) white      (b) grey

(c) black      (d) not grey

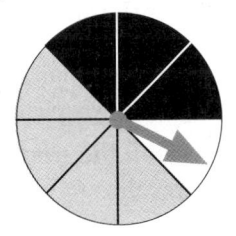

**A4** For each of the bags below find the probability of

(i) choosing a black bead      (ii) choosing a white bead

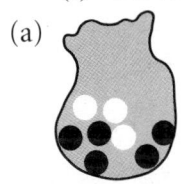

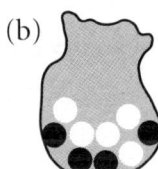

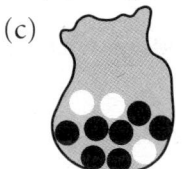

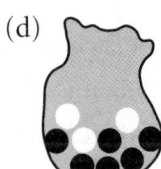

(a)      (b)      (c)      (d)

27 Probability • 81

## B  Off the table

**Old Blue Eyes**

A class is carrying out a survey on their hair colour and eye colour.
They produce these results.

| Hair colour | Frequency |
|---|---|
| Brown | 16 |
| Black | 8 |
| Blonde | 5 |
| Auburn | 1 |
| Total | 30 |

| Eye colour | Boys | Girls |
|---|---|---|
| Blue | 3 | 5 |
| Brown | 9 | 13 |

The names of the students in the class are written on pieces of paper and placed in a bag.
If a name is chosen at random what is the probability that the person chosen

- has blonde hair
- is a boy
- has blue eyes

**B1** A class carries out a survey on colours of cars in the school car park.

This table shows their results.

(a) How many cars did they survey altogether?

(b) If a car is chosen at random from those in the survey, what is the probability that the car

  (i) is blue (ii) is white
  (iii) is not red (iv) is brown

| Car colour | Frequency |
|---|---|
| White | 15 |
| Black | 6 |
| Silver | 8 |
| Red | 12 |
| Blue | 3 |
| Green | 6 |

**B2** If you push back your hair your hairline is either straight or a 'V' shape.
The 'V' shape is called a 'widow's peak.

Kaya carried out a survey on the students in her class. These are her results.

(a) How many students were in Kaya's class?

(b) How many students had a widow's peak?

(c) What is the probability that a student, chosen at random, has a widow's peak?

(d) If a student is chosen at random, what is the probability that

  (i) the student is male (ii) the student is female
  (iii) the student has a straight hairline

| Hairline | Straight | Widow's peak |
|---|---|---|
| Male | 9 | 6 |
| Female | 6 | 4 |

## C Listing outcomes

**C1** A class has to choose two students to appear on a TV chat show.
The names of three boys Aaron, Baljit and Colin are written on pieces of paper.
The names of four girls Donna, Evelyn, Fatima and Gill are also written on pieces of paper.

A boy and a girl are then chosen at random.

(a) Copy and complete this list of possible choices.
(b) How many different choices are there altogether?
(c) What is the probability that
   (i) Baljit and Fatima are chosen
   (ii) Aaron is one of those chosen
   (iii) Evelyn is not chosen

| Boy | Girl |
|---|---|
| Aaron | Donna |
| Aaron | Evelyn |
| Aaron | Fatima |

**C2** Two fair spinners with red, blue and green on them are spun.

(a) Make a list of all the possible outcomes.
(b) Find the probability that
   (i) both point to red
   (ii) both point to the same colour
   (iii) they point to different colours

**C3** A game is played with two sets of cards.

Set A have the numbers 1, 2 and 3 on them.
Set B have the numbers 4, 5, 6 and 7 on them.

A card is chosen from each set at random.
The scores on the two cards chosen are added.

Set A: 1 2 3
Set B: 4 5 6 7

(a) Copy and complete this grid to show all the possible total scores.

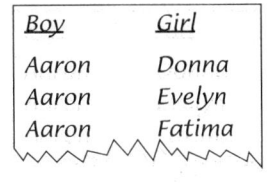

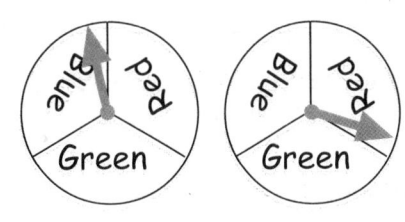

|  | + | 4 | 5 | 6 | 7 |
|---|---|---|---|---|---|
| Set A | 1 |   |   |   | 8 |
|  | 2 | 6 |   |   |   |
|  | 3 |   |   |   |   |

Set B

(b) Find the probability that the total score is
   (i) 6
   (ii) 8
   (iii) more than 8
   (iv) less than 8
   (v) more than 4

## D Experiments

### Going potty

If you hold up a cottage cheese or similar shaped carton at nose height and drop it, it can land in one of three ways.

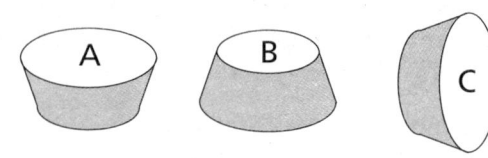

Which way is it most likely to land?
Which way is the least likely?

- Drop a carton 10 times and record how many times it lands each way.
  Write down the probability it lands each of the ways A, B and C.

- Now drop the carton another 15 times and record the results for the 25 drops in total.
  Write down the probability it lands each of the ways A, B and C using the 25 results.

- Finally drop the carton another 25 times and record the results.
  Write down the probability it lands each of the ways A, B and C using the 50 results.

Compare your results with others in the class – do you get roughly the same answers?

Which are the most accurate estimates of the probabilities for each of the ways?

Gavin has dropped a pot 25 times and found that it landed way A 6 times.

Gavin finds the probability of landing way A as a decimal.

Probability of landing way A = $\frac{6}{25} = \frac{24}{100} = 0.24$ (×4)

- After 50 times Gavin's pot had landed way A 14 times.
  What is this as a decimal?

- Is this a higher or lower probability than after 25 times?

**D1** Jenni is doing an experiment dropping pieces of toast to see if they land 'jam-down' or 'jam-up'.

(a) After 25 tries the toast has landed 'jam-down' 17 times.
Copy and complete this statement:

After 25 tries the probability of the toast landing 'jam-down' = $\frac{17}{25} = \frac{\phantom{00}}{100} = 0.\phantom{00}$

(b) After 50 tries the toast has landed 'jam-down' 36 times.
  (i) Write the probability of landing 'jam-down' as a fraction.
  (ii) Write the probability as a decimal.

**D2** After 100 tries the toast has landed 'jam-down' 69 times.

(a) Write this probability as a decimal.

(b) Which of Jenni's results is likely to be the most accurate estimate of the probability of landing 'jam-down'?

**D3** Lisa drops a drawing pin and notes if it lands point up.
Write these probabilities as decimals
(a) $\frac{2}{5}$  (b) $\frac{3}{10}$  (c) $\frac{8}{20}$  (d) $\frac{13}{25}$  (e) $\frac{23}{50}$

**D4** Kirsten is recording which direction cars go when they reach a junction in the road near her school.
She writes right (R) or left (L) for each car.

Here are her results in order:

R R L R L R R L L L     R R R L L R L R L R     L R L L R R R R R L
L R L R L R R R L R     R L R R R L L R R  R

(a) Estimate the probability of a car turning right after these number of results (write your answer as a decimal)
  (i) after the first 10 cars have passed
  (ii) after 20 cars have passed
  (iii) after 50 cars have passed

(b) Kirsten's local Council have also carried out a survey at this junction. They observed over 1000 cars and say that the probability of a car turning right is 0.62.
Do you think Kirsten's results agree with this?

(c) Whose result do you think is more accurate, Kirsten's or the Council's?

**D5** Anwar is carrying out an experiment dropping a spoon.
He records whether the spoon lands up or down.

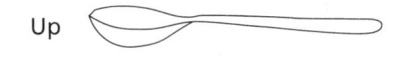

(a) Copy and complete this table of Anwar's results.

| Number of drops | 5 | 10 | 20 | 25 | 50 | 100 |
|---|---|---|---|---|---|---|
| Number of times landed up | 3 | 7 | 11 | 15 | 32 | 63 |
| Probability | 0.6 | 0.7 | | | | |

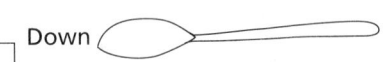

(b) Use the table to copy and complete this graph.
(c) What do you think would be a reasonable estimate for the probability of a spoon landing up?

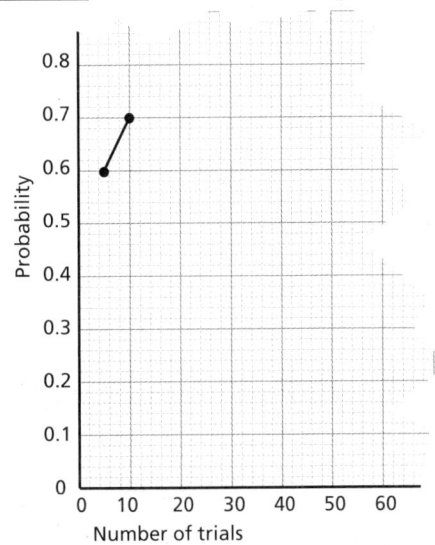

27 Probability • 85

# E Theory or experiment?

**Bear necessities**

Sheet P174 has two sets of cards A and B.
Two players each take one set of cards.

Each player shuffles their pack and turns a card over at random.

Set A

Bear beats running man.
Rifle beats bear.
Any other combination is a draw.

Set B

Is the game fair?

**Chinese dice**

A set of Chinese dice consists of three dice numbered:-

A: 6 6 2 2 2 2    B: 5 5 5 5 1 1    C: 4 4 4 3 3 3

One player chooses a dice to play with.

Then the second player chooses a dice to play with.

Both players roll their dice and the highest score wins.

It is said that by choosing their dice second a player can have a higher chance of winning. Is this true?

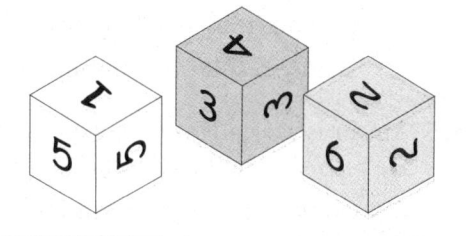

**E1** Shakib makes a spinner with the colours red, blue, green, yellow and white on it.

(a) If the spinner is fair, what is the probability of it pointing to blue?

Write this as a decimal.

(b) Shakib thinks his spinner might be biased.
He spins the spinner 50 times and records the results.

Copy and complete this table.

| Colour | Red | Blue | Green | Yellow | White |
|---|---|---|---|---|---|
| Frequency | 8 | 13 | 10 | 7 | 12 |
| Estimated Probability | $\frac{8}{50}$ = 0.16 | | | | |

(c) Which colours came up less times than expected?

(d) Which colours came up more than expected?

(e) What could Shakib do to have a better check if his spinner was biased?

86 • 27 Probability

## F Sum to 1

Peter records whether the first 50 pupils who come through the school gate are on foot or not. He estimates that the probability of a pupil chosen at random being on foot is 0.72.

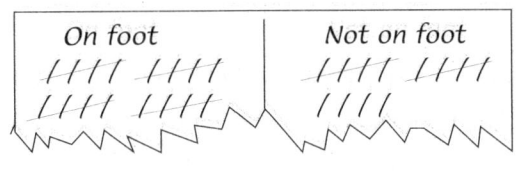

| On foot | Not on foot |
|---|---|
| //// //// //// //// | //// //// //// |

Since the total probability in any situation is 1, the probability the pupil **is not** on foot = 1 − 0.72 = 0.28.

**F1** In Peter's class the probability of a randomly chosen student being a boy is 0.56.

What is the probability of a randomly chosen student being a girl?

**F2** Neeta's grandfather gives her a coin that is biased.
After testing a large number of times she estimates the probability of tails is 0.35.

What is the probability of heads?

**F3** John makes a biased spinner with black, white and grey sections.
After many trials he estimates the probability of black = 0.41 and the probability of white = 0.34.

What is the probability of grey?

**F4** Isobel is testing whether a normal six-sided dice is biased.
These are some of her results.

| Number | 1 | 2 | 3 | 4 | 5 | 6 |
|---|---|---|---|---|---|---|
| Probability | 0.15 | 0.19 | 0.13 | 0.10 | 0.17 | |

(a) What is the probability of getting a 6?
(b) What is the probability of getting a 7?

**F5** There are black, blue and red pens in a box and one is to be chosen at random.
The probability of choosing black is 0.5 and blue 0.3.

(a) What is the probability of choosing a red pen?
(b) There are 80 pens in the box altogether.
How many of these are black?

**F6** Ewan is carrying out a probability experiment with a large bag containing red, white and black beads.
He calculates that the probability of getting red is 0.27, white 0.42 and black 0.28.

Explain why these answers cannot be right.

**F7** Another student doing the same experiment as Ewan calculates the probability of red as 0.31, white 0.48 and black 0.24.

Explain why these answers cannot be right.

## G Mixed questions

**G1** Find the probability, as a fraction, of

(a) getting a number less than 3 on an ordinary six-sided dice

(b) picking an orange sweet at random from a bag containing 3 orange, 5 strawberry and 2 blackcurrant sweets

(c) picking an even number card from cards with the numbers 1 to 7 on them

**G2** In a game a fair spinner is used with numbers 1, 2, 3, 4, 5.
The spinner is spun once.

(a) What is the probability it lands on an odd number?

(b) What is the probability it lands on a number greater than 5?

Two of these spinners are spun and the scores are subtracted.

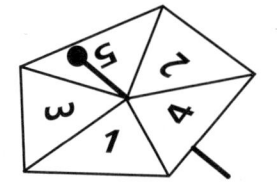

(c) Copy and complete this table showing the **differences**.

|  | Differences |  |  |  |  |
|---|---|---|---|---|---|
| **Second spinner** 5 |  |  |  |  |  |
| 4 |  |  |  |  |  |
| 3 | 2 | 1 |  |  |  |
| 2 | 1 | 0 | 1 |  |  |
| 1 | 0 | 1 | 2 | 3 | 4 |
|  | 1 | 2 | 3 | 4 | 5 |
|  | First spinner |  |  |  |  |

(d) Use the grid to find the probability that

(i) both spinners show the same number

(ii) the difference is 1

(iii) the difference is more than 1

**G3** (a) A national survey of 1000 people found the probability of being left-handed is 0.1. What is the probability of being right-handed?

(b) This table shows the results of a class survey of 25 children.

|  | Boys | Girls |
|---|---|---|
| Left-handed | 3 | 5 |
| Right-handed | 9 | 13 |

A child is chosen at random from the class.
What is the probability that the child is left-handed?

(c) Which of the two surveys, in (a) or (b), is likely to be more reliable?
Give a reason for your answer.

*AQA 2003 Specimen*

**G4** There are blue, red and yellow discs in a bag.
When a disc is picked out at random, the probability of it being red is 0.4, and the probability of it being blue is 0.3.

(a) What is the probability of picking a yellow disc?

There are 60 discs in the bag.

(b) Work out how many of them are red.

*OCR*

## Test yourself with these questions

**T1** The table shows information about some cars.

A car is chosen from the list at random.

(a) What is the probability it has a mileage more than 10 000?

(b) What is the probability it is a white Ford?

(c) A Vauxhall car is chosen at random. The probability that it is blue is 0.25.

What is the probability it is **not** blue?

| Make | Colour | Mileage |
|---|---|---|
| Vauxhall | blue | 8 606 |
| Ford | white | 12 214 |
| Vauxhall | white | 5 567 |
| Rover | red | 11 984 |
| Rover | blue | 9 085 |
| Vauxhall | red | 6 984 |
| Ford | blue | 8 763 |
| Vauxhall | white | 14 675 |

AQA(SEG) 1999

**T2** Alan throws a fair coin 600 times.

(a) How many times would you expect to get Heads?

Here is a 5-sided spinner.
Its sides are labelled 1, 2, 3, 4, 5.

Alan spins the spinner and throws a coin.
One possible outcome is (3, Heads)

(b) List all the possible outcomes.

The spinner is biased.
The probability that the spinner will land on each of the numbers 1 to 4 is given in the table.

| Number | 1 | 2 | 3 | 4 | 5 |
|---|---|---|---|---|---|
| Probability | 0.36 | 0.1 | 0.25 | 0.15 | |

Alan spins the spinner once.

(c) (i) Work out the probability the spinner will land on 5.

(ii) Work out the probability the spinner will land on 6.

(iii) Write down the number that the spinner is most likely to land on.  Edexcel

**T3** A bag contains discs of different colours.
In an experiment Murinder took one disc out at random, noted its colour, then put it back into the bag.

He repeated this 50 times.
Here are Murinder's results.

| Colour | Frequency |
|---|---|
| Blue | 10 |
| Green | 12 |
| Yellow | 8 |
| Red | 20 |

Estimate the probability that the next time Murinder takes a disc it will be red.

OCR

# 28 Using a calculator 2

You will revise
- how to round to the nearest integer, to one decimal place and so on

You will learn
- how to use a calculator for complex calculations

## A Rounding: review

**A1** Round to the nearest integer    (a) 46.8   (b) 133.43   (c) 29.57   (d) 37.28

**A2** Round to one decimal place    (a) 3.42   (b) 17.156   (c) 20.98   (d) 6.024

**A3** Round to two decimal places    (a) 0.578   (b) 9.037   (c) 6.4027   (d) 13.8571

**A4** (a) Round 3.1854 to one decimal place.    (b) Round 15.947 to two decimal places.
     (c) Round 7.2971 to two decimal places.    (d) Round 2.0753 to one decimal place.

## B Order of operations

Multiply first, **before** adding or subtracting.

$$3 + 2 \times 4$$
$$= 3 + 8$$
$$= 11$$

$$11 - 3 \times 2$$
$$= 11 - 6$$
$$= 5$$

Check that your calculator follows these rules.

**B1** (a) Use the 'multiply first' rule to do $7 + 4 \times 3$ in your head.
     (b) Check that your calculator gives the same result.

**B2** Do each of these in your head. Then check each one using a calculator.
     (a) $2 + 6 \times 4$   (b) $10 - 3 \times 3$   (c) $5 \times 4 - 1$   (d) $7 + 5 \times 3$   (e) $40 - 10 \times 2$

**B3** Do each of these on a calculator.
     (a) $34 + 16 \times 9$   (b) $84 - 26 \times 3$   (c) $17 \times 38 - 24$   (d) $762 - 23 \times 22$

**B4** (a) Use a calculator to work out $53.6 + 2.4 \times 5.5$ .
     (b) Round the answer to the nearest integer.
     (c) Work out $17.4 - 2.7 \times 0.86$ and round the answer to one decimal place.

**B5** Do these on a calculator. Round each answer to the nearest integer.
    (a) 29.4 + 13.6 × 2.7    (b) 83.4 – 16.5 × 1.4    (c) 25.3 + 76.4 × 0.35

**B6** Do these on a calculator. Round each answer to one decimal place.
    (a) 18.6 × 2.6 + 41.7    (b) 27.4 + 9.5 × 13.2    (c) 65.4 – 7.4 × 2.6

**B7** Do these on a calculator. Round each answer to two decimal places.
    (a) 68.13 – 8.16 × 5.3    (b) 81.55 + 20.2 × 3.52    (c) 108.49 – 21.5 × 3.88

## C Division

| Written down | On the calculator | |
|---|---|---|
| $6 + \dfrac{8}{2}$ | 6 + 8 ÷ 2 = | The calculator divides before adding or subtracting. |
| $9 - \dfrac{6}{3}$ | 9 – 6 ÷ 3 = | |

**C1** (a) Do $12 - \dfrac{8}{2}$ in your head.

    (b) Now do it on a calculator and check that you get the same result.

**C2** Do each of these first in your head and then on a calculator.
Check that the results are the same.
    (a) $4 + \dfrac{6}{2}$    (b) $\dfrac{12}{4} - 2$    (c) $20 - \dfrac{16}{4}$    (d) $8 + \dfrac{15}{3}$    (e) $24 - \dfrac{28}{7}$

**C3** Do each of these on a calculator.
    (a) $\dfrac{275}{25} + 38$    (b) $77 - \dfrac{286}{22}$    (c) $45 + \dfrac{578}{34}$    (d) $47 - \dfrac{738}{18}$    (e) $345 + \dfrac{9018}{54}$

**C4** Calculate these. Round each answer to the nearest integer.
    (a) $45.2 + \dfrac{78.2}{6.8}$    (b) $112 - \dfrac{58.5}{15.6}$    (c) $\dfrac{34.6}{3.7} + 5.18$    (d) $23.6 - \dfrac{13.2}{0.72}$

**C5** Calculate these. Give each answer correct to one decimal place.
    (a) 34.6 – 3.4 × 7.8    (b) $38.9 + \dfrac{71.4}{1.28}$    (c) $2.65 - \dfrac{1}{0.47}$

**C6** Calculate these. Give each answer correct to two decimal places.
    (a) $2.6 \times 5.4 + \dfrac{25.8}{6.4}$    (b) $\dfrac{11.34}{1.46} + \dfrac{23.54}{2.57}$    (c) $\dfrac{10.8}{3.56} + 0.65 \times 62.5$

## D Brackets

| Written down | On the calculator |
|---|---|
| (4 + 5) × 3 | `( 4 + 5 ) × 3 =`  or  `4 + 5 = × 3 =` |
| 7 × (8 – 2) | `7 × ( 8 – 2 ) =`  or  `8 – 2 = × 7 =` |
| $\dfrac{7 + 8}{5}$ | `( 7 + 8 ) ÷ 5 =`  or  `7 + 8 = ÷ 5 =` |

**D1** (a) In your head, work out 3 × (6 – 2).

(b) Now do the same calculation on a calculator and check that you get the same result.

**D2** Do these on a calculator. Round the answers to one decimal place.

(a) (5.67 + 2.95) × 3.24   (b) 2.64 × (3.21 – 0.88)   (c) 0.057 × (34.2 + 12.8)

(d) $\dfrac{12.55 - 3.68}{2.69}$   (e) $\dfrac{14.32 + 6.05}{0.15}$   (f) $\dfrac{9.86 \times 3.28}{1.43}$

**D3** Do these on a calculator. Round the answers to 2 decimal places.

(a) 1.236 × (0.207 + 0.866)   (b) $\dfrac{1.864 - 0.767}{0.388}$   (c) $\dfrac{3.67 - 2.94}{1.82} + 4.77$

## E Squares and other powers

| Written down | On the calculator |
|---|---|
| $7^2$ | `7 x² =`  or  `7 × 7 =` |
| $9 + 5^2$ | `9 + 5 x² =`  or  `9 + 5 × 5 =` |
| $(9 + 5)^2$ | `( 9 + 5 ) x² =`  or  `9 + 5 = x² =` |

**E1** Calculate these, giving each answer correct to 2 decimal places.

(a) $4.74^2$   (b) $0.85^2$   (c) $(1.56 - 0.28)^2$   (d) $1.85^2 - 0.72$

**E2** Calculate these, giving each answer correct to 2 decimal places.

(a) $3.12 + 1.64^2$   (b) $(7.39 + 0.47)^2$   (c) $7.26 - 1.24^2$   (d) $3.44^2 - 1.63^2$

$6^3$ means 6 × 6 × 6     $5^4$ means 5 × 5 × 5 × 5     … and so on.

**E3** Calculate each of these. Round each answer to 2 decimal places.

(a) $1.7^3$   (b) $4.8^4$   (c) $0.96^3$   (d) $2.1 \times 4.3^3$   (e) $6.4 + 3.7^3$

# F Square roots

The **square root** of 9 is 3, because $3^2 = 9$.
The sign for 'square root' is $\sqrt{\phantom{x}}$, so we write $\sqrt{9} = 3$.
On some calculators, you press the square root key after the number, on others before.

**F1** (a) Use a calculator to find $\sqrt{18.49}$.

(b) Square your answer to (a) and check that the result is 18.49.

**F2** Use a calculator to find (a) $\sqrt{784}$ (b) $\sqrt{0.2916}$ (c) $\sqrt{1049.76}$

**F3** Use a calculator to evaluate these.

(a) $26.4 + \sqrt{57.76}$ (b) $3.8 - \sqrt{3.61}$ (c) $5.5 \times \sqrt{77.44}$ (d) $\dfrac{\sqrt{12.96}}{1.6}$

(e) $4.5^2 + \sqrt{2.89}$ (f) $3.3^2 - \sqrt{7.84}$ (g) $\dfrac{\sqrt{10.24}}{0.8}$ (h) $0.92 - \sqrt{0.2916}$

### More complicated expressions

The square root sign applies only to the number it is written by.
$\sqrt{9} + 7$ means 'square root of 9, then add 7' which comes to $3 + 7 = 10$.
$\sqrt{9 + 7}$ means 'do $9 + 7$ first, then find the square root.'

**F4** Evaluate each of these expressions.

(a) $\sqrt{576} + 100$ (b) $\sqrt{576 + 100}$ (c) $\sqrt{289} - \sqrt{64}$ (d) $\sqrt{289 - 64}$

(e) $\dfrac{\sqrt{3.24}}{6.25}$ (f) $\sqrt{\dfrac{3.24}{6.25}}$ (g) $\dfrac{\sqrt{3.24}}{\sqrt{6.25}}$ (h) $2.8 + \sqrt{6.3 - 3.74}$

**F5** Do these on a calculator. Give your answers correct to 2 decimal places.

(a) $\sqrt{4.56 - 1.29} + 3.12$ (b) $3.5 + \sqrt{8.03 - 1.74}$ (c) $\sqrt{6.64 - 1.3^2}$

### Test yourself with these questions

**T1** (a) Work out $\sqrt{7}$. Give your answer correct to 2 decimal places.

(b) Work out $7^3$.

AQA (SEG) 2000

**T2** Work out (a) $\dfrac{14.6 - 8.72}{0.014}$ (b) $(5.1)^2 \times \sqrt{6.2 - 3.6}$

Edexcel

**T3** Calculate the following:

(a) $\sqrt{57.76}$ (b) $4.2^4$ (c) $\dfrac{3.9 - 0.65}{0.013}$

# 29 Transformations

You will revise
- how to reflect, rotate, translate and enlarge shapes

You will learn
- how to carry out transformations on a coordinate grid
- about congruent shapes

## A Patterns

This is a piece of the pattern on sheet P175.

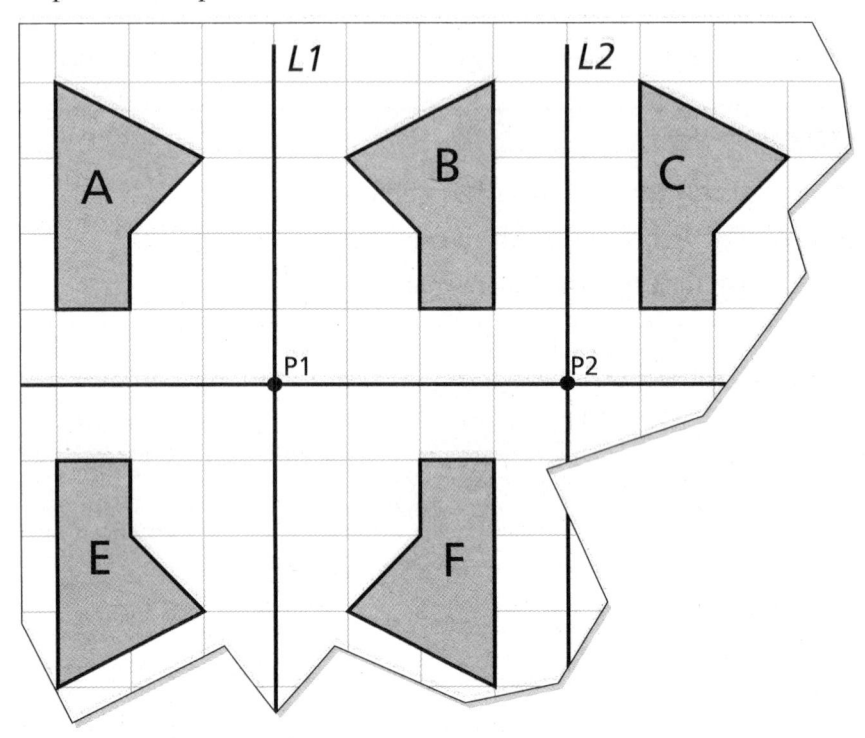

- Which shape on the pattern is
  (a) the reflection of shape C in the line *L2*
  (b) a half turn of shape B with centre P1
  (c) a translation of shape J by 8 squares right and 10 squares up
- Describe the transformation which maps
  (a) shape A onto shape B   (b) shape C onto shape F   (c) shape B onto shape L
- What other transformations can be used to map these shapes onto one another?

**A1** Using the pattern on sheet P175, what shape is the image of
  (a) reflecting shape G in line *L5*
  (b) reflecting shape E in line *L2*
  (c) rotating shape K a half turn using centre P6
  (d) rotating shape P a half turn using centre P5
  (e) translating shape E by 8 squares right and 10 squares down
  (f) translating shape B by 10 squares down

**A2** Describe these transformations from sheet P175.
  (a) Shape D to shape H        (b) Shape K to shape N
  (c) Shape N to shape H        (d) Shape B to shape M
  (e) Shape C to shape O        (f) Shape I to shape K

**A3** On sheet P176, what shape would be the image after
  (a) rotating shape B a half turn, centre (6, 14)
  (b) rotating shape G a quarter turn clockwise, centre (9, 9)
  (c) translating shape J by 10 across and 6 up
  (d) rotating shape K a quarter turn anticlockwise, centre (12, 4)
  (e) rotating shape A a half turn, centre (5, 10)
  (f) rotating shape I a quarter turn clockwise, centre (9, 9)

**A4** What transformations on sheet P176 will map
  (a) shape C to shape H        (b) shape J to shape K
  (c) shape B to shape J        (d) shape C to shape G
  (e) shape E to shape D        (f) shape E to shape K

**A5** Copy this diagram onto the middle of a sheet of centimetre squared paper.
Draw the reflection of shape A in line *h*. Label this B.

**A6** Rotate shape A a half turn centre O. Label this C.

**A7** Translate shape A by 10 right and 2 up. Label this D.

**A8** Rotate shape A a quarter turn clockwise with centre O. Label this E.

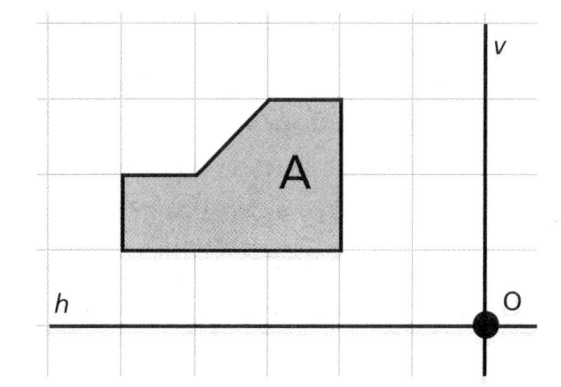

**A9** (a) Describe the transformation that takes shape C onto shape B.
  (b) Shape C can be moved onto shape D by a half turn
      Mark the centre of rotation and label it P.

**Summary**

To describe a **reflection** you need to say where the mirror line is.

To describe a **rotation** you need to say
- where the centre of rotation is
- through how much it is rotated ($\frac{1}{2}$ turn, $\frac{1}{4}$ turn)
- whether it is clockwise or anticlockwise

To describe a **translation** you need to say how far left or right and how far up or down the shape is moved.

## B *Reflecting coordinates*

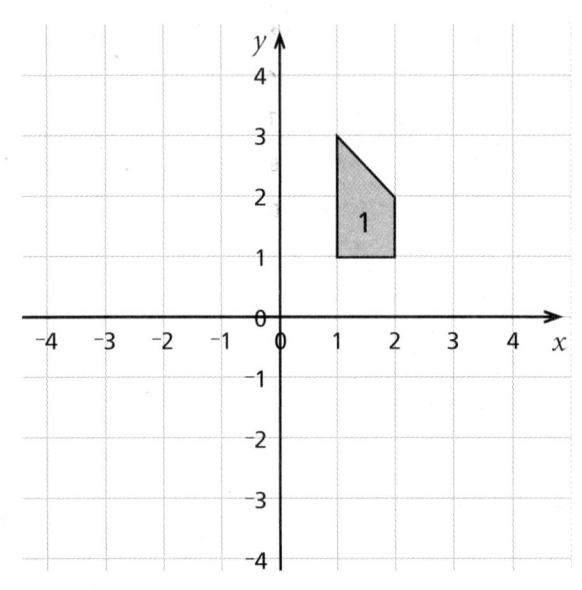

**B1** Write down the coordinates of the four corners of trapezium 1.

**B2** Copy this diagram onto centimetre square paper.

Draw the reflection of shape 1 in the *y*-axis on your diagram. Label this 2.

**B3** Draw the reflection of shape 1 in the *x*-axis on your diagram. Label this 3.

**B4** (a) Draw a grid on centimetre square paper with both axes going from −5 to 5. Draw the shape with corners at E(2, 1), F(4, 1), G(4, 2) and H(3, 3).

(b) Reflect the shape in the *x*-axis. Label this 'reflection in x-axis'

(c) Copy and complete this table

| Original shape | Reflection in x-axis |
|---|---|
| E (2, 1) | E' (2, −1) |
| F (4, 1) | F' ( , ) |
| G (4, 2) | G' ( , ) |
| H (3, 3) | H' ( , ) |

(d) Where would these points move to after a reflection in the *x*-axis?

    (i) (5, 3)      (ii) (4, 0)      (iii) (15, 10)      (iv) (3, −2)

**B5** (a) On the same diagram as B4 reflect the shape in the *y*-axis.
Label this *'reflection in y-axis'*

(b) Copy and complete this table

| Original shape | Reflection in y-axis |
|---|---|
| E (2, 1) | E' (−2, 1) |
| F (4, 1) | F' ( , ) |
| G (4, 2) | G' ( , ) |
| H (3, 3) | H' ( , ) |

(c) Where would these points move to after a reflection in the *y*-axis?

(i) (4, 5)　　(ii) (0, 3)　　(iii) (12, 15)　　(iv) (3, −2)

**B6** There are 4 lines on this graph *a*, *b*, *c* and *d*.
Below are six equations of lines.

Match the right equation to each line.

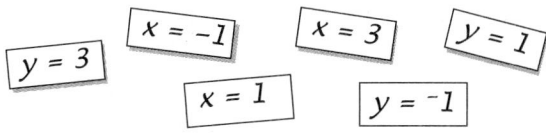

$x = -1$　$x = 3$　$y = 1$　$y = 3$　$x = 1$　$y = -1$

**B7** Copy and complete this statement:

*The x-axis has the equation ... = 0, and the y-axis has the equation ... = 0*

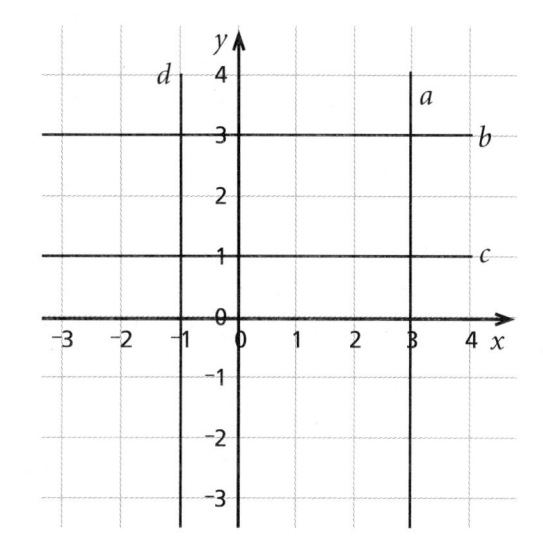

**B8** In this diagram what is the reflection of

(a) shape E in the line $y = 3$
(b) shape B in the line $x = 3$
(c) shape F in the line $y = 0$

**B9** Which line would be the mirror line in these reflections?

(a) Shape I onto shape H
(b) Shape A onto shape D
(c) Shape G onto shape H

## C Translations

**C1** Which shape is reached after these translations?
 (a) Shape 3 by 6 right and 1 up
 (b) Shape 1 by 4 left and 2 up
 (c) Shape 2 by 7 left and 6 down

**C2** Describe the translations which take
 (a) shape 1 to shape 2
 (b) shape 3 to shape 1
 (c) shape 1 to shape 4

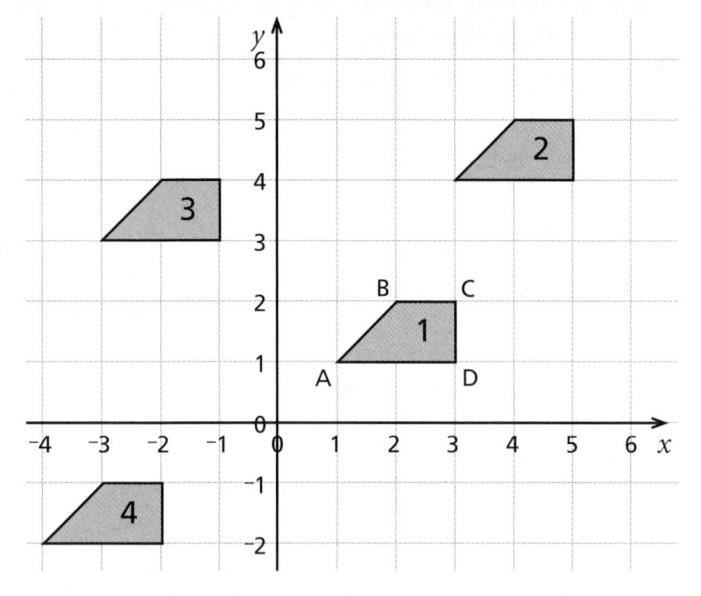

**C3** Copy this grid and shape 1 onto centimetre square paper.
Draw and label shape 5 which is a translation of shape 1 by 3 right and 2 up.

**C4** Copy and complete this table for points A, B, C and D.

| Shape 1 | Shape 5 |
| --- | --- |
| A (1, 1) | A' ( , ) |
| B (2, 2) | B' ( , ) |
| C ( , ) | C' ( , ) |
| D ( , ) | D' ( , ) |

**C5** Where would these points go to after a translation of '3 right and 2 up'?
 (a) (4, 2)  (b) (12, 9)  (c) (−3, 4)  (d) (5, 0)
 (e) (2, −5)  (f) (0, 4)  (g) (−6, −4)  (h) (−3, −2)

**C6** Where would the point (5, 3) go to after these translations?
 (a) 4 right and 3 up  (b) 2 left and 2 up  (c) 8 left and 3 up
 (d) 2 right and 5 down  (e) 7 left and 4 down  (f) 5 left and 3 down

## D Rotations

### The L method

When rotating a shape on a grid, using an 'L' to rotate each corner can be useful.
Here is how you would rotate a shape through a $\frac{1}{4}$ turn anticlockwise about point P.

Draw an 'L' using the grid from the centre P to any corner of the shape.

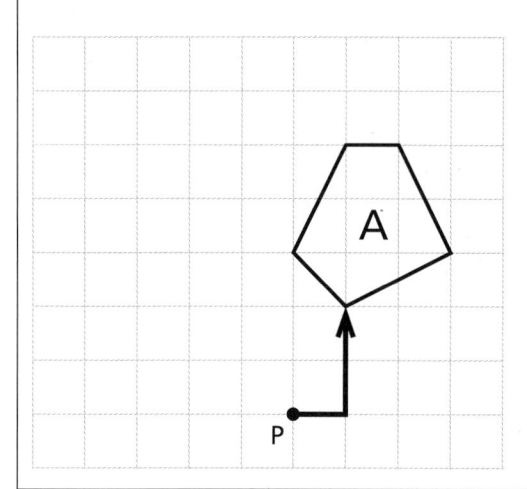

Rotate the L a $\frac{1}{4}$ turn anticlockwise. The end of the L marks the new position of this corner.

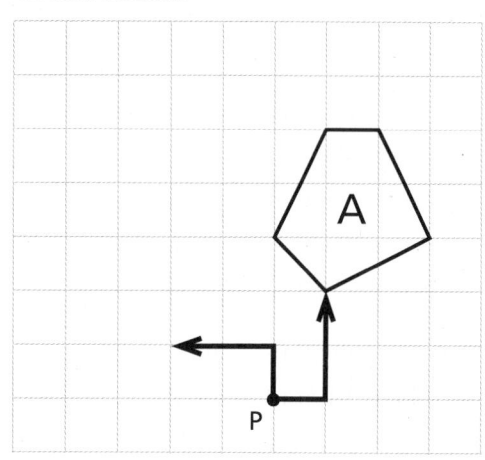

**D1** Sheet P149 has a copy of the shape above and point P.
Use the L method to rotate A a $\frac{1}{4}$ turn anticlockwise centre P.

**D2** Use the L method to draw the images of these rotations on sheet P149.
(a) B rotated $\frac{1}{4}$ turn clockwise, centre Q
(b) C rotated $\frac{1}{4}$ turn clockwise, centre R
(c) D rotated $\frac{1}{4}$ turn anticlockwise, centre S
(d) E rotated $\frac{1}{2}$ turn clockwise, centre T

**D3** (a) Draw a grid with both axes going from ⁻6 to 6.
Draw the shape with coordinates (2, 1), (5, 1), (5, 2), (4, 3), (2, 2).
Label this shape A.
(b) Draw the shape which is a $\frac{1}{4}$ turn anticlockwise rotation of shape A with centre (0, 0). Label this shape B.
(c) Draw the shape which is a $\frac{1}{2}$ turn rotation of shape A with centre (0, 0). Label this shape C.
(d) Describe the transformation that takes shape C onto shape B.

### Using angles

A $\frac{1}{2}$ turn is the same as a 180° rotation.

A $\frac{1}{4}$ turn is the same as a 90° rotation.

You still need to say whether it is clockwise or anticlockwise.

**D4** In this diagram, which shape is the image of each of these rotations?

(a) Rotation of shape G through 90° clockwise using centre (0, 0)

(b) Rotation of shape A through 180° using centre (0, 0)

(c) Rotation of shape D through 90° anticlockwise using centre (0, 0)

(d) Rotation of shape G through 180° using centre (0, 0)

**D5** Describe fully these transformations.

(a) Shape E onto shape C
(b) Shape D onto shape H
(c) Shape F onto shape H
(d) Shape C onto shape A

**D6** Describe fully these transformations.

(a) Shape M onto shape P
(b) Shape N onto shape M
(c) Shape P onto shape Q

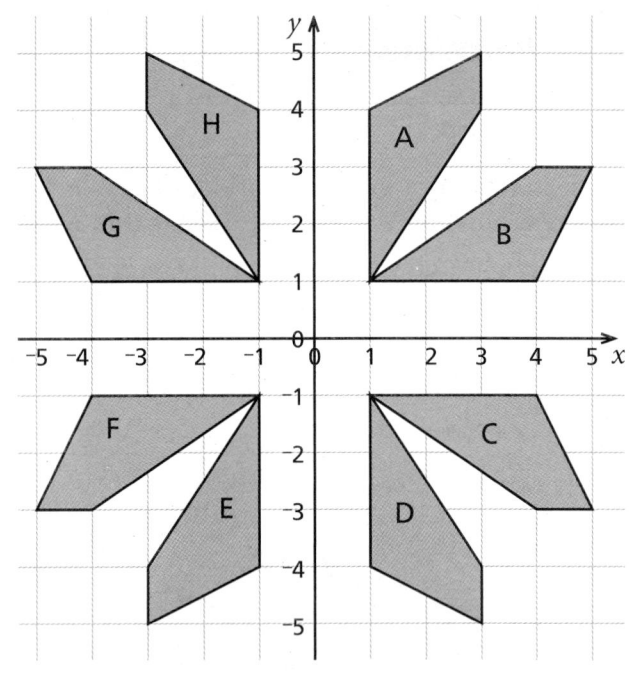

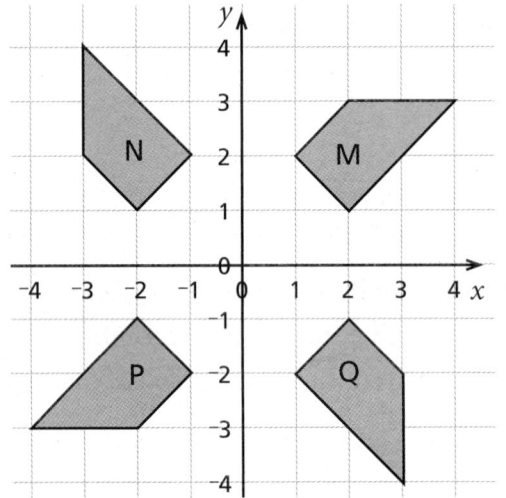

**D7** This pattern has been made by rotating the flag about the centre O using 60° rotations.

What flag is the image of these rotations?

(a) Flag B rotated 180° with centre O
(b) Flag F rotated 60° clockwise, centre O
(c) Flag D rotated 60° anticlockwise, centre O
(d) Flag C rotated 120° anticlockwise, centre O

**D8** Describe the transformation that maps

(a) flag B onto flag C
(b) flag A onto flag E

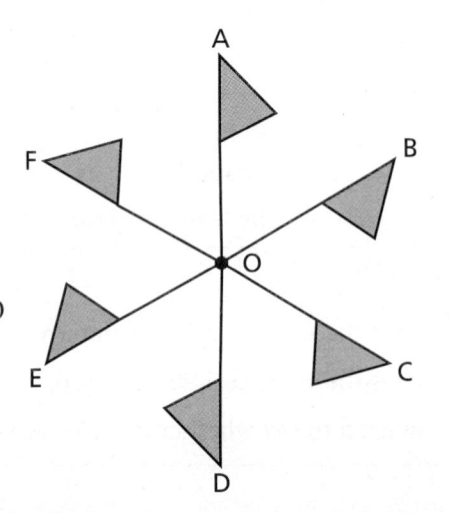

# E Enlargements

There are two ways to enlarge a shape by scale factor 2 using a given centre.

If there is no grid, draw lines from the centre to each corner and make the lines twice as long.

If there is a grid draw an 'L' from the centre to each corner. Repeat each L to get the new corner.

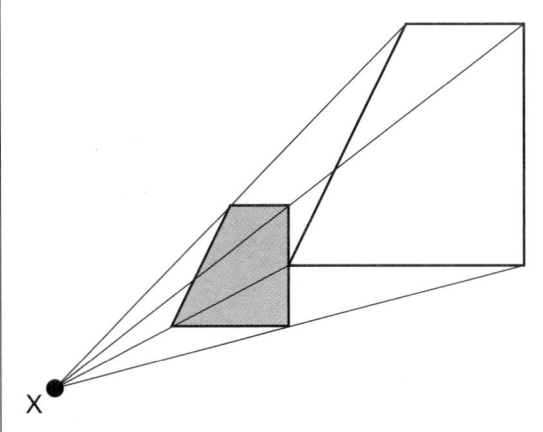

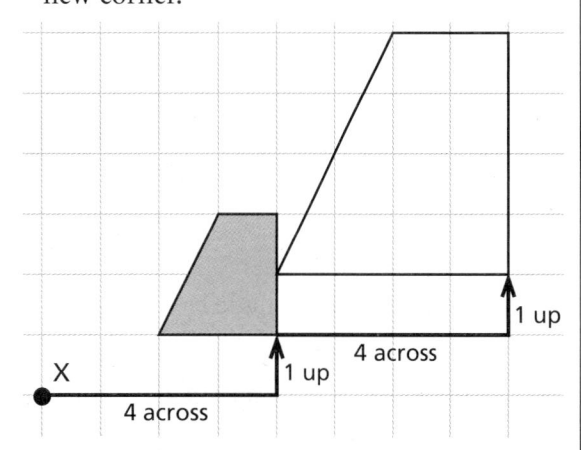

To enlarge a shape by scale factor 3
- in the ray method make the lines 3 times longer
- in the 'L' method repeat each L again

**E1** (a) Draw a grid with both axes going from 0 to 10. Draw the triangle shown here on your grid.

(b) Enlarge the triangle by scale factor 2 with centre (0, 0). Label this 'scale factor 2'

(c) Enlarge the triangle by scale factor 3 with centre (0, 0). Label this 'scale factor 3' (Your shapes may overlap!)

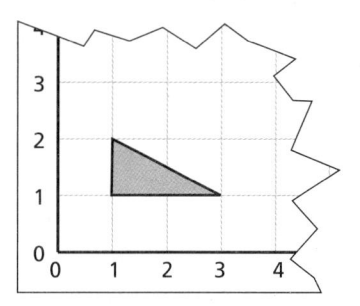

**E2** (a) On another grid the same size as E1 draw the shape with corners at A(1, 1), B(3, 1), C(1, 2) and D(0, 2).

(b) Enlarge the shape ABCD by scale factor 2 with centre (0, 0)

(c) Enlarge the shape ABCD by scale factor 3 with centre (0, 0)

(d) Copy and complete this table

| Original | Enlarged by scale factor 2 | Enlarged by scale factor 3 |
|---|---|---|
| A (1, 1) | A' ( , ) | A" ( , ) |
| B (3, 1) | B' ( , ) | B" ( , ) |
| C (1, 2) | C' ( , ) | C" ( , ) |
| D (0, 2) | D' ( , ) | D" ( , ) |

(e) Describe what happens to coordinates after enlargement scale factor 2 centre (0, 0).

(f) Describe what happens to coordinates after enlargement scale factor 3 centre (0, 0).

## F Mixed transformations

**F1** In the grid below describe fully the transformation which maps
  (a) shape A onto shape B
  (b) shape A onto shape C
  (c) shape A onto shape D
  (d) shape A onto shape G
  (e) shape G onto shape C
  (f) shape A onto shape F
  (g) shape A onto shape E
  (h) shape G onto shape F

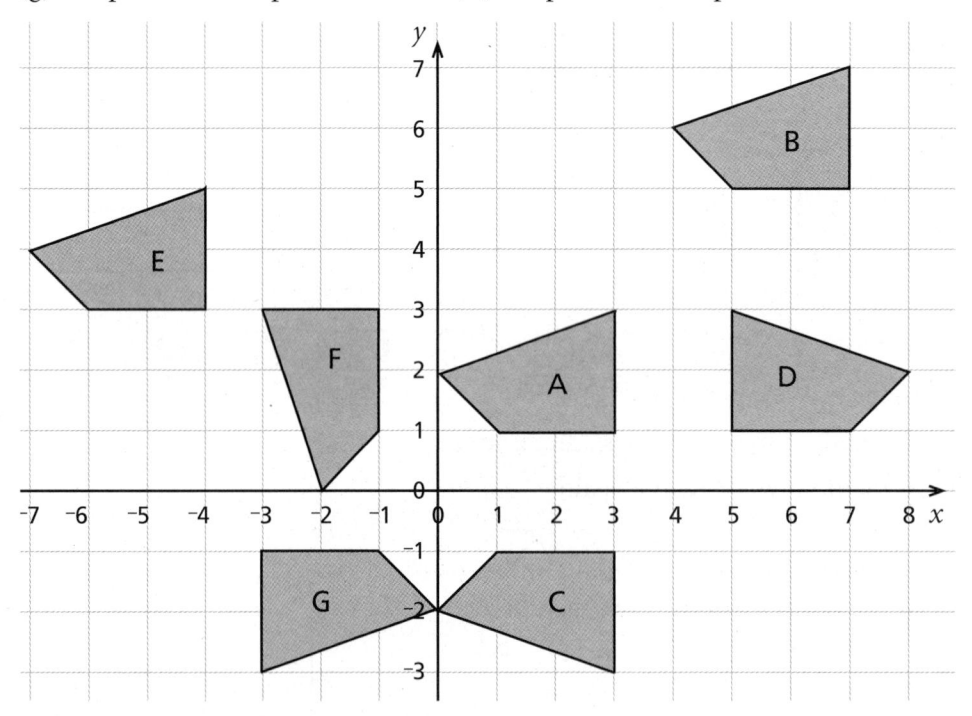

**F2** Copy this diagram onto squared paper.
  (a) Triangle A is a reflection of the shaded triangle.
   Draw the mirror line for this reflection on the diagram.
  (b) Describe fully the transformation that maps the shaded triangle onto triangle B.

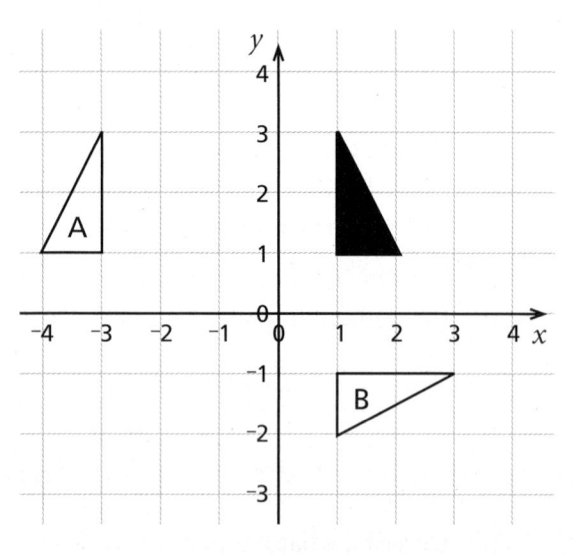

AQA(NEAB) 1998

**F3** Draw a grid on centimetre square paper with both axes going from −5 to 10. Copy shapes 1, 2 and 3 from this diagram.

(a) Describe fully the transformation which takes shape 1 onto shape 2.

(b) Describe fully the transformation which takes shape 1 onto shape 3.

(c) Draw the image of shape 1 after a 90° clockwise rotation, centre (0, 0)

(d) Draw the image of shape 1 after an enlargement scale factor 3, centre (0, 0)

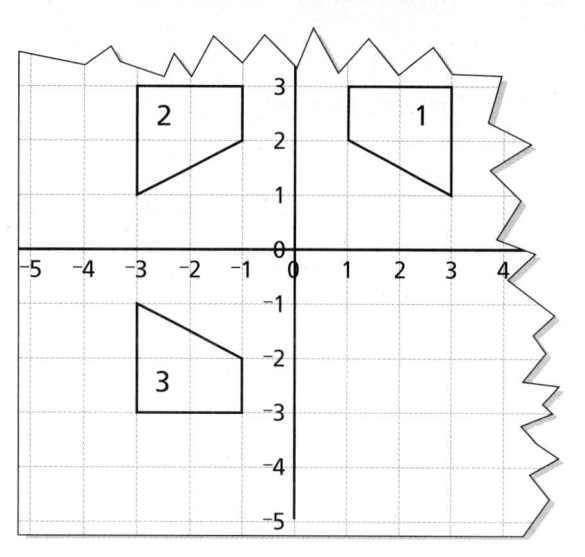

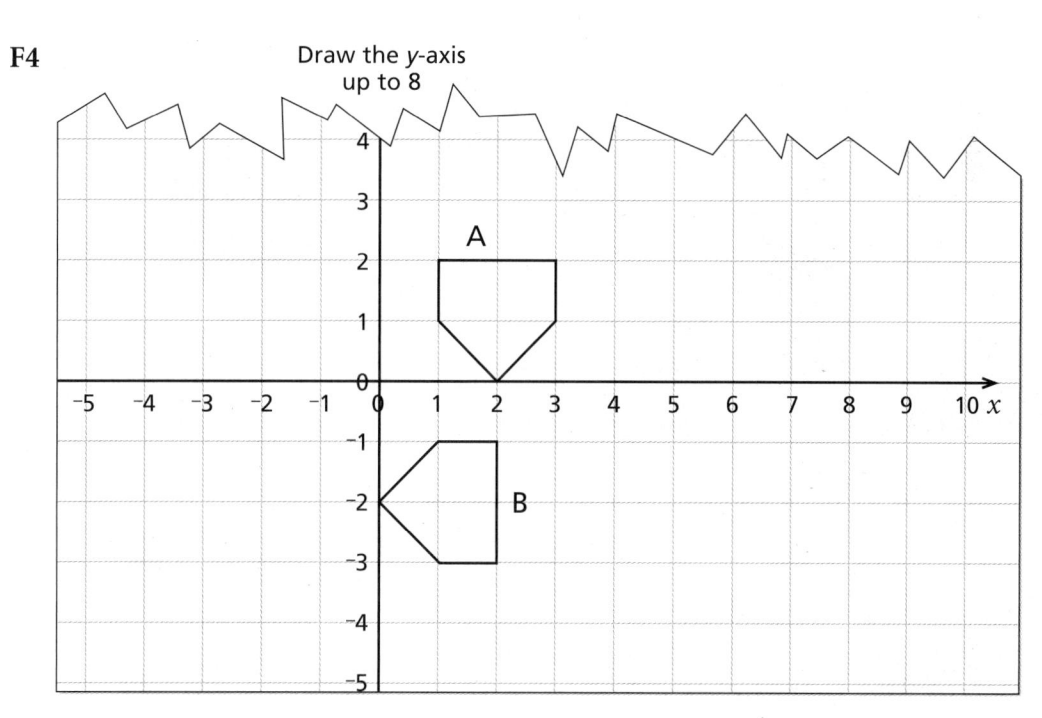

**F4**

Draw the y-axis up to 8

This diagram shows shapes A and B.

Copy the diagram onto centimetre square paper.

(a) Describe fully the single transformation that maps shape A onto shape B.

(b) Draw the image of shape B after a reflection in the y-axis. Label this shape C.

(c) Draw the image of shape A after an enlargement. Use (0, 0) as the centre and scale factor 3. Label this shape D.

OCR

## G  Congruence

Two shapes which are identical in shape and size are said to be **congruent**. The image of a shape after a translation, reflection or rotation is congruent to the original shape.

**G1** (a) Which of the shapes below are congruent to shape A?

(b) Which of the shapes below are congruent to shape B?

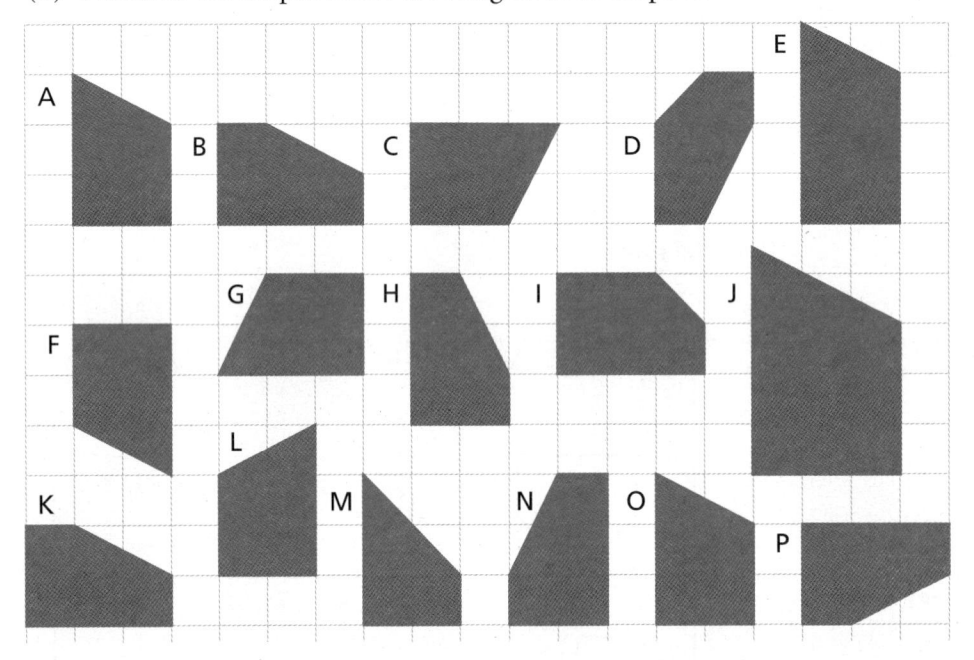

**G2** Which of the triangles below are congruent to triangle A?

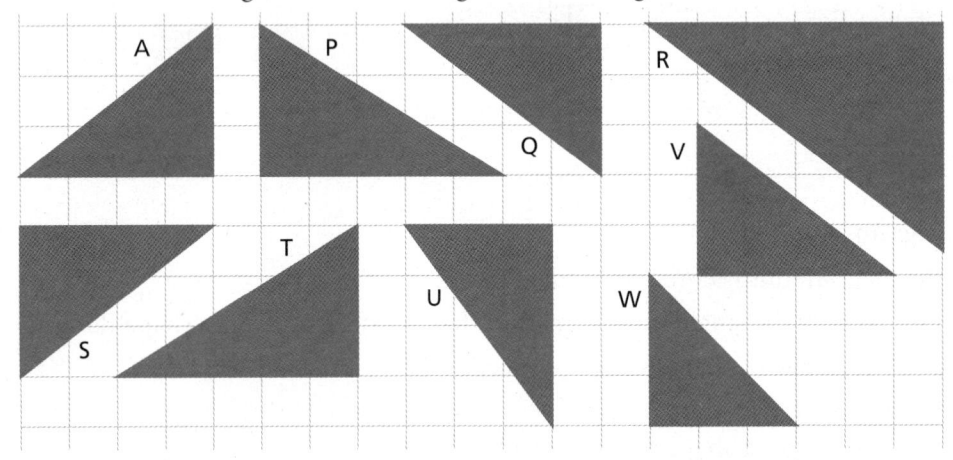

**G3** An image which is the same shape but an enlargement is said to be **similar**. In G1 which shape is similar to A.

## Test yourself with these questions

**T1** This question is on sheet P177. *OCR*

**T2** This diagram shows shapes P and Q.

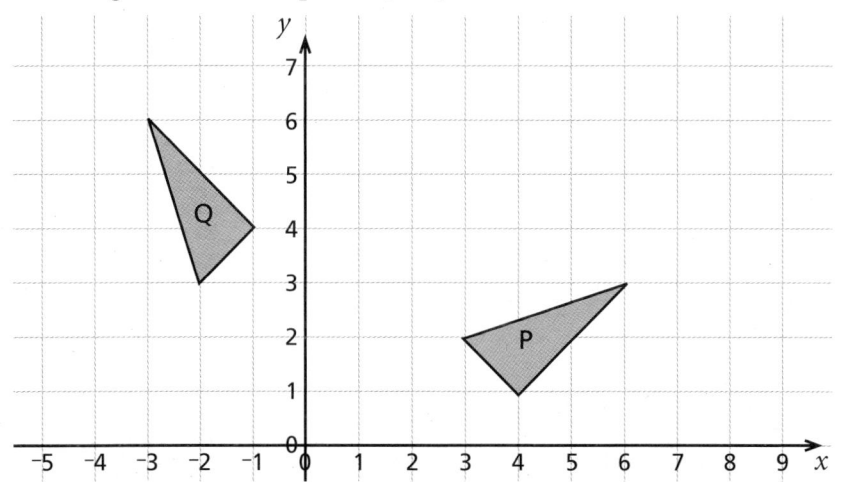

Describe fully the single transformation which takes P onto Q. *AQA 2003 Specimen*

**T3** Draw a grid with both axes going from −4 to 6. Copy shape A onto your grid.

(a) Draw the reflection of shape A in the *y*-axis. Label this B.

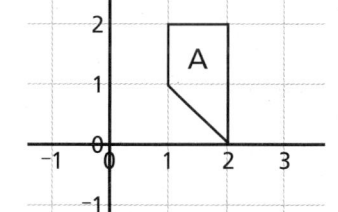

(b) Draw image of shape A after a $\frac{1}{4}$ turn clockwise rotation centre (0, 0). Label this C

(c) Draw the enlargement of shape A scale factor 2 with centre (0, 0). Label this D.

**T4** Here are eight shapes.

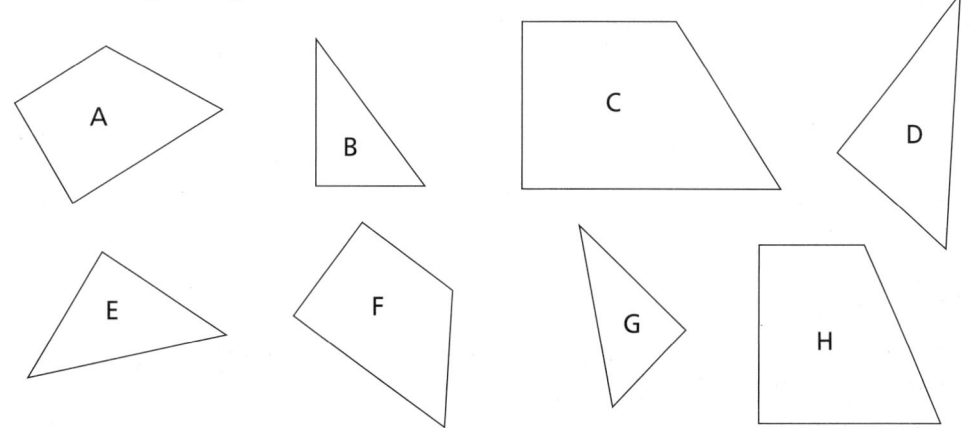

Write down the letters of the two pairs of congruent shapes. *Edexcel*

# 30 Calculating with decimals 2

You will revise
- how to add and subtract decimals
- how to multiply and divide decimals by integers
- how to multiply simple decimals by decimals
- how to multiply by a two-digit number

You will learn
- how to multiply any decimals

## A Review

**Reminders**

6.8 + 2.35

```
  6.80
+ 2.35
  ----
  9.15
  1
```

6.2 − 3.15

```
  6.¹2̸¹0
− 3.1 5
  -----
  3.0 5
```

24.5 × 5

```
  24.5
×    5
  ----
 122.5
  2 2
```

24.5 ÷ 5

```
    4.9
5)2 4.⁴5
```

**A1** Work these out
(a) 7.2 + 0.45   (b) 9.38 − 1.25   (c) 10.4 − 1.25   (d) 7.62 + 8

**A2** Work these out
(a) 15.8 × 7   (b) 1.34 × 8   (c) 10.4 ÷ 4   (d) 9.06 ÷ 3

**A3** Choose numbers from the loop to make these calculations correct.
You can use each number more than once.

(a) ☐ + ☐ = 8.4   (b) ☐ − ☐ = 4.1
(c) ☐ − ☐ = 0.9   (d) ☐ × ☐ = 5.8
(e) ☐ × ☐ = 9.8   (f) ☐ ÷ ☐ = 2.75
(g) ☐ ÷ ☐ = 0.2   (h) ☐ + ☐ = 5.7

(  2.8   5.5   2.9
   2     7     1.4  )

**A4** Here are two large cheeses.
(a) What is the total weight of the two cheeses?
(b) What is the difference in weight of the two cheeses?
(c) How much would six of these Stilton cheeses weigh?
(d) The Cheddar cheese is split into four equal pieces.
How much does each piece weigh?

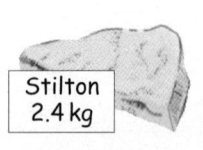

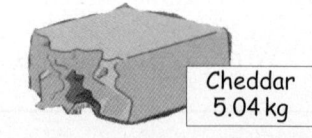

Stilton 2.4 kg

Cheddar 5.04 kg

**Multiplying by a two-digit whole number**

Here are some different ways to work out 24 × 35

|    | 20  | 4   |
|----|-----|-----|
| 30 | 600 | 120 |
| 5  | 100 | 20  |

```
  600
  120
  100
+  20
  840
```

```
   24
 × 35
  120
  720
  840
```

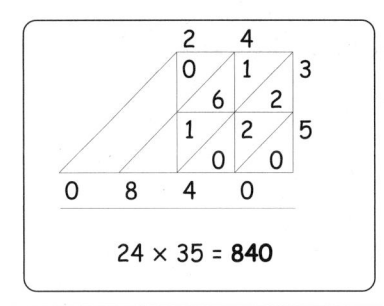

24 × 35 = **840**

**A5** Work these out

(a) 45 × 15   (b) 72 × 18   (c) 29 × 21   (d) 36 × 62

**A6** Work these out

(a) 120 × 18   (b) 256 × 27   (c) 340 × 23   (d) 603 × 54

**A7** Selina can type at a rate of 55 words per minute.
How many words does she type in 15 minutes?

**A8** A box of tiles contains 25 tiles.
Chris buys 28 boxes of tiles.

How many tiles has he bought altogether?

**A9** Martha is buying new furniture for her office.
She needs to buy 18 desks, 21 chairs and 12 filing cabinets.

(a) How much will the desks cost?
(b) How much will the chairs cost?
(c) How much will the filing cabinets cost?
(d) Martha has a budget of £7500 for office furniture.
How much money has she got left to spend on other items?

**Office supplies**

Chairs £68

Desks £125

Filing cabinets £140

**A10** A bag of building sand weighs 25 kg. A pallet holds 42 bags.
What is the weight of a pallet of sand?

## B Multiplying with decimals

Find the area of a rug measuring 1.3 m by 2.2 m.

> **To multiply numbers involving decimals**
>
> Count the decimal places in the calculation.
>
>     1.3 × 2.2    (2 decimal places)
>
> Ignore decimal points and multiply.
>
> |   | 10 | 3 |
> |---|---|---|
> | 20 | 200 | 60 |
> | 2 | 20 | 6 |
>
>     200
>      60
>      20
>    + 6
>    286
>
> *answer could be...*
> *28.6   2.86*
> *0.286....*
>
> Put back the same number of decimal places.
>
>     2.86
>
> So 1.3 × 2.2 = **2.86**
>
> *check this answer using estimation....*
> *1 × 2 = 2*

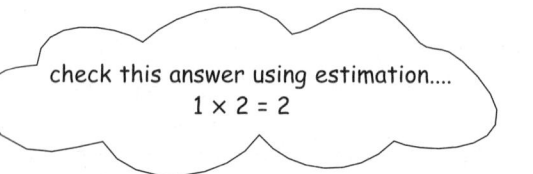

**B1** Work out a rough estimate for each of these.

(a) 0.62 × 5.2   (b) 3.5 × 4.2   (c) 18 × 0.72   (d) 280 × 1.6   (e) 0.18 × 0.23

**B2** Use the fact that 48 × 11 = 528 to write down the answer to

(a) 4.8 × 1.1   (b) 4.8 × 11   (c) 48 × 1.1   (d) 4.8 × 0.11   (e) 0.48 × 0.11

**B3** Use the fact that 26 × 34 = 884 to write down the answer to

(a) 2.6 × 3.4   (b) 2.6 × 34   (c) 26 × 3.4   (d) 0.26 × 3.4   (e) 0.26 × 0.34

**B4** You are told that 47 × 35 = 1645
Find four matching pairs of multiplications that give the same answer.
Give the answer to each pair.

For example, **A** and **F** both give 164.5.

| A | 4.7 × 35 | B | 4.7 × 3.5 | C | 4.7 × 0.35 | D | 0.47 × 0.35 |

| E | 0.047 × 3.5 | F | 47 × 3.5 | G | 0.47 × 35 | H | 0.47 × 3.5 |

**B5** Work these out

(a) 3.4 × 5.6   (b) 2.6 × 5.7   (c) 4.5 × 5.3   (d) 1.4 × 3.5   (e) 7.5 × 3.6

**B6** Work these out

(a) 3.6 × 21   (b) 43 × 5.6   (c) 0.24 × 5.6   (d) 2.6 × 0.27   (e) 0.34 × 2.5

**B7** Find the area of these rugs in m².

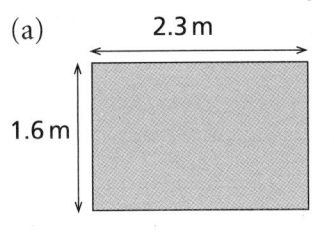

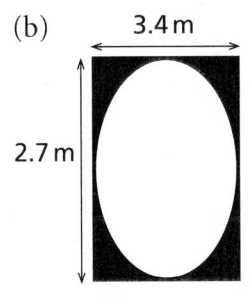

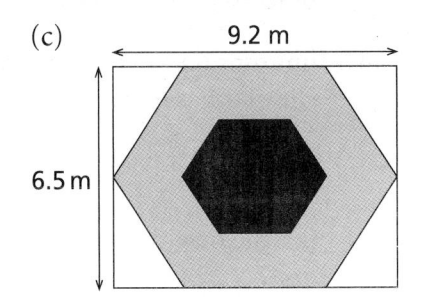

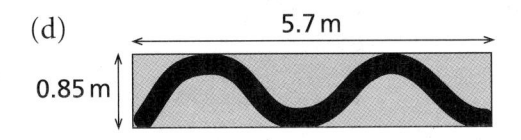

(a) 2.3 m × 1.6 m

(b) 3.4 m × 2.7 m

(c) 9.2 m × 6.5 m

(d) 5.7 m × 0.85 m

**B8** Gareth worked for 27 hours one week.
He is paid at a rate of £6.40 per hour.

How much was he paid altogether that week?

**Conversions**

This table shows some Imperial measurements and their metric equivalents.

Use this information to answer the question below.

| Imperial | Metric |
|---|---|
| 1 pound | 0.45 kg |
| 1 mile | 1.6 km |
| 1 inch | 2.5 cm |
| 1 foot | 0.3 m |
| 1 pint | 0.57 litres |
| 1 gallon | 4.5 litres |

**B9** Convert these quantities into metric units.

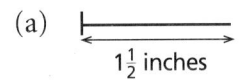

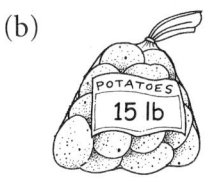

(a) $1\frac{1}{2}$ inches

(b) 15 lb potatoes

(c) COVENTRY 20 miles

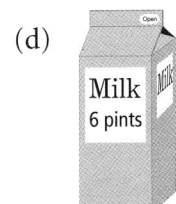

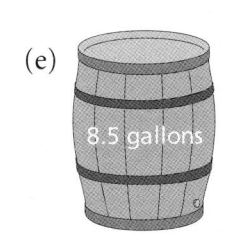

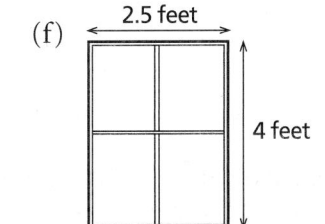

(d) Milk 6 pints

(e) 8.5 gallons

(f) 2.5 feet × 4 feet

## C Mixed questions

**C1** Jim runs 6.8 km each day for a week.
How far has he run altogether?

**C2** This shows a picture in a frame.
Work out

(a) the height of the picture
(b) the width of the picture
(c) the perimeter of the frame
(d) the perimeter of the picture

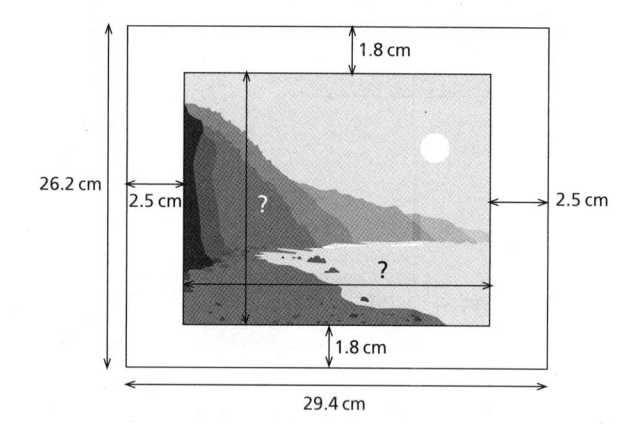

**C3** Work out the cost of these items

(a) 1 kg of bananas and 1 kg of grapes
(b) 0.4 kg of grapes
(c) 1.2 kg of apples
(d) 2 kg of pears and 1 kg of bananas

Apples £0.95 per kilo
Grapes £1.90 per kilo
Bananas £1.08 per kilo
Pears £1.28 per kilo

**C4** Liz buys 1.6 kg of apples and 0.5 kg of bananas.
She pays with a £10 note.

How much change does she get?
Show all your working.

**C5** Anna keeps copies of her favourite magazine.
Each copy of the magazine is 0.6 cm thick.
She has a magazine file 7.5 cm thick.

Could she keep 12 copies of the magazine in this magazine file?

**C6** Tosca the cat weighs 2.58 kg.
Murdo the cat weighs 3.4 kg.

(a) What is the total weight of the two cats?
(b) What is the difference in the weight of the two cats?

**C7** (a) Roughly how many kilometres are there in one mile?

(b) Heather lives 7.5 miles away from school.
How many kilometres is this?

**C8** A cricket pitch is 66 feet long.
Roughly how long is this in metres?

**C9** A Smart car is 2.5 m long.
How many would you fit, bumper to bumper, on a car ferry deck 20 m long?

---

### Test yourself with these questions

**T1** An electrician used two pieces of wire each 1.6 m long.

(a) Find the total length of wire he used.

He cut the two pieces from a 10 m length of wire.

(b) How much wire did he have left over?  OCR

**T2** Henry bought
2 pencils at 28p each,
4 pads of paper at £1.20 each and
1 magazine at £2.95.

He paid with a £10 note.
How much change should Henry get from £10?  Edexcel

**T3** Ashfield School held a Christmas disco.

(a) 224 pupils paid £1.50 each.
How much was paid altogether?

(b) Cans of drink and packets of crisps were sold at the disco.
220 cans at 30p each were sold.

| Cans | 30p |
| Crisps | 25p |

(i) How much was spent on drinks?

(ii) A total of £111 was spent on drinks and crisps.
The crisps cost 25p a packet.
How many packets of crisps were sold?  OCR

**T4** A supermarket has some part-time jobs for people aged under 18.
These are the hourly rates for the different jobs.

| Job | Hourly rate |
|---|---|
| Cleaner | £3.15 |
| Car park attendant | £3.25 |
| Shelf filler | £3.50 |
| Cashier | £3.80 |

Andy has a job as a shelf filler. He is 17 years old.
One week he works 3 hours on Thursday, 7 hours on Friday and 8 hours on Saturday.

How much is he paid altogether?  OCR

# 31 The solution is clear

You will revise how to solve simple equations

The work will help you learn how to solve more interesting equations.

## A Review

**A1** Write an equation for each puzzle. Solve it to find the weight of each animal.

(a) (b) (c) (d)

**A2** Solve each of these equations and check your answers.

(a) $2x + 5 = 17$     (b) $4x - 2 = 10$     (c) $3x + 1 = 10$

(d) $6 + 4x = 18$     (e) $5 = x - 3$     (f) $27 = 5x + 2$

**A3** Use balancing to solve these equations.

(a) $5n + 2 = 2n + 14$     (b) $3w + 1 = 11 + w$     (c) $2m + 14 = 5m + 2$

(d) $3x - 4 = x + 2$     (e) $n + 8 = 4n - 10$     (f) $6h - 12 = 8 + 4h$

**A4** The angles of a triangle add up to 180°.
Use this fact to write an equation involving $x$ for each triangle.
Solve each equation.

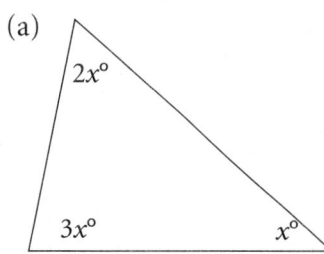

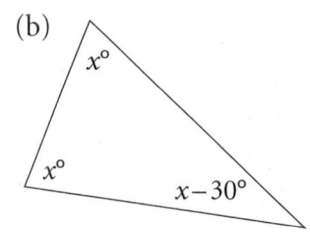

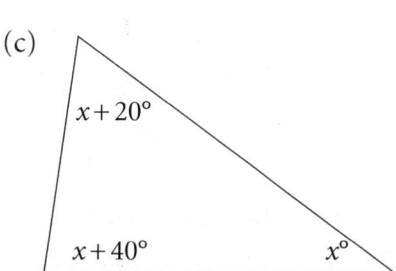

(a) Triangle with angles $2x°$, $3x°$, $x°$

(b) Triangle with angles $x°$, $x°$, $x - 30°$

(c) Triangle with angles $x + 20°$, $x + 40°$, $x°$

## B  x subtracted

Some equations may involve terms like '– 2x'.
But we can solve them just as before.

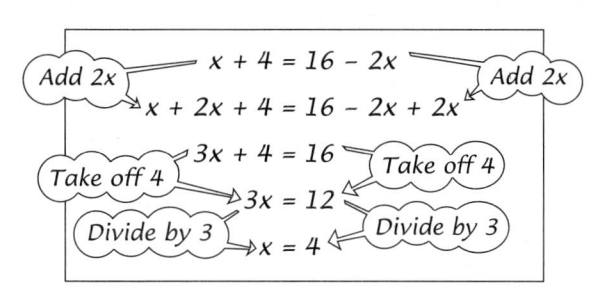

*Add 2x* → $x + 4 = 16 - 2x$ ← *Add 2x*
$x + 2x + 4 = 16 - 2x + 2x$
*Take off 4* → $3x + 4 = 16$ ← *Take off 4*
$3x = 12$
*Divide by 3* → $x = 4$ ← *Divide by 3*

**B1** Copy and complete this working to solve $2x + 7 = 19 - 4x$.

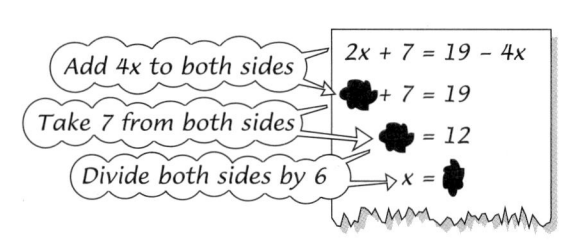

*Add 4x to both sides* → $2x + 7 = 19 - 4x$
■ $+ 7 = 19$
*Take 7 from both sides* → ■ $= 12$
*Divide both sides by 6* → $x = $ ■

**B2** Solve each of these equations.
(a) $3x = 15 - 2x$
(b) $7r = 18 - 2r$
(c) $2p = 20 - 3p$
(d) $x = 12 - 2x$
(e) $8 - 3x = x$
(f) $20 - 3x = 2x$

**B3** Solve
(a) $3n + 2 = 22 - 2n$
(b) $2q + 4 = 29 - 3q$
(c) $7s + 1 = 28 - 2s$
(d) $16 - x = 1 + 2x$
(e) $16 - 2x = 1 + 3x$
(f) $3 + 4x = 35 - 4x$

**B4** Solve these equations.
(a) $5n - 1 = 17 - n$
(b) $3n - 6 = 10 - n$
(c) $15 - 3n = 4n - 6$
(d) $2n - 5 = 15 - 3n$
(e) $16 - 2n = 7n - 20$
(f) $n - 1 = 1 - n$

**B5** (a) Solve $2 = 8 - 3a$ (first add $3a$ to both sides)
(b) Solve $20 - 2b = 12$ by first adding $2b$ to both sides.

**B6** Solve
(a) $2 = 12 - 2x$
(b) $1 = 15 - e$
(c) $25 - 3x = 7$

**B7** This question is puzzle A on sheet P178.

**B8** (a) By forming an equation, work out what $x$ stands for.
(b) What is the length of the plank?

$2x + 1$
$10 - x$

**B9** Work out what $x$ stands for in each of these.

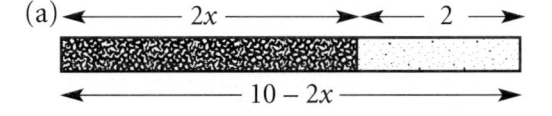

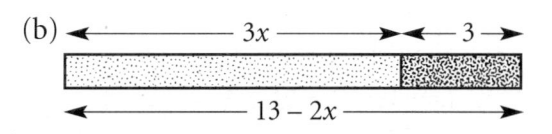

(a) $2x$ | $2$
$10 - 2x$

(b) $3x$ | $3$
$13 - 2x$

**B10** Solve these. Some answers may be negative.
(a) $3x + 10 = 7$   (b) $8 = 6 - n$   (c) $2 = 14 - 4r$   (d) $3f + 8 = {}^-1$

**B11** Solve these. The answers may include fractions.
(a) $2n + 5 = 10$   (b) $4m = m + 2$   (c) $x = 7 - x$   (d) $3 - 2d = 2d$

## C Brackets

Some equations involve brackets.

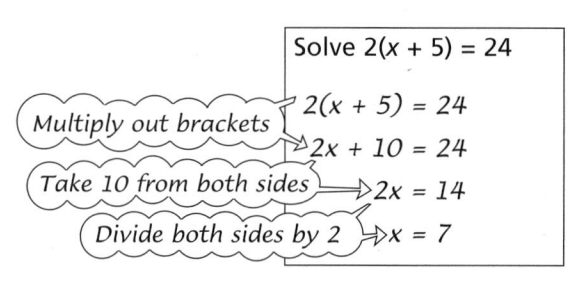

> Solve $2(x + 5) = 24$
> $2(x + 5) = 24$
> Multiply out brackets → $2x + 10 = 24$
> Take 10 from both sides → $2x = 14$
> Divide both sides by 2 → $x = 7$

**C1** Solve each of these equations by first multiplying out the brackets.
(a) $3(x + 1) = 15$   (b) $4(x - 2) = 12$   (c) $2(x - 6) = 20$
(d) $5(4 + n) = 25$   (e) $14 = 2(1 + n)$   (f) $3(n + 5) = 36$

**C2** Solve each of these equations.
(a) $2(p + 5) = 3p$   (b) $5(q - 2) = 3q$   (c) $2(r + 7) = 3r$
(d) $3(s - 2) = 2s$   (e) $4(t - 3) = 2t$   (f) $u = 3(u - 2)$

**C3** Solve these.
(a) $4(6 - d) = 2d$   (b) $f = 3(8 - f)$   (c) $8 = 2(10 - v)$

**C4** Copy and complete this working to solve $3(2x - 5) = 9$

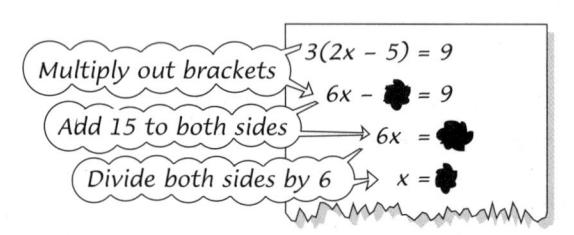

> $3(2x - 5) = 9$
> Multiply out brackets → $6x - \blacksquare = 9$
> Add 15 to both sides → $6x = \blacksquare$
> Divide both sides by 6 → $x = \blacksquare$

**C5** Solve each of these equations.
(a) $2(3n - 1) = 22$   (b) $4(2n - 5) = 28$   (c) $5(3n + 7) = 80$

**C6** This question is puzzle B on sheet P178.

**C7** (a) Simplify $3x + 4y - 2x + 7y$
(b) Solve the equations
(i) $2(3x - 2) = 50$   (ii) $7x = 6 + 3x$   OCR

**C8** Solve these equations
(a) $3x + 2 = 2x + 5$   (b) $2(x + 3) = 15$   OCR

**C9** The solution to each equation below stands for a letter.
Use the table on the right to find the letters.
Rearrange them into the name of an animal.

$3(x + 2) = 12$    $2(8 - x) = 6$
$21 - 3x = 2x + 11$    $4(x + 1) = 16$
$2(3x - 1) = 4$    $3(2x - 3) = 5x$

| 1 | T |
| 2 | B |
| 3 | A |
| 4 | B |
| 5 | R |
| 6 | G |
| 7 | E |
| 8 | S |
| 9 | I |

**C10** Copy and complete this working to solve $2(x + 5) = 17 + x$.

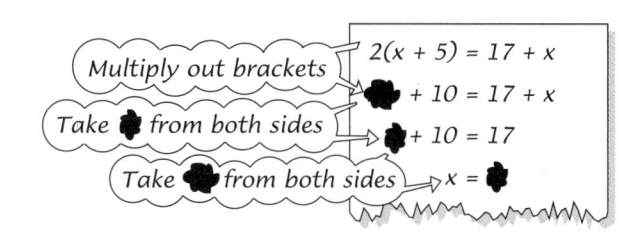

Multiply out brackets: $2(x + 5) = 17 + x$
✿ $+ 10 = 17 + x$
Take ✿ from both sides: ✿ $+ 10 = 17$
Take ✿ from both sides: $x = $ ✿

**C11** Solve

(a) $3(x - 1) = x + 11$    (b) $n - 5 = 2(n - 6)$    (c) $3(f - 1) = 2(f + 1)$

**\*C12** To solve an equation with fractions in it, first multiply to get rid of fractions.

Copy and complete this working to solve $\frac{x - 5}{2} = 3$.

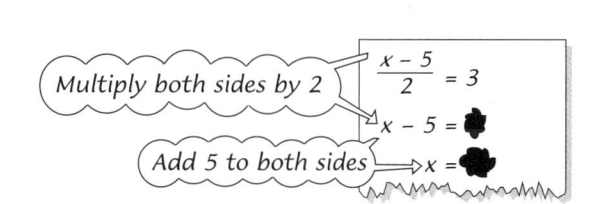

Multiply both sides by 2: $\frac{x - 5}{2} = 3$
$x - 5 = $ ✿
Add 5 to both sides: $x = $ ✿

**\*C13** Solve each of these equations.

(a) $\frac{h}{3} = 6$    (b) $\frac{x + 2}{4} = 5$    (c) $\frac{2j - 1}{3} = 5$

## D Mixed questions

**D1** Solve these equations.  (a) $x - 5 = 12$    (b) $5x = 40$    OCR

**D2** Solve these equations.  (a) $5x = 35$    (b) $x - 19 = 4$    OCR

**D3** Solve these equations.  (a) $3x + 2 = 14$    (b) $4 = 10 - x$    OCR

**D4** Solve these equations.
(a) $2x = 12$    (b) $4x + 1 = 13$    (c) $5x - 2 = 3x + 9$    OCR

**D5** Solve these equations.
(a) $3p = 21$    (b) $q + 8 = 5$    (c) $5r - 2 = 11$    AQA 2003 Specimen

**D6** Solve    (a) $3x - 5 = 16$    (b) $5(y + 3) = 40$    Edexcel

**D7** Solve the equations  (a) $2q + 7 = {-1}$  (b) $12a + 2 = 2a - 6$  *Edexcel*

**D8** (a) What do the interior angles of a quadrilateral add up to?

(b) Write down and simplify an expression for the sum of the interior angles of this quadrilateral, in degrees.

(c) Use your answers to parts (a) and (b) to form an equation in $x$.

(d) Solve your equation for $x$.

(e) Hence write down the size of angles A and B, in degrees.

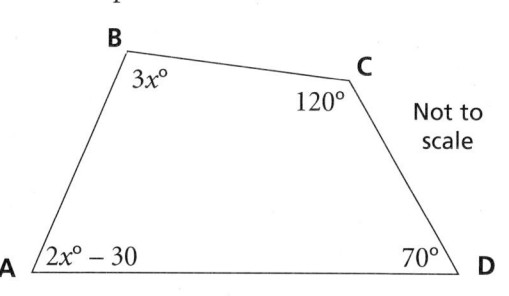

**D9** This question is puzzle C on sheet P178.

**D10** (a) Simplify this expression.  $6a - 5b + 2a + b$

(b) Solve this equation.  $8x - 5 = 5x + 13$

(c) Multiply out this expression.  $7(x - 3)$  *OCR*

**D11** The angles of a triangle are $2x°$, $3x°$ and $4x°$.

(a) Write an expression, in terms of $x$, for the sum of the angles. Give your answer in its simplest form.

(b) By forming an equation, find the value of $x$.

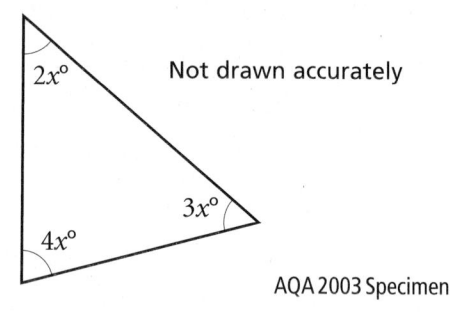

*AQA 2003 Specimen*

**D12** The length of the sides of a triangle are $(x + 1)$ cm, $(x + 3)$ cm and $(x - 2)$ cm, as shown.

(a) Write an expression, in terms of $x$, for the perimeter of the triangle. Give your answer in its simplest form.

The perimeter is 23 cm.

(b) Write down an equation in $x$ and use it to find the value of $x$.  *AQA(SEG) 2000 Specimen*

## Test yourself with these questions

**T1** Solve these equations.
- (a) $2n + 1 = 11$
- (b) $16 = 3m + 4$
- (c) $4n + 1 = n + 13$
- (d) $2n - 3 = 3$
- (e) $2n + 10 = 5n - 8$
- (f) $5h - 10 = 3h + 10$

**T2** Solve
- (a) $4a = 15 - a$
- (b) $2b + 5 = 25 - 3b$
- (c) $20 - 2c = 3c$
- (d) $26 - 4d = d + 1$
- (e) $5e = 27 - 4e$
- (f) $1 = 28 - 3f$

**T3** (a) Work out what $h$ stands for.
(b) What is the length of the plank?

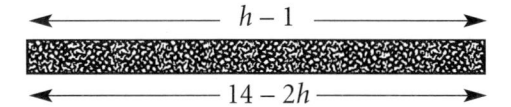

(Plank labelled $h - 1$ above and $14 - 2h$ below)

**T4** Solve each of these equations.
- (a) $2(n + 1) = 14$
- (b) $3(n - 2) = 18$
- (c) $2(n - 6) = 30$
- (d) $3(2n - 1) = 15$
- (e) $2(3n + 1) = 32$
- (f) $n = 3(8 - n)$

**T5** (a) Solve the equation $2x + 3 = 16$
(b) Where $y = 4x + 1$
 (i) find the value of $y$ when $x = {}^-2$
 (ii) find the value of $x$ when $y = 19$   OCR

**T6** Solve these equations.
- (a) $5x - 2 = 13$
- (b) $3(2x - 1) = 9$    AQA(SEG) 2000

**T7** Solve these equations.
- (a) $4x = 12$
- (b) $5x + 2 = 9$
- (c) $3 - x = 7$
- (d) $4x - 3 = 2x + 11$    OCR

**T8** (a) Write down an equation involving $x$.
(b) Solve your equation to find the value of $x$.

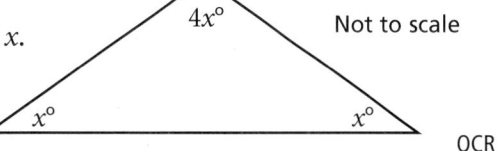

(Triangle with angles $4x°$, $x°$, $x°$. Not to scale)   OCR

**T9** ABCD is a quadrilateral.
Work out the value of $x$.

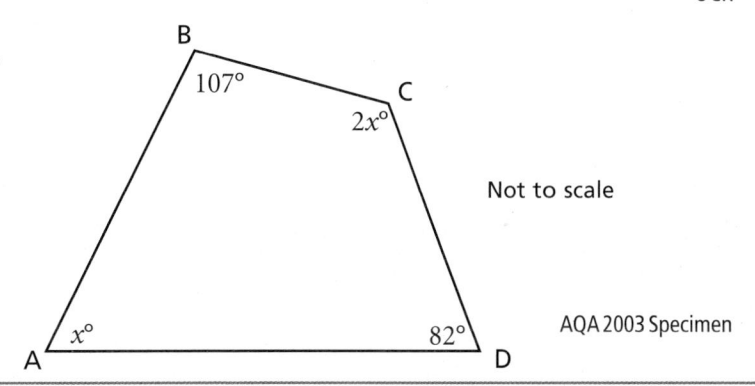

(Quadrilateral ABCD with angle at A = $x°$, angle at B = $107°$, angle at C = $2x°$, angle at D = $82°$. Not to scale)   AQA 2003 Specimen

# 32 Calculating with fractions 2

**You should know how to**
- multiply a fraction by an integer
- work with mixed numbers
- find a fraction of a quantity when the result is a whole number

**You will learn how to**
- divide a fraction by an integer
- find a fraction of a quantity when the result is a fraction or mixed number
- multiply a fraction by a unit fraction

## A Review

**A1** Work these out.
(a) $\frac{1}{2}$ of 8 (b) $\frac{1}{4}$ of 12 (c) $\frac{1}{3}$ of 9 (d) $\frac{1}{5}$ of 50

**A2** Jane eats half a bar of chocolate that weighs 60 grams.
What weight of chocolate has she eaten?

**A3** Katy has £20.
She spends a quarter of her money on a book.
What was the cost of the book?

**A4** Work these out.
(a) $\frac{3}{4}$ of 8 (b) $\frac{2}{3}$ of 9 (c) $\frac{4}{5}$ of 15 (d) $\frac{5}{8}$ of 16

**A5** Out of a class of 28 students, $\frac{3}{4}$ of them bring a packed lunch to school.
How many of these students have a packed lunch?

**A6** About two thirds of our body weight is water.
Estimate the weight of water in a person weighing 60 kg.

**A7** Jan uses $\frac{1}{4}$ litre of milk to make a milkshake.
Which calculation gives how much milk she would need to make 10 milkshakes?

A  $\frac{1}{4} + 10$   B  $10 - \frac{1}{4}$   C  $\frac{1}{4} \times 10$   D  $\frac{1}{4} \div 10$

**A8** On a picnic, each child eats $\frac{1}{2}$ of a pizza.
How many pizzas in total will 12 children eat?

**A9** Work these out.
(a) $\frac{1}{4} \times 8$ (b) $12 \times \frac{1}{3}$ (c) $\frac{1}{5} \times 20$ (d) $\frac{1}{10} \times 50$ (e) $\frac{1}{7} \times 14$

**A10** Ron does a $\frac{3}{4}$ hour walk each day as his exercise.
How many hours does he walk in

(a) 2 days  (b) 6 days  (c) a week

**A11** Work these out.

(a) $\frac{3}{4} \times 4$  (b) $\frac{2}{3} \times 6$  (c) $10 \times \frac{3}{5}$  (d) $\frac{2}{3} \times 12$  (e) $\frac{2}{5} \times 15$

**A12** Work these out.
Give your answers as mixed numbers.

(a) $\frac{1}{2} \times 3$  (b) $\frac{1}{4} \times 5$  (c) $\frac{1}{3} \times 7$  (d) $10 \times \frac{1}{6}$  (e) $\frac{1}{5} \times 7$

## B  Finding a fraction of a quantity: fractional results 1

$\frac{1}{3}$ of $4 = 4 \div 3$

Share 4 cakes equally between 3 people.

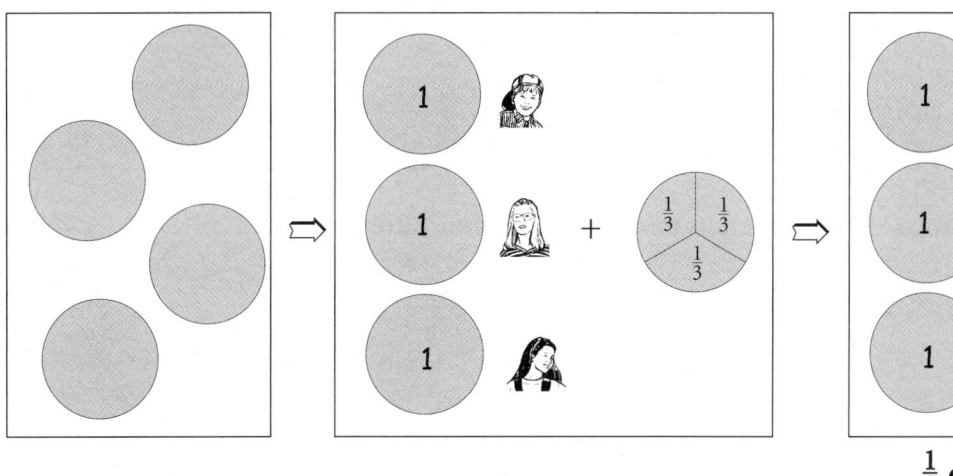

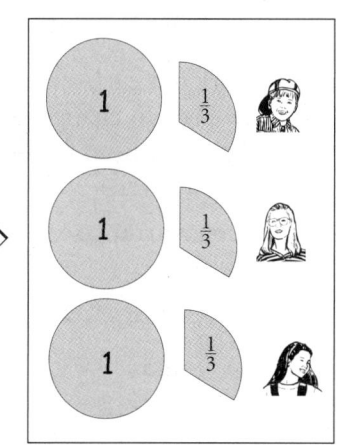

$\frac{1}{3}$ of $4 = 1\frac{1}{3}$

**B1** Three buns are shared equally between two people.
How many buns did each person get?

**B2** Find four pairs of matching calculations.

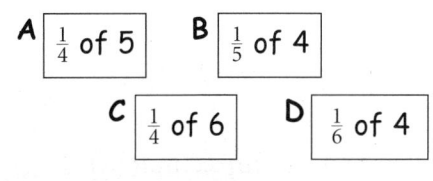

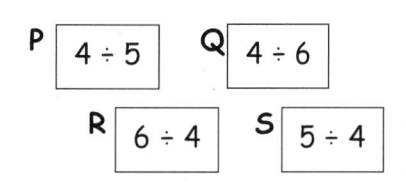

A  $\frac{1}{4}$ of 5   B  $\frac{1}{5}$ of 4   P  $4 \div 5$   Q  $4 \div 6$
C  $\frac{1}{4}$ of 6   D  $\frac{1}{6}$ of 4   R  $6 \div 4$   S  $5 \div 4$

**B3** Work these out.
Write your answers as mixed numbers.

(a) $\frac{1}{2}$ of 7   (b) $\frac{1}{4}$ of 5   (c) $\frac{1}{3}$ of 10   (d) $\frac{1}{4}$ of 14
(e) $\frac{1}{5}$ of 6   (f) $\frac{1}{3}$ of 16  (g) $\frac{1}{4}$ of 21   (h) $\frac{1}{8}$ of 12

## C  Finding a fraction of a quantity: fractional results 2

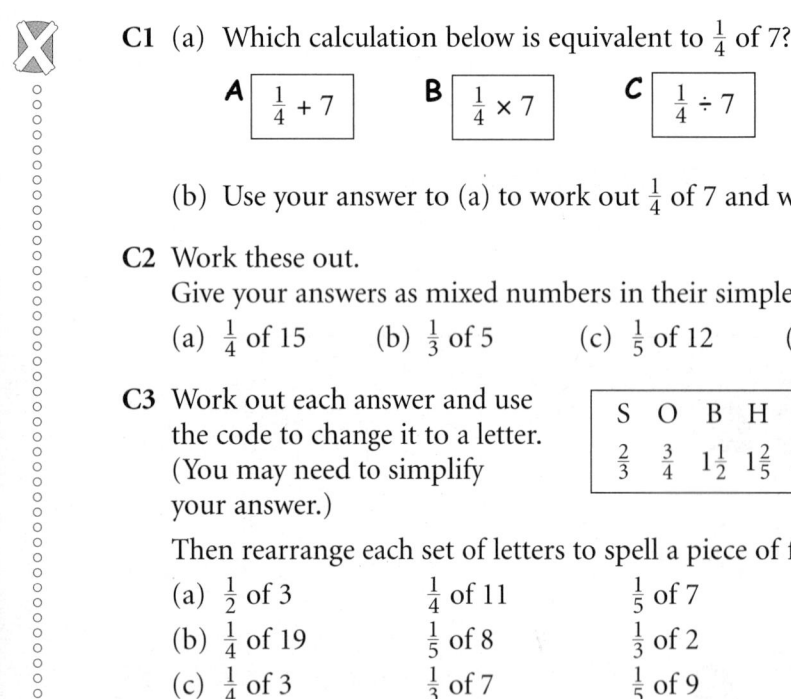

$\frac{1}{3}$ of 5

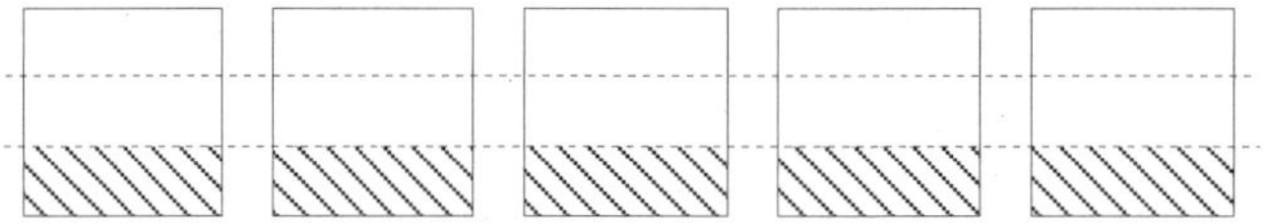

$\frac{1}{3}$ of $5 = \frac{1}{3} \times 5$
$= \frac{5}{3}$
$= 1\frac{2}{3}$

**C1** (a) Which calculation below is equivalent to $\frac{1}{4}$ of 7?

   A  $\frac{1}{4} + 7$   B  $\frac{1}{4} \times 7$   C  $\frac{1}{4} \div 7$   D  $7 - \frac{1}{4}$

   (b) Use your answer to (a) to work out $\frac{1}{4}$ of 7 and write it as a mixed number.

**C2** Work these out.
Give your answers as mixed numbers in their simplest form.

   (a) $\frac{1}{4}$ of 15   (b) $\frac{1}{3}$ of 5   (c) $\frac{1}{5}$ of 12   (d) $\frac{1}{4}$ of 18   (e) $\frac{1}{8}$ of 14

**C3** Work out each answer and use the code to change it to a letter.
(You may need to simplify your answer.)

| S | O | B | H | K | L | T | E | A | C | N | D |
|---|---|---|---|---|---|---|---|---|---|---|---|
| $\frac{2}{3}$ | $\frac{3}{4}$ | $1\frac{1}{2}$ | $1\frac{2}{3}$ | $1\frac{3}{5}$ | $1\frac{4}{5}$ | $2\frac{1}{3}$ | $2\frac{1}{2}$ | $2\frac{2}{3}$ | $2\frac{3}{4}$ | $3\frac{3}{4}$ | $4\frac{3}{4}$ |

Then rearrange each set of letters to spell a piece of furniture.

   (a) $\frac{1}{2}$ of 3     $\frac{1}{4}$ of 11    $\frac{1}{5}$ of 7     $\frac{1}{4}$ of 15    $\frac{1}{2}$ of 5
   (b) $\frac{1}{4}$ of 19    $\frac{1}{5}$ of 8     $\frac{1}{3}$ of 2     $\frac{1}{4}$ of 10
   (c) $\frac{1}{4}$ of 3     $\frac{1}{3}$ of 7     $\frac{1}{5}$ of 9     $\frac{1}{8}$ of 6     $\frac{1}{6}$ of 4

$\frac{3}{4}$ of 5

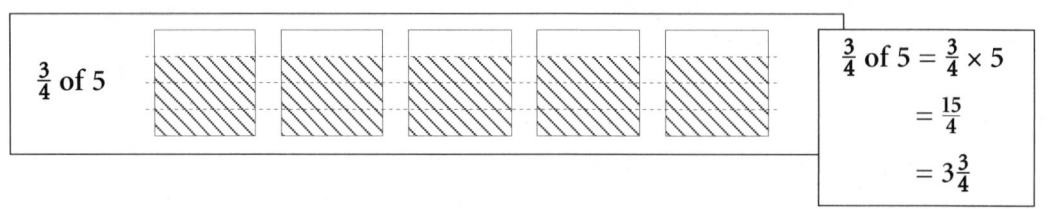

$\frac{3}{4}$ of $5 = \frac{3}{4} \times 5$
$= \frac{15}{4}$
$= 3\frac{3}{4}$

**C4** (a) Which calculation below is equivalent to $\frac{3}{4}$ of 3?

   A  $\frac{3}{4} \div 3$   B  $3 + \frac{3}{4}$   C  $3 \div \frac{3}{4}$   D  $\frac{3}{4} \times 3$

   (b) Use your answer to (a) to work out $\frac{3}{4}$ of 3 and write it as a mixed number.

**C5** Work these out.
Give your answers as mixed numbers.

   (a) $\frac{2}{3}$ of 4   (b) $\frac{3}{4}$ of 7   (c) $\frac{2}{5}$ of 4   (d) $\frac{3}{4}$ of 6   (e) $\frac{2}{3}$ of 10

**C6** Work out each answer and use the code to change it to a letter.

Then rearrange each set of letters to spell an item of food.

| R | A | D | S | C | B | E | H | I | F | T | P |
|---|---|---|---|---|---|---|---|---|---|---|---|
| $\frac{6}{7}$ | $1\frac{1}{5}$ | $1\frac{1}{3}$ | $1\frac{1}{2}$ | $1\frac{2}{3}$ | $2\frac{1}{4}$ | $2\frac{2}{5}$ | $2\frac{4}{5}$ | $3\frac{1}{5}$ | $3\frac{1}{3}$ | $3\frac{3}{4}$ | $6\frac{3}{4}$ |

(a) $\frac{2}{3}$ of 2    $\frac{2}{5}$ of 3    $\frac{3}{4}$ of 3    $\frac{2}{5}$ of 6    $\frac{3}{7}$ of 2

(b) $\frac{3}{4}$ of 2    $\frac{2}{5}$ of 8    $\frac{2}{3}$ of 5    $\frac{2}{5}$ of 7

(c) $\frac{3}{4}$ of 9    $\frac{5}{8}$ of 6    $\frac{3}{8}$ of 4    $\frac{3}{5}$ of 2    $\frac{3}{10}$ of 4

## D  Dividing a unit fraction by a whole number

This is $\frac{1}{2}$ ...    ... and this is $\frac{1}{2} \div 3$ 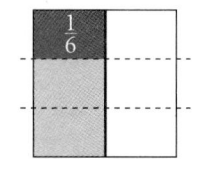 ...    ... so $\frac{1}{2} \div 3 = \frac{1}{6}$.

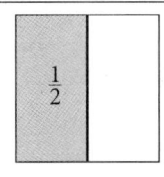

**D1** (a) Which diagram below matches $\frac{1}{4} \div 2$?

A 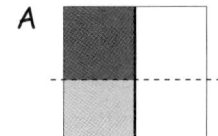    B 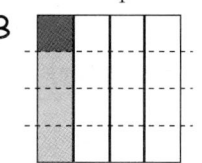    C     D

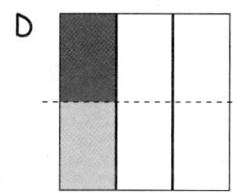

(b) Work out $\frac{1}{4} \div 2$.

**D2** (a) Match each calculation to a diagram.

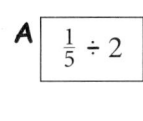

A  $\frac{1}{5} \div 2$

B  $\frac{1}{3} \div 3$

C  $\frac{1}{4} \div 3$

D  $\frac{1}{3} \div 5$

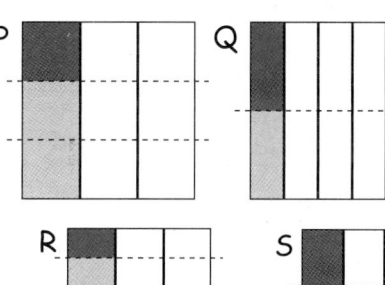

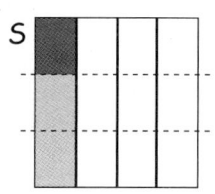

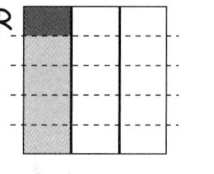

(b) Work out the result of each calculation.

**D3** Work these out.

(a) $\frac{1}{2} \div 2$    (b) $\frac{1}{5} \div 3$    (c) $\frac{1}{6} \div 2$    (d) $\frac{1}{3} \div 4$    (e) $\frac{1}{2} \div 4$

**D4** Moira has a quarter of a bar of chocolate. She shares it equally with her friend Iain.

What fraction of the bar do they each get?

*32 Calculating with fractions 2*

This is $\frac{1}{5}$ ... ... and this is $\frac{1}{2}$ of $\frac{1}{5}$ 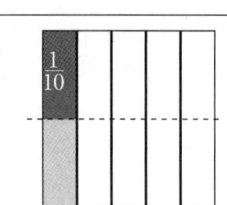 ... ... $\frac{1}{2}$ of $\frac{1}{5} = \frac{1}{5} \div 2 = \frac{1}{10}$.

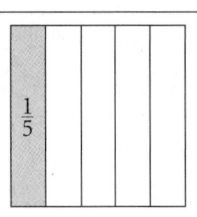

**D5** (a) Which diagram below matches $\frac{1}{2}$ of $\frac{1}{3}$?

   A 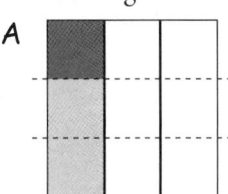   B 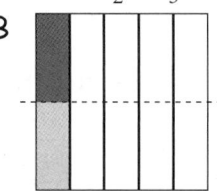   C 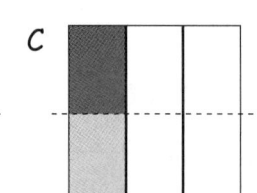   D

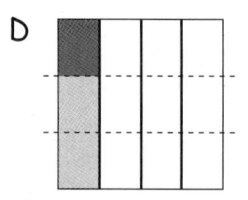

   (b) Work out $\frac{1}{2}$ of $\frac{1}{3}$.

**D6** Work these out.

   (a) $\frac{1}{2}$ of $\frac{1}{4}$    (b) $\frac{1}{2}$ of $\frac{1}{8}$    (c) $\frac{1}{2}$ of $\frac{1}{6}$    (d) $\frac{1}{3}$ of $\frac{1}{2}$    (e) $\frac{1}{4}$ of $\frac{1}{2}$

## E Dividing a fraction by a whole number

This is $\frac{3}{4}$ ... ... and this is $\frac{3}{4} \div 2$ 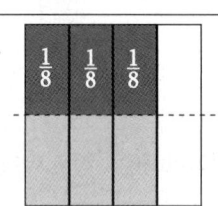 ... ... so $\frac{3}{4} \div 2 = \frac{3}{8}$.

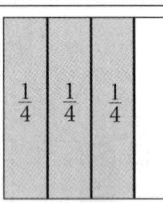

This is $\frac{2}{3}$ ... ... and this is $\frac{1}{5}$ of $\frac{2}{3}$ 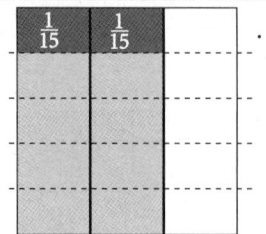 ... ... $\frac{1}{5}$ of $\frac{2}{3} = \frac{2}{3} \div 5 = \frac{2}{15}$.

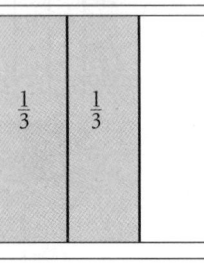

**E1** (a) Which diagram below matches $\frac{2}{3} \div 3$?

   A 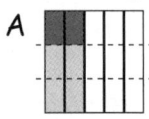   B 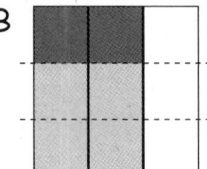   C 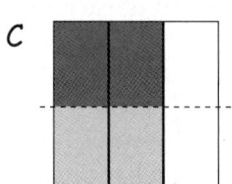   D

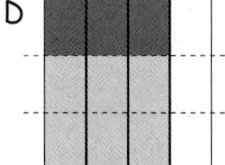

   (b) Work out $\frac{2}{3} \div 3$.

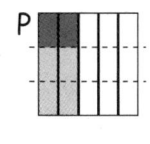

**E2** (a) Match each calculation to a diagram.

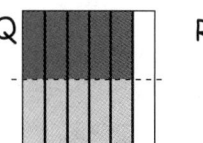

A  $\frac{3}{5} \div 2$   B  $\frac{5}{6} \div 2$   C  $\frac{2}{5} \div 3$

(b) Work out the result of each calculation.

**E3** Cath has $\frac{4}{5}$ of a cake and has to share it equally between two people. What fraction of the cake do they each get?

**E4** Work these out.

(a) $\frac{2}{3} \div 2$   (b) $\frac{2}{3} \div 4$   (c) $\frac{3}{4} \div 3$   (d) $\frac{3}{4} \div 4$

**E5** Work these out.

(a) $\frac{1}{2}$ of $\frac{2}{5}$   (b) $\frac{1}{2}$ of $\frac{3}{5}$   (c) $\frac{1}{2}$ of $\frac{5}{8}$   (d) $\frac{1}{4}$ of $\frac{2}{3}$

## F Multiplying fractions

Here is John's working for $\frac{1}{2} \times \frac{1}{3}$.

$\frac{1}{2} \times \frac{1}{3} = \frac{1}{2}$ of $\frac{1}{3}$
$= \frac{1}{3} \div 2$
$= \frac{1}{6}$

Can you calculate these?

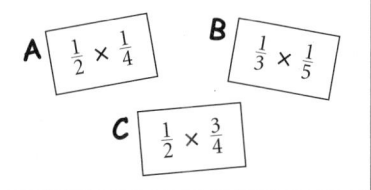

A  $\frac{1}{2} \times \frac{1}{4}$   B  $\frac{1}{3} \times \frac{1}{5}$   C  $\frac{1}{2} \times \frac{3}{4}$

**F1** Work these out.

(a) $\frac{1}{2} \times \frac{1}{5}$   (b) $\frac{1}{2} \times \frac{1}{8}$   (c) $\frac{1}{3} \times \frac{1}{4}$   (d) $\frac{1}{3} \times \frac{2}{5}$

**F2** Work out each answer and use the code to change it to a letter.

Then rearrange each set of letters to spell a city.

| S | G | R | I | O | A | D | P | W | L | E | M |
|---|---|---|---|---|---|---|---|---|---|---|---|
| $\frac{1}{12}$ | $\frac{1}{10}$ | $\frac{1}{9}$ | $\frac{1}{8}$ | $\frac{1}{6}$ | $\frac{3}{16}$ | $\frac{1}{5}$ | $\frac{1}{4}$ | $\frac{3}{8}$ | $\frac{1}{2}$ | $\frac{2}{5}$ | $\frac{3}{4}$ |

(a) $\frac{4}{5} \div 2$   $\frac{1}{2}$ of $\frac{2}{9}$   $\frac{1}{2}$ of $1\frac{1}{2}$   $\frac{5}{6} \div 5$

(b) $\frac{1}{10} \times \frac{5}{6}$   $\frac{1}{3}$ of $\frac{3}{4}$   $\frac{1}{16}$ of 3   $\frac{3}{8} \div 3$   $2 \times \frac{1}{18}$

(c) $\frac{3}{5} \div 3$   $\frac{1}{2} \times \frac{2}{5}$   $\frac{1}{4}$ of 3   $\frac{1}{3} \times \frac{1}{3}$   $\frac{3}{8} \div 2$   $\frac{1}{4} \times \frac{1}{2}$

(d) $\frac{1}{2}$ of $\frac{3}{4}$   $\frac{1}{2}$ of $\frac{1}{5}$   $\frac{1}{3}$ of $1\frac{1}{2}$   $\frac{1}{8}$ of $\frac{2}{3}$   $\frac{1}{4} \times \frac{2}{3}$   $\frac{1}{4} \times \frac{3}{4}$   $\frac{1}{5} \times \frac{1}{2}$

**Test yourself with these questions**

**T1** On a school trip, each child is given $\frac{1}{4}$ of a bar of chocolate.
How many bars of chocolate are needed for 20 children?

**T2** Fiona's dog eats $\frac{2}{3}$ of a tin of dog food each day.
How many tins does she need to feed her dog for 9 days?

**T3** Three apples are shared equally between six people.
What fraction of an apple does each person get?

**T4** Three sausages are shared equally between four people.
How much does each person get?

**T5** Work these out.
Write your answers as mixed numbers.
(a) $\frac{1}{3}$ of 7    (b) $\frac{1}{5}$ of 7

**T6** Work out $\frac{3}{4}$ of 9 and write your answer as a mixed number.

**T7** Helen shares $\frac{1}{2}$ of a cake equally between her two sons.
What fraction does each son get?

**T8** Work out $\frac{1}{5} \div 4$.

**T9** What is $\frac{1}{2}$ of $\frac{1}{6}$?

**T10** Calculate $\frac{1}{3} \times \frac{3}{4}$.

**T11** Calculate
(a) $\frac{3}{8} \times \frac{1}{2}$    (b) $\frac{3}{8} \div 6$

OCR

# 33 Constructions

You will learn
- how to draw accurate diagrams using compasses, a ruler and an angle measurer
- how to draw triangles from side lengths and angles

## A Using lengths

To draw a triangle with these lengths

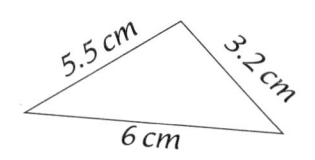

5.5 cm, 3.2 cm, 6 cm

Draw the longest side (6 cm) with a ruler.

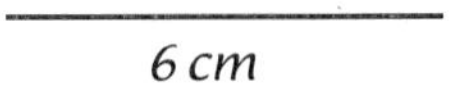

Draw part of a circle with radius 5.5 cm from the left-hand end.

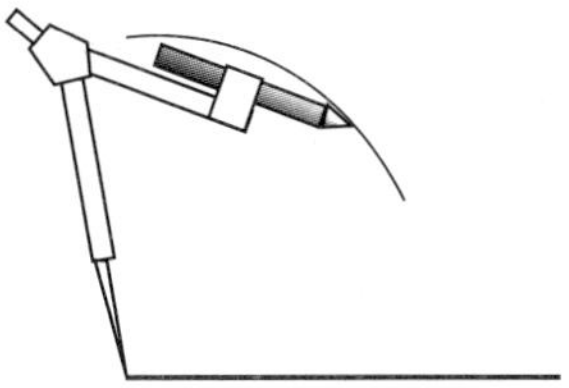

6 cm

Do the same with a circle radius 3.2 cm from the other end.

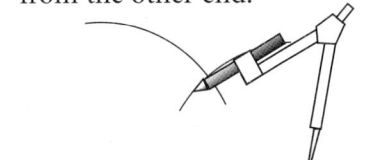

Draw a line from each end to where the two part circles cross

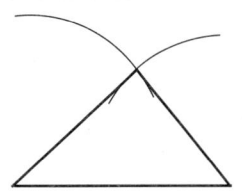

### Triangle puzzle

These are rough sketches of five triangles. Make accurate copies of these on paper or card. Can you fit the pieces together to make a square?

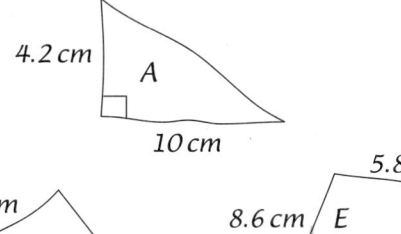

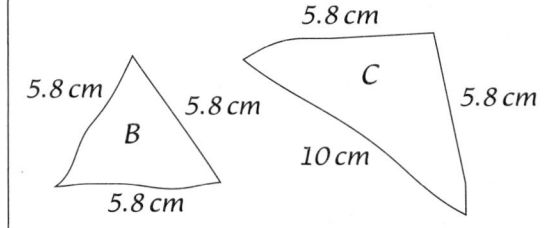

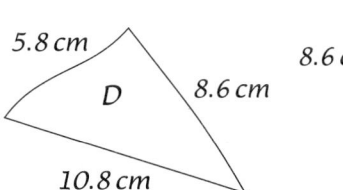

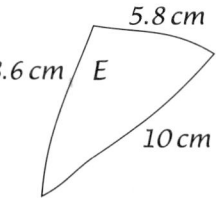

Triangle A: 4.2 cm, 10 cm, right angle
Triangle B: 5.8 cm, 5.8 cm, 5.8 cm
Triangle C: 5.8 cm, 5.8 cm, 10 cm
Triangle D: 5.8 cm, 8.6 cm, 10.8 cm
Triangle E: 5.8 cm, 8.6 cm, 10 cm

- What special types of triangle are (i) C (ii) D?
- Why can you not draw a triangle with side lengths 10.4 cm, 3.7 cm and 5.3 cm?

**A1** (a) Draw a triangle with corners A, B and C so that
AB = 13 cm, BC = 12 cm and CA = 5 cm.

(b) What type of angle is ACB?

(c) Calculate the area of the triangle.

**A2** A triangle ABC has sides of length BC = 10 cm, AC = 10 cm and AB = 12 cm.

(a) Draw a line AB, 12 cm long on a piece of paper.
**Using ruler and compasses only**, make an accurate drawing of the triangle.

(b) Measure and write down the size of angle B of the triangle.

(c) What is the name given to this type of triangle?

(d) Work out the area of this triangle.

AQA 2003 Specimen

**A3** (a) Make an accurate drawing of the sketch.

(b) On your drawing, measure the size of the angle marked $x°$.

5.4 cm

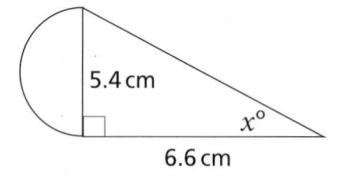

6.6 cm

$x°$

Edexcel

**A4** (a) In the middle of a piece of paper draw a line PQ = 5 cm long.
Complete the triangle PQR, with QR = 5 cm and RP = 7 cm

(b) Using RP as the base draw another triangle where RS = PS = 8 cm, and point S is on the opposite side of line RP to Q.

(c) What type of quadrilateral have you drawn?

---

**An impossible shape!**

The object shown here is a well known 'impossible' object.
The drawing looks like a solid object that cannot be made.

Here is how to draw one.

First draw an equilateral triangle with sides 11 cm long.

Mark points 1 cm and 2 cm from each point on the sides.

Join the points to make this diagram.

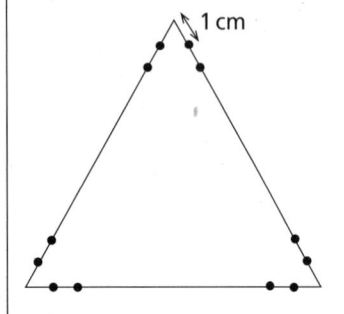

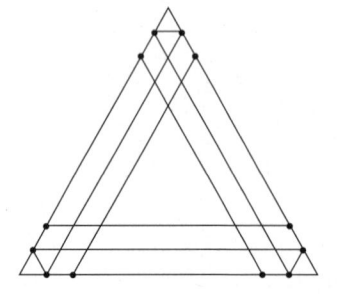

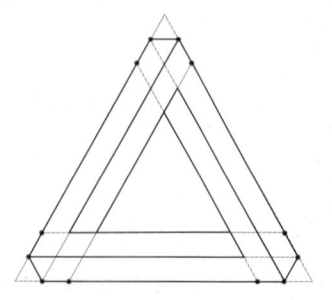

Make these lines thicker or go over them in ink.

1 cm

Now shade the drawing in to give it a solid appearance.

126 • 33 Constructions

## B Using angles

Triangles can also be drawn using a side and the angle at each end.

*Draw a triangle ABC where AB = 8 cm and CAB = 40° and ABC = 77°*

Draw a line 8 cm long    Mark angle 40° at A    Mark angle 77° at B
Complete the triangle.

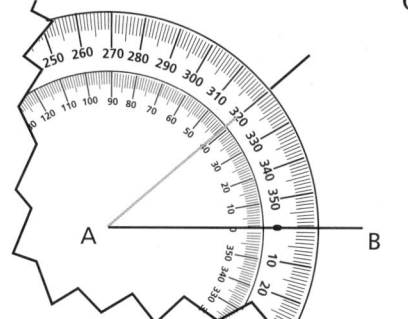

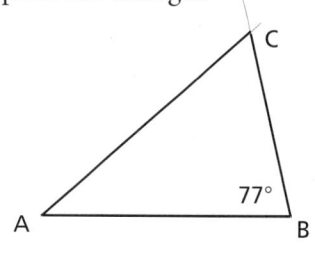

Make an accurate copy of this triangle.
- What is the angle BCA?
- What is the perpendicular height from line AB to point C?

Does everyone get the same result?

**B1** Make accurate copies of these triangles.

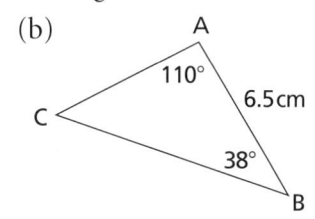

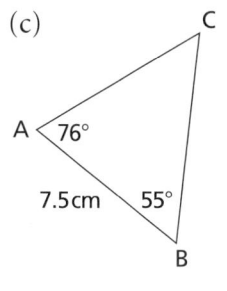

(a) angle A = 57°, angle B = 35°, AB = 8 cm
(b) angle A = 110°, angle B = 38°, AB = 6.5 cm
(c) angle A = 76°, angle B = 55°, AB = 7.5 cm

For each triangle measure length BC and angle BCA.
Check your result against others in the class.

**B2** (a) Try to draw a triangle where AB = 8 cm and angle CAB = 55° and angle ABC = 135°.
What happens in this case? Explain why this happens.

(b) If length AB was 8 cm, which of these pairs of angles could be used to draw a triangle?

(i) CAB=50° and ABC=130°
(ii) CAB=45° and ABC=140°
(iii) CAB=30° and ABC=120°
(iv) CAB=125° and ABC=60°

**B3** (a) Make an accurate copy of the quadrilateral in this sketch.

(b) What special type of quadrilateral is this?

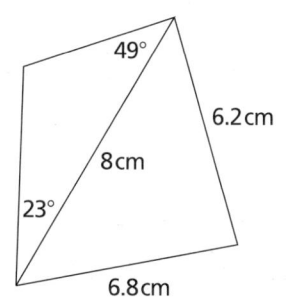

(Quadrilateral: 49°, 6.2 cm, 8 cm, 23°, 6.8 cm)

## C  Two sides and an angle

- Make accurate copies of these two triangles.

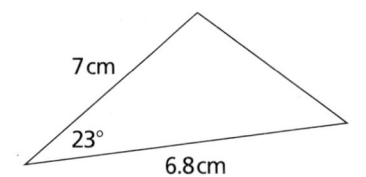

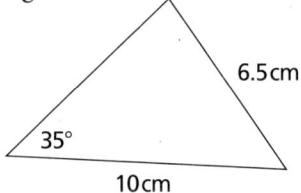

  (triangle with sides 7 cm, 6.8 cm and angle 23°)

  (triangle with sides 6.5 cm, 10 cm and angle 35°)

- Measure the remaining side and angles in each case.
  Does everyone get the same result?

- What is different about the information given in the two cases above?

**C1** (a) Make accurate copies of these triangles.

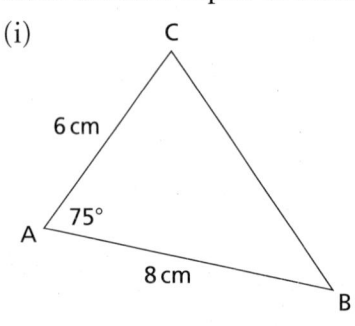

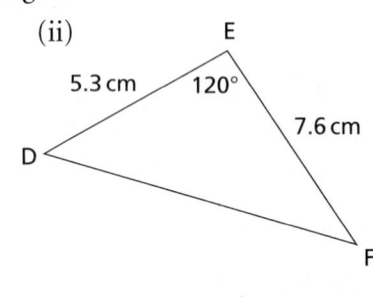

  (i) Triangle ABC with AC = 6 cm, AB = 8 cm, angle A = 75°

  (ii) Triangle DEF with DE = 5.3 cm, EF = 7.6 cm, angle E = 120°

  (b) Measure the missing sides and angles and write them on your drawings.
  Would anyone who used these instructions draw exactly the same triangle as you?

**C2** Draw two different triangles that have the measurements shown in this sketch

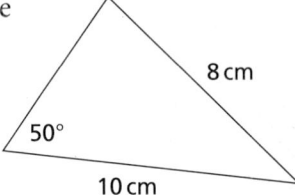

  (triangle with sides 8 cm, 10 cm and angle 50°)

**C3** (a) Make an accurate drawing of this right-angled triangle.

  (b) Is there more than one right-angled triangle with these measurements?

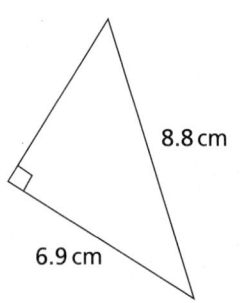

  (right-angled triangle with sides 8.8 cm and 6.9 cm)

128 • 33 Constructions

## D Scale drawings

**D1** A surveyor needs to draw an accurate plan of this awkward shaped field.
A scale of 1 cm represents 10 m is to be used.

(a) What lengths will these distances be shown as on the plan?

   (i) AB         (ii) BC

(b) Draw an accurate scale drawing of this field on a sheet of plain paper.

**D2** A draughtsman is drawing plans for a building. She needs to draw an accurate plan of this side elevation.

(a) Using a scale of 1 cm = 1 m draw an accurate plan of this side elevation.

(b) The local Council say that new buildings in the area cannot be more than 8 m tall.
Does this building meet this regulation?

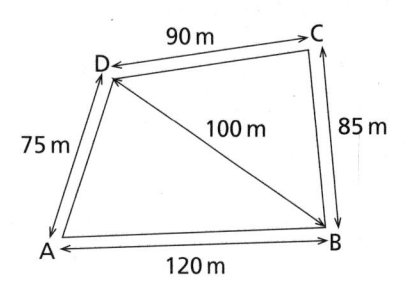

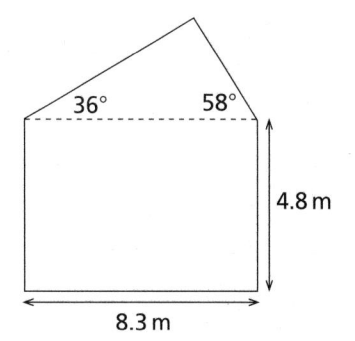

---

### Test yourself with these questions

**T1** The diagram shows a sketch of a triangle.

(a) Make an accurate drawing of the triangle.

(b) (i) On your drawing, measure the size of the angle marked $x°$.

    (ii) What type of angle is the angle marked $x°$?

(c) Work out the area of the triangle
State the units of your answer.

*Edexcel*

**T2** In triangle PQR, PQ = 7.2 cm, PR = 4.5 cm and the angle at P is 75°.

(a) Make an accurate drawing of the triangle.

(b) Measure and write down the length of QR.

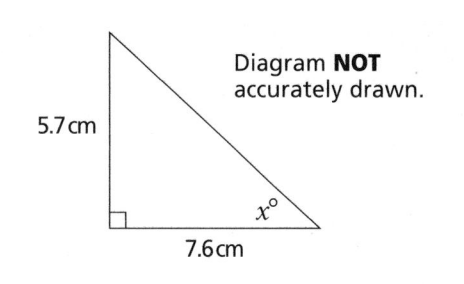

*AQA(SEG) 1999*

33 Constructions • 129

# 34 Navigation

You will revise
- how to use scales
- how to give directions using compass points

You will learn
- how to use four-figure grid references
- how to use bearings to give positions and to describe journeys

## A Grid references

This is a map of the island of Tiree off the north west coast of Scotland.
The grid lines are 1 km apart.

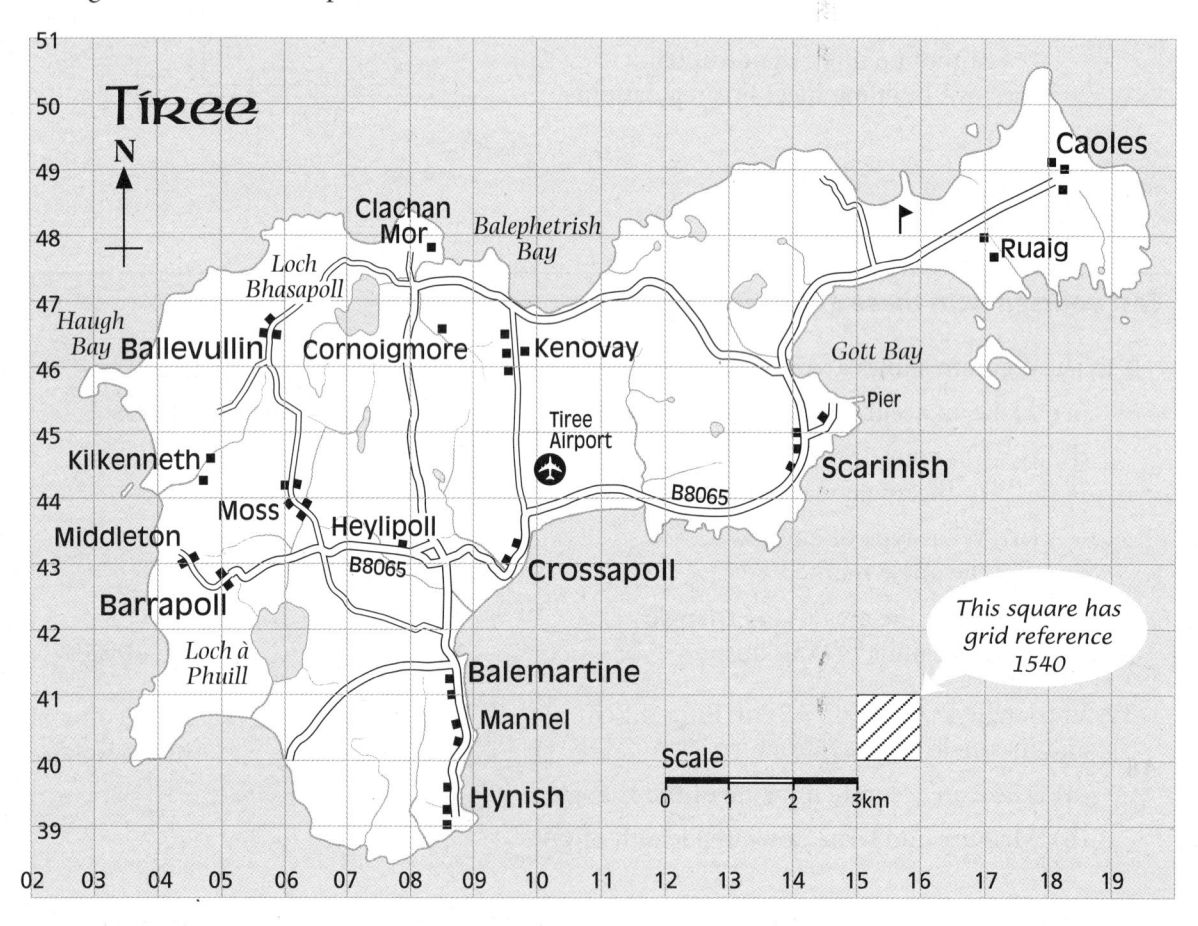

*This square has grid reference 1540*

To describe a place on a map, grid references can be used.

The shaded square on the map opposite has grid reference 1540.
The reference across the page is always given first.

On this map, like many in real life, the grid lines are 1 km apart.

Answer these questions using the map opposite.

**A1** What are the names of the villages in grid squares
- (a) 0839
- (b) 1747
- (c) 0546
- (d) 1444

**A2** In what grid squares are these
- (a) the pier
- (b) the airport (shown by a plane)
- (c) Mannel
- (d) the golf course (shown by a flag)?

**A3** A helicopter takes off from the airport.
In what compass direction would it fly on to go over
- (a) Balephetrish Bay
- (b) Scarinish
- (c) Kilkenneth
- (d) Loch a Phuill
- (e) Loch Bhasapoll
- (f) the golf course

**A4** In which compass direction would a helicopter be flying
if it flew directly between these places:
- (a) Clachan Mor to Hynish
- (b) Ruaig to Scarinish
- (c) Moss to Kenovay
- (d) Ballevullin to Crossapoll

**A5** Use the scale to find, to the nearest kilometre, the distance as the crow flies between
- (a) the airport and the golf course
- (b) Middleton and Crossapoll
- (c) the crossroads by Clachan Mor and Hynish village
- (d) Kilkenneth and Ruaig.

**A6** The B8065 runs between Middleton and Scarinish.
Roughly how far is it between Middleton and Scarinish along this road?

**A7** A canoeist wants to canoe around this island keeping close to the coast.
Find the rough distance around the island.

**A8** Name the places described here.
- (a) 3 km due west of Balemartine
- (b) 5 km due north of Crossapoll
- (c) 4 km north-west of the airport
- (d) 3 km south-west of Ruaig

**A9** Give the compass direction and distance a helicopter would have to fly to travel from
- (a) Crossapoll to Kenovay
- (b) Ruaig to Hynish
- (c) Middleton to Clachan Mor

## B Scales

This shows part of a scale drawing of the ground floor of a house.

The complete drawing is on sheet P179.

The scale of the drawing is 1 cm represents 1 m.

On the plan the width of the kitchen is 4 cm.
In real life the kitchen is 4 m wide.

Use the sheet to answer these questions.

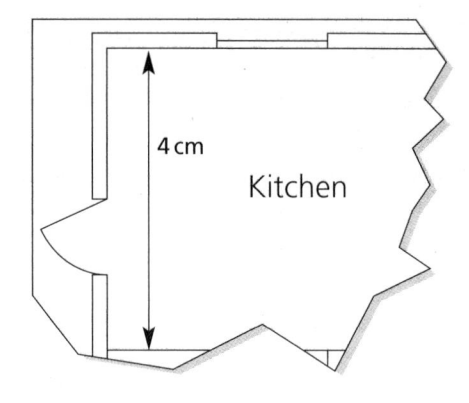

**B1** What is the overall width and length of this house in real life?

**B2** Find the length and width of these rooms in real life.
- (a) the living room
- (b) the dining room
- (c) the bedroom
- (d) the W.C.

**B3** Add these features to the plan of the house
- (a) A porch around the front door which is 4 m along the side of the house and 2 m deep
- (b) A carpet in the middle of the living room measuring 4 m by 6 m
- (c) A double bed in the bedroom measuring 2 m long by 1.5 m wide
- (d) A table in the dining room measuring 1 m by 2 m.

Sheet P180 shows a scale drawing of Harton School.
The scale of the drawing is 1 cm represents 10 m.

Use the sheet to answer these questions.

**B4** What are these measurements in real life (to the nearest 5 m)
- (a) the width of the playground
- (b) the width of the sports pitch
- (c) the distance from the side entrance to the oak tree?

**B5** (a) A fence is to be erected along the edge of the school field from A to B. How long will this fence be?
- (b) Fencing is sold in 2 m wide sections. How many sections would be needed to fence from A to B?
- (c) The panels cost £15. How much would it cost in total for fence panels from A to B?

**B6** Add a cycle rack 10 m wide by 20 m long at the edge of the car park to the plan.

Sheet P181 shows the whole of Great Britain and part of Ireland.
The scale of the map is 1 cm represents 50 km.

Answer these questions using the map.

**B7** In what compass direction would you be travelling if you flew directly from
  (a) Cardiff to London
  (b) London to Belfast
  (c) Cardiff to Land's End
  (d) Edinburgh to John o'Groats

**B8** By measuring to the nearest centimetre, find the real life distances from
  (a) Dublin to Leicester
  (b) London to Belfast
  (c) Belfast to Edinburgh
  (d) Land's End to John o'Groats.

**B9** A courier firm in Manchester says it will guarantee same day delivery to anywhere within 300 km.
Which of the places on the map are within 300 km as the crow flies of Manchester?

Sheet P182 is part of an Ordnance Survey map of Great and Little Cumbrae in Scotland.
The scale of the map is 1 cm represents $\frac{1}{2}$ km.

Answer these questions using the map.

**B10** What features can be found in these grid squares?
  (a) 1855
  (b) 1452
  (c) 1759
  (d) 1658

**B11** The scale of this map is 1 cm represents $\frac{1}{2}$ km.
How far apart are the grid lines on this map in real life?

**B12** Find the distances, to the nearest $\frac{1}{2}$ kilometre in a straight line from
  (a) Sheanawally Point (1552) to Farland Point (1753)
  (b) Trail Isle (1551) to Clashfarland Point (1856)
  (c) the telephone (1858) to the Marine Station (1754)
  (d) Sherrif's Port (1555) to Skate Point (1658)

**B13** What feature will you find
  (a) 3 km north of Broad Islands (1551)
  (b) 3 km east of Sheriff's Port (1555)
  (c) $2\frac{1}{2}$ km west of the Marine Station (1754)
  (d) $4\frac{1}{2}$ km south west of Clashfarland Point (1856)

**Do it yourself!**
- Draw a scale map of your school playground to a scale of 1 cm represents 1 m.
  Add any features such as sports areas which are marked out.
- Get an Ordnance Survey map which is 1:50 000 (1 cm represents $\frac{1}{2}$ km) for your area.

Make up some questions of your own about these maps.

## C Using angles

**C1** This is a picture of an Elizabethan clock.
It has only an hour hand.
What angle does the hand turn through from midday to
(a) 3 p.m.
(b) 6 p.m.
(c) 9 p.m.
(d) 1 p.m.
(e) 7 p.m.
(f) 8 p.m.

**C2** Describe each of the angles below using one of these statements

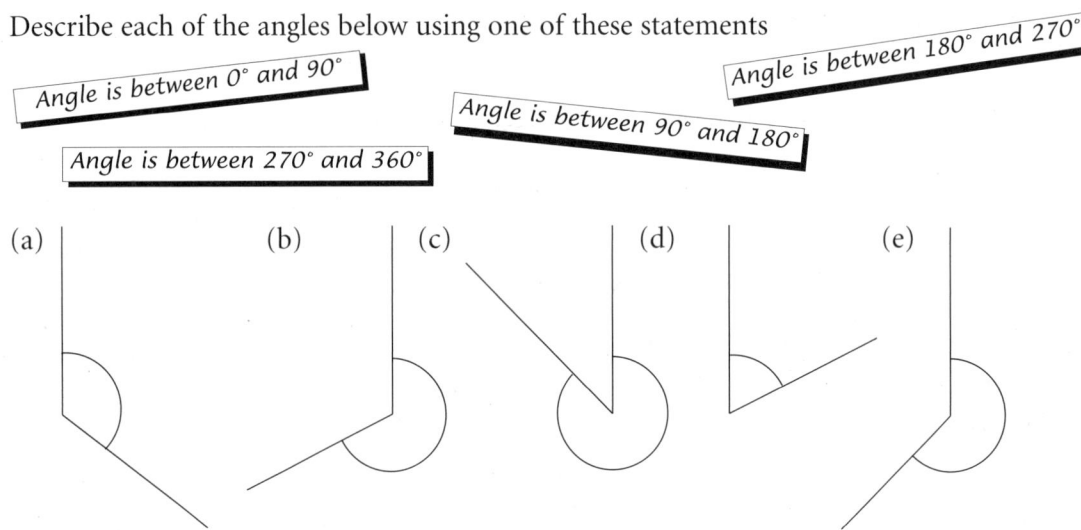

*Angle is between 0° and 90°*

*Angle is between 90° and 180°*

*Angle is between 180° and 270°*

*Angle is between 270° and 360°*

(a) (b) (c) (d) (e)

**C3** What angle would you have turned through clockwise **from North** to face
(a) west
(b) south
(c) south-east
(d) north-west

**C4** Which compass direction would you be facing if you turned clockwise **from North** through
(a) 90°
(b) 45°
(c) 225°

**C5** Copy and complete this compass 'rose' which shows the angles measured clockwise **from north** to each point.

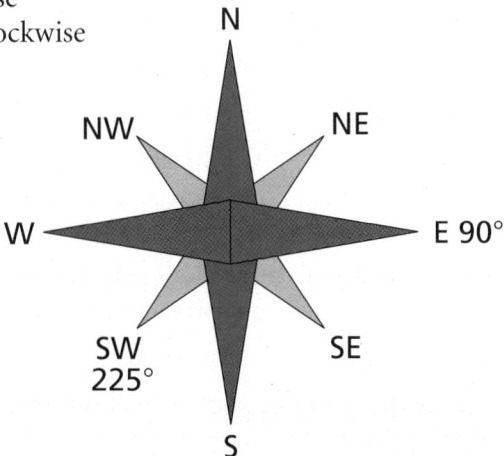

0° N
NW
NE
W
E 90°
SW 225°
SE
S

134 • 34 Navigation

## D Bearings

**Bearings**

For accurate navigation compass directions like north, south-east and so on are not enough.

A **bearing** is the angle measured clockwise from a North line to a given direction.

Bearings are always given as three numbers to avoid mistakes.

*To approach the runway, turn to a bearing of zero-three-five.*

This is how you can measure a bearing on a map.

*Find the bearing from A to B on this map.*

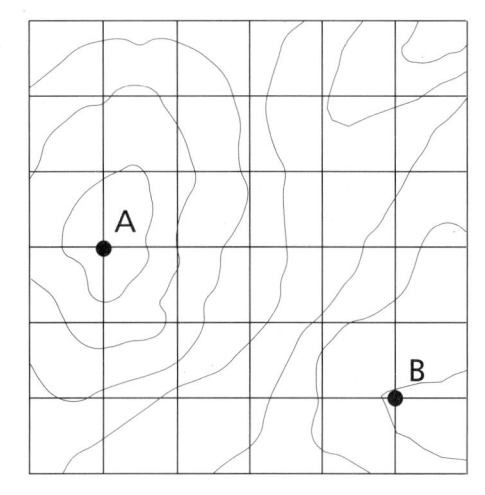

Draw the North line vertically from point A. Use the grid lines on the map to help. Draw a line from A to B.

Use an angle measurer to measure the **clockwise** angle between the lines.

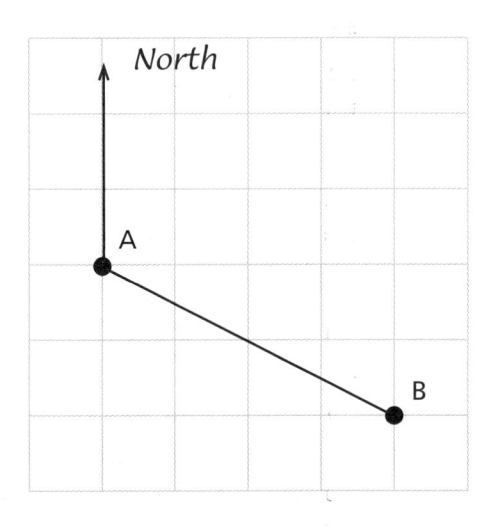

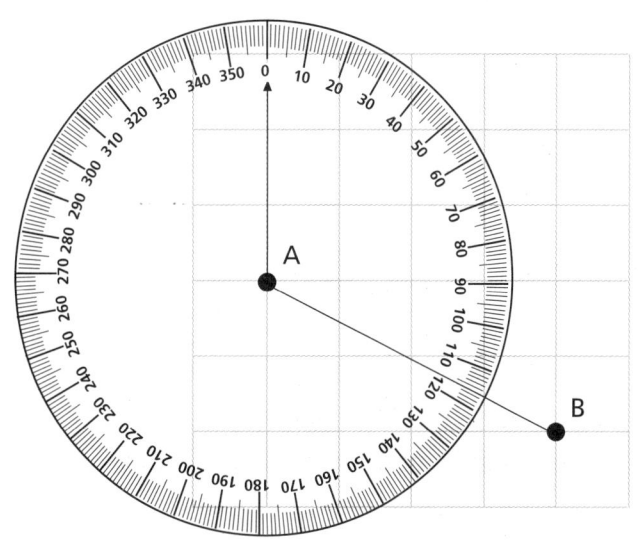

*The bearing from A to B is 116°*

34 Navigation • 135

Use the map on sheet P183 and an angle measurer for questions D1 to D4.

**D1** What is the bearing from point A to

(a) point B  (b) point C  (c) point E

**D2** What are the bearings from

(a) point B to point C  (b) point C to point E  (c) D to point A

**D3** Which point is on a bearing of

(a) 166° from point D  (b) 255° from point B  (c) 332° from point C

**D4** The scale of this map is 1 cm represents 2 km.
Find the real life distances, to the nearest kilometre, from

(a) A to B  (b) E to B  (c) D to C

---

**Seeing from the Eye**

Going on the London Eye enables you to see much of Central London.

Sheet P184 shows a map of London with the London Eye and some places you can see when you are at the top.

Use the map to make a simple diagram like the one here to show what bearing you would have to look on to see places.

The places marked on the map are

|   |   |   |   |
|---|---|---|---|
| A | St. Paul's Cathedral | B | Imperial War Museum |
| C | Tower Bridge | D | Big Ben |
| E | Tate Britain | F | Covent Garden |
| G | Buckingham Palace | H | BT Tower |
| I | Nelson's Column | | |

North ↑
Tower Bridge 087° →

---

**D5** The map on sheet P185 shows an island drawn on a scale of 1 cm represents 2 km.
Find the real life distance and bearing of

(a) the Jetty from Folly Farm
(b) the Lighthouse from Seal Point
(c) Seal Point from Sandcombe Bay
(d) Sandcombe Bay from the Lighthouse
(e) Folly Farm from Sandcombe Bay
(f) Sandcombe Bay from the Jetty.

**D6** (a) A new pier is to be placed on the coast on a bearing of 250° from Folly Farm.
Mark the position of the pier with a cross and label it P.

(b) A radio mast is to be placed 8 km from the Jetty on a bearing of 025°.
On the map put a cross where the mast will be and label this R.

(c) A coastguard standing at Seal Point spots a yacht in trouble on a bearing of 295° and at a distance of 6 km.
Mark a cross where the yacht is and label Y.

**D7** (a) A large boat is spotted at 1400 hours on a bearing of 193° from the Lighthouse.
Draw a line at a bearing of 193° from the lighthouse.

(b) At the same time the boat is seen on a bearing of 236° from the jetty.
Mark the position of the boat with a dot, label this 1400.

(c) At 1500 hours the boat is on a bearing of 139° from the lighthouse and 198° from the jetty.
Mark the position of the boat and label this 1500.

(d) If the boat continues on exactly the same course and speed, mark where the boat will be at 1600 hours.

(e) On what bearing will someone at the jetty see the boat at 1600 hours?

(f) How far will the boat be from the jetty at 1600 hours?

**Test yourself with these questions**

**T1** Here is an outline map of an island.
It is drawn to a scale of 1 cm to 5 km.

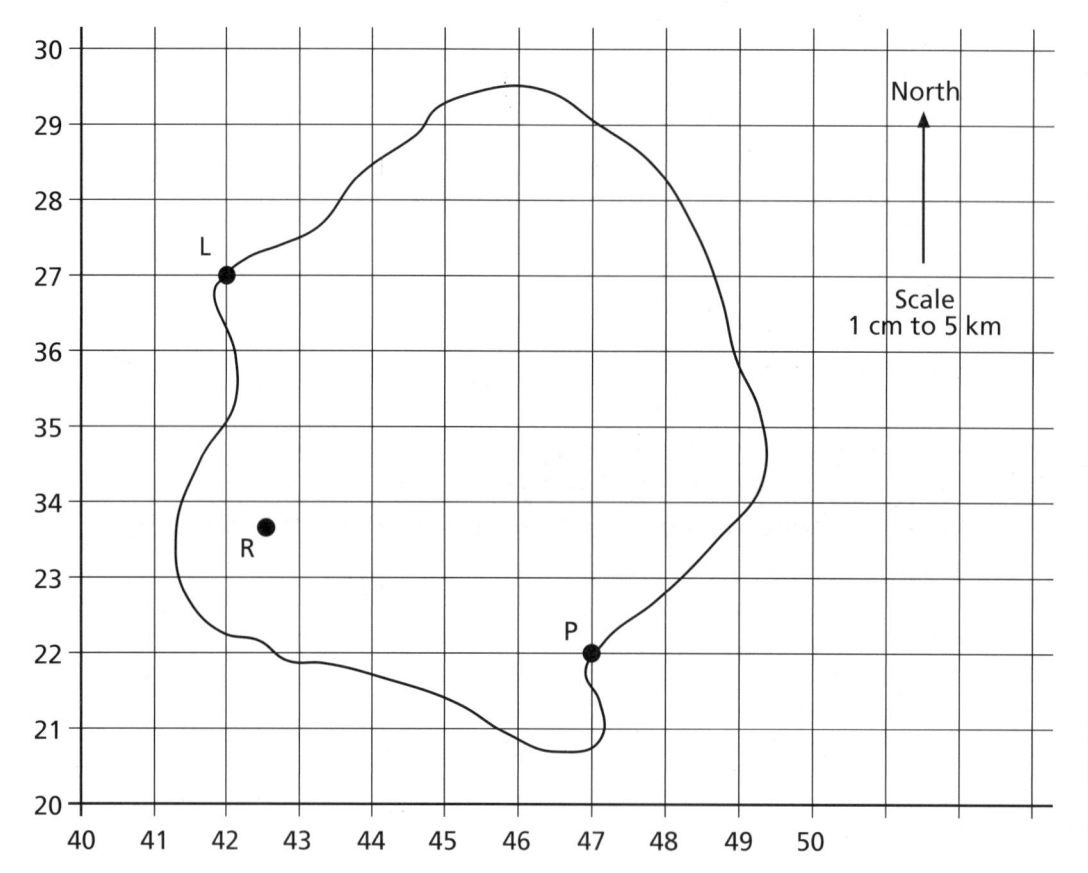

(a) Write down the four-figure grid reference of the square containing the Radio Mast (R).

(b) A party of visitors walks straight across the island from the Port (P) to the Life-boat Station (L).

    (i) In which direction do they walk from P to L?

    (ii) How far is it from P to L?
       Give your answer to the nearest kilometre.

OCR

**T2** Sheet P186 shows the map of an island drawn to a scale of 3 cm to represent 1 km.

(a) The port is at A and the airport is at B.
Use the map to find the distance AB in kilometres.

(b) The Lion Hotel is 2 km from A on a bearing of 150°.
Use a cross to mark the position of the hotel on the map.

AQA 2003 Specimen

# 35 Percentage calculations 2

You will revise
- how to work out percentages of quantities

You will learn how to
- work out percentage increase and decrease
- use percentage in real life situations
- work out increase and decrease by a fraction

## A Review

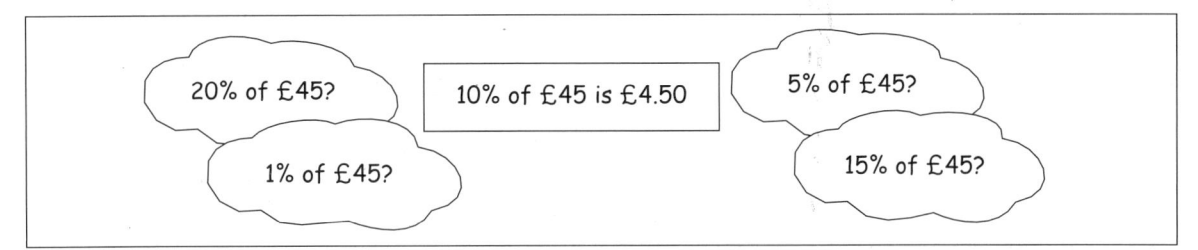

- 20% of £45?
- 10% of £45 is £4.50
- 5% of £45?
- 1% of £45?
- 15% of £45?

**A1** Work out
(a) 10% of £24 (b) 5% of £24 (c) 15% of £24 (d) 20% of £24

**A2** Work out 5% of
(a) £36 (b) 60 kg (c) £70 (d) 16 m (e) £5

**A3** Work out 20% of
(a) £14 (b) 40 cm (c) £350 (d) £4000 (e) 25 kg

**A4** Work out
(a) 50% of 68 km (b) 25% of £12 (c) 25% of 28 m (d) 50% of 37 kg

1% is the same as $\frac{1}{100}$.
To work out 1% of something - divide by 100.
   1% of 350 = 350 ÷ 100 = 3.5

Once you know what 1% is you can easily work out 2%, 3% ......
   2% of 350 = 2 × 3.5 = 7
   3% of 350 = 3 × 3.5 = 10.5

**A5** Work out
(a) 1% of £200 (b) 1% of £8 (c) 1% of £650 (d) 1% of £1260

**\*A6** Work out
(a) 2% of £500 (b) 3% of £1400 (c) 4% of £25 (d) 6% of £2400

## B  Percentage increase

The price of a camera is to be increased by 10%.
If the original cost was £140, what will its new price be?

Increase is 10% of £140 = £14
New price = old price + increase
          = £140 + £14
          = £154

**BUY NOW!**
Prices go up **10%** next week

**B1** The price of a television increases by 10%.
  (a) How much is 10% of £250?
  (b) What is the new price of the television?

**B2** A bottle of cola contains 500 ml. A special offer bottle will have 10% extra free.
  (a) How much is 10% of 500 ml?
  (b) How much cola is in the special offer bottle?

**B3** Anna's pocket money is £3.50 per week. It goes up by 10%.
  (a) How much is 10% of £3.50?
  (b) How much pocket money will Anna now receive?

**B4** How much will each of these amounts be when they have been increased by 10%?
  (a) £240    (b) £600    (c) £18    (d) £5400    (e) £1.90

**B5** Pete earns £6 per hour. He gets a pay rise of 5%.
  (a) How much is 5% of £6?
  (b) What is Pete's new rate of pay?

**Investing money**

When you save money in a bank or building society they pay you interest on the money in your account. The interest rate is given as a percentage.

A rate of 5% per annum (p.a.) means you get an extra 5% of your savings added to your account at the end of the year.

**B6** Sanjay has £1200 invested. If the interest rate is 5% per annum, find
  (a) how much interest he will receive after 1 year
  (b) how much his investment will be worth after one year

**B7** A test is due to last 90 minutes.
    The teacher allows Kevin 20% extra time because of a broken arm.
  (a) How much extra time will Kevin be allowed?
  (b) How long can he take in total to complete the test?

**B8** At present a school has 1500 pupils.
The school plans to increase its pupil numbers by 10%.

How many pupils will it have after the increase?

**B9** A roll of kitchen foil normally contains 50 m.
How much foil is there on this special offer roll?

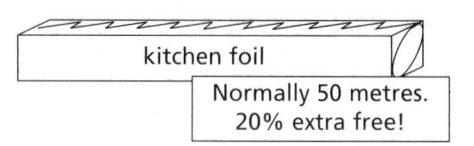

kitchen foil
Normally 50 metres.
20% extra free!

**B10** For each pair, find which gives the greater amount after the increase.

(a) £20 increased by 5% or £18 increased by 10%

(b) £12 increased by 50% or £15 increased by 20%

(c) £40 increased by 15% or £42 increased by 10%

(d) £2000 increased by 25% or £2200 increased by 10%

## C *Percentage decrease*

The price of a television is to be reduced by 10%.
If the original cost was £240, what will its new price be?

Decrease is 10% of £240 = £24
New price = old price − decrease
              = £240 − £24
              = £216

Special Offer
10% off all prices

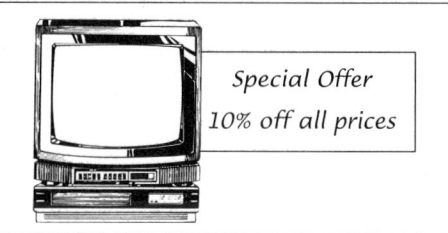

**C1** A jacket originally cost £40. The price is reduced by 10% in a sale.

(a) Find 10% of £40.

(b) Find the sale price of the jacket.

**C2** The population of a village is 5600.
It is expected that the population will decrease by 10% over the next five years.

What is the population expected to be in five years?

**C3** Jan used to work for 40 hours each week. She now works 5% less hours.

How many hours does she work now?

**C4** Match these up.

| | | | | |
|---|---|---|---|---|
| A | Decrease £10 by 30% | | P | £3 |
| B | Increase £4 by 25% | | Q | £4 |
| C | Increase £2 by 50% | | R | £5 |
| D | Decrease £5 by 20% | | S | £6 |
| E | Decrease £8 by 25% | | T | £7 |

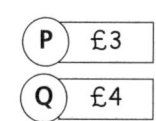

**C5** Find the sale price of each item.

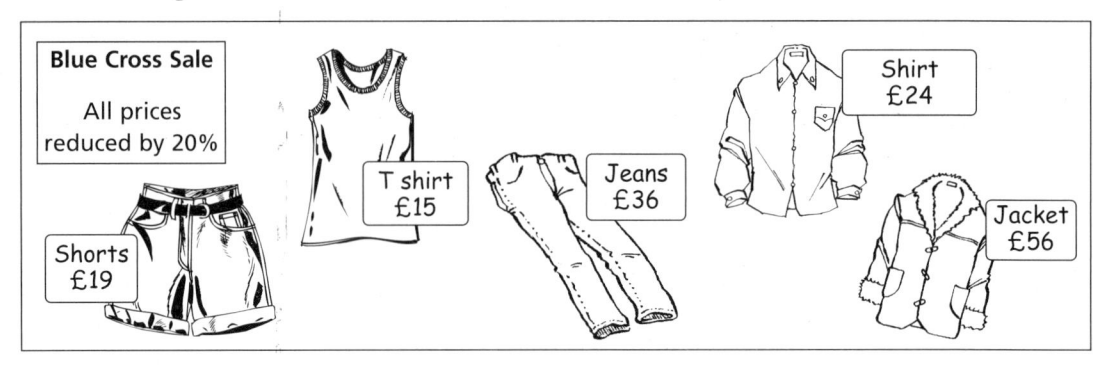

**Blue Cross Sale**
All prices reduced by 20%

Shorts £19
T shirt £15
Jeans £36
Shirt £24
Jacket £56

## D  Increase and decrease with fractions

The price of a jumper is to be reduced by $\frac{1}{4}$ in a sale.
If the original price of the jumper is £24, what will the sale price be?
Decrease is $\frac{1}{4}$ of £24 = £24 ÷ 4 = £6
New price = old price − decrease
= £24 − £6
= £18

**D1** Prices are to be **reduced** by $\frac{1}{4}$ in a sale. Find the sale prices of each of these items.
   (a) a skirt costing £32
   (b) a pair of trousers costing £40
   (c) a jacket costing £60
   (d) a t-shirt costing £14

**D2** A packet of pasta normally contains 500 g.
   (a) How much **extra** pasta is in the special offer packet?
   (b) How much pasta is there altogether in the special offer packet?

Special offer Pasta
$\frac{1}{2}$ EXTRA FREE

**D3** Find the total amount in each of these special offers.
   (a) Cereal Normally 1.5 kg — $\frac{1}{3}$ EXTRA FREE
   (b) Orange juice Normally 500 ml — $\frac{1}{4}$ EXTRA FREE
   (c) Tea Normally 125 g — $\frac{1}{5}$ EXTRA FREE

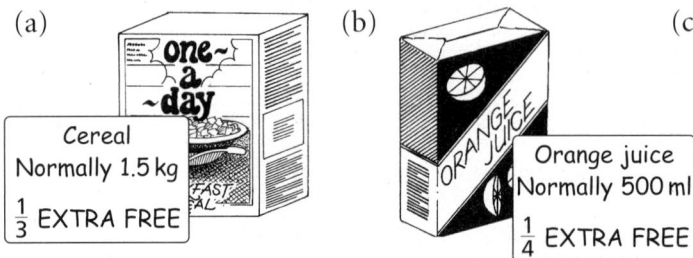

**D4** The price of a computer is £840.
In a sale the price is **reduced** by one third.
What is the sale price of the computer?

## E Percentages on a calculator

Tom worked this out on his calculator.    38% of £64 = £24.32 ✓

| 38 ÷ 100 × 64 | 64 ÷ 100 × 38 | 0.38 × 64 |

Check that you can get the right answer on your calculator.

**E1** Calculate
   (a) 42% of £54
   (b) 35% of 48 kg
   (c) 49% of £2500
   (d) 17% of £95
   (e) 8% of 3750
   (f) 2% of 318 000

**E2** Calculate the following, rounding your answers to the nearest penny.
   (a) 9% of £7.50
   (b) 12% of £8.60
   (c) 15% of £24.99

**E3** There are 1250 pupils in a school.
   (a) 14% of the pupils wear glasses. How many pupils wear glasses?
   (b) 52% of the pupils walk to school. How many pupils walk to school?
   (c) 46% of the pupils have school dinners. How many pupils is this?

**E4** Find
   (a) 4% of 160 litres
   (b) 28% of 1270 g
   (c) 87% of 190 cm
   (d) 13% of 245 ml
   (e) 42% of 95 kg
   (f) 65% of 3500 m

**E5** Angie's salary was £12 000 per year. It was then increased by 7%.
   (a) How much was her salary increased by?
   (b) What is her new salary?

**E6** The value of the Jones' house was £85 000. House prices then rose by 12%.
   (a) By how much has value of their house increased?
   (b) What is the new value of their house?

**E7** After advertising in the local paper, visitor numbers at a Wildlife Centre increased by 7%. There were 2300 visitors the previous month. How many visitors came after the advertisement?

**E8** Sam's car cost £11 300 when new. When it was one year old it had depreciated in value by 23%. (This means that the value has gone down by 23%.)
   (a) By how much has its value gone down?
   (b) What is the value when it is one year old?

**E9** The numbers of blackbirds in British gardens has dropped by 31%.
In an area where there used to be 2500 blackbirds, how many would there be now?

# F In the real world

**VAT**

VAT is short for Value Added Tax.
You usually pay it when you buy something or when you pay for a service.
VAT is a percentage of the cost of something. The Government sets the percentage.
VAT is currently set at $17\frac{1}{2}$%.

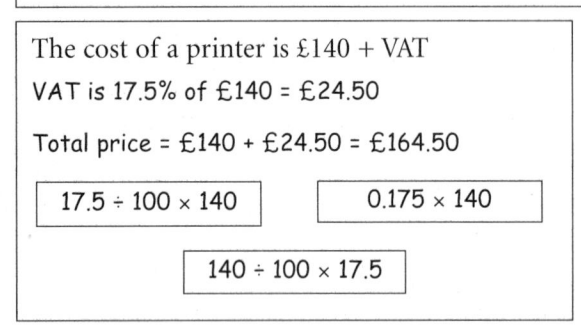

---

The cost of a printer is £140 + VAT

VAT is 17.5% of £140 = £24.50

Total price = £140 + £24.50 = £164.50

| 17.5 ÷ 100 × 140 | 0.175 × 140 |

| 140 ÷ 100 × 17.5 |

---

Anita invested £260 for 1 year at an interest rate of 3.5% per annum.

Interest is 3.5% of £260 = £9.10

Total investment = £260 + £9.10 = £269.10

| 3.5 ÷ 100 × 260 | 0.035 × 260 |

| 260 ÷ 100 × 3.5 |

---

**F1** Work out the prices of each of these items if the rate of VAT is $17\frac{1}{2}$%.
Round each answer to the nearest penny.

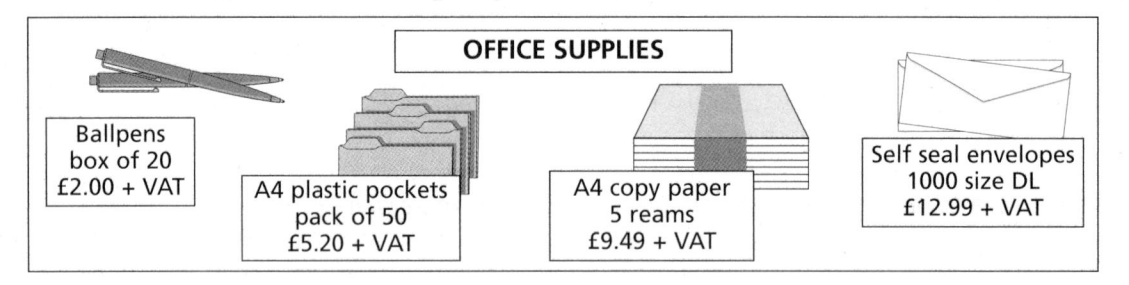

**OFFICE SUPPLIES**

Ballpens
box of 20
£2.00 + VAT

A4 plastic pockets
pack of 50
£5.20 + VAT

A4 copy paper
5 reams
£9.49 + VAT

Self seal envelopes
1000 size DL
£12.99 + VAT

**F2** At which shop is this television cheaper?

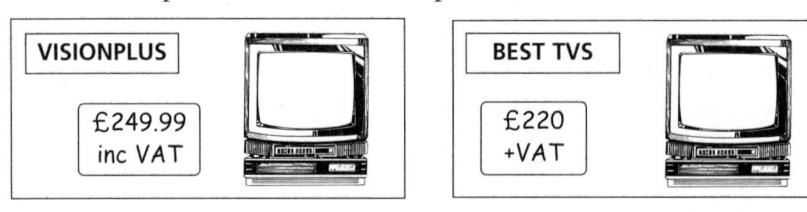

VISIONPLUS
£249.99
inc VAT

BEST TVS
£220
+VAT

**F3** Hilda invested £3800 in an account with an interest rate of 3.2% per annum.

(a) How much interest will her investment have earned after one year?

(b) How much in total will her investment now be worth?

**F4** Which of these sofas is cheaper?

A  Normally £650
Now
40% off!

B  SALE
Was £500
Save 25%!

**F5** Sonia works in a shop where she gets 12% staff discount.

How much would she pay if she bought one duvet cover, one sheet and two pillow cases?

| Price list | |
|---|---|
| Duvet covers | £29.50 |
| Sheets | £14.50 |
| Pillows | £8.99 |
| Pillowcases | £3.25 |

**F6** Patrick gets paid £8.60 an hour.
He gets paid 'time and a quarter' for any overtime he works.

How much would he get paid for 6 hours overtime?

**F7** A shop has this special offer on packets of biscuits.
Randeep buys two packets of biscuits.

How much does he pay altogether?

> SPECIAL OFFER
> Normally 68p
> BUY ONE GET THE SECOND HALF PRICE!

**F8** (a) An adult pays £9.90 to get into a theme park.
Children pay half price.
A family of two adults and three children go to the theme park.

How much do they pay altogether?

(b) At the park the family buy a gift.
The gift costs £5.20 plus VAT.
The VAT rate is 17.5%.

What is the total cost of the gift?

AQA(SEG) 2000

**F9** Barry buys 300 mountain bikes for £15 000 and he starts to sell them at £110 each.
After he has sold $\frac{3}{4}$ of the bikes, Barry reduces the price by 20%.

(a) What is the new selling price of a bike?

Barry sells $\frac{3}{4}$ of the bikes at £110 each.
He then sells the remaining bikes at the reduced price.

(b) What is the total amount that Barry receives from selling the 300 bikes?  AQA(SEG) 2000

**F10** An electricity company supplies electricity to a family with the following charges:

　　Standing charge: 9.13 pence per day

　　Electricity used: 6.19 pence per unit

　　VAT of 5% is added to the total

The Green family receives a bill for 91 days.
In that time they had used a total of 1272 units of electricity.
Calculate the amount the Greens have to pay. Show your working clearly.　　OCR

**F11** In 1997 Mrs Patel earned £16 640 for a 52 week year.
At the start of 1998 she was given a rise of 3%.

Calculate how much she will earn **per week** in 1998.

OCR(MEG)

**Test yourself with these questions**

**T1** Ben invests £60 in a bank account.
Interest of 5% is added at the end of each year.

Work out the money in Ben's account after one year.

*Edexcel*

**T2** Karen sees an advertisement for a suede jacket.
Calculate the final cost of the suede jacket.

> Our price
> 30% off Recommended Price of £130

*AQA(SEG)2000*

**T3** Work out the sale price of this dress.

> Price £45

> SALE ALL PRICES REDUCED BY 20%

*OCR(MEG)*

**T4** A school buys a trampoline.
The school is given a discount of $\frac{1}{8}$ of the price.

(a) Write $\frac{1}{8}$ as

   (i) a decimal    (ii) a percentage.

The price of the trampoline is £3218.

(b) Work out the amount the school actually has to pay.

*Edexcel*

**T5** The cash price of the saxophone is £740.
Tom buys the saxophone using a Credit Plan.
He pays a deposit of 5% of the cash price and 12 monthly payments of £65.

> Saxophone £740 for cash
> Credit Plan available

Work out the difference between the cost when he used the Credit Plan and the cash price.

*Edexcel*

**T6** Sam wants to buy a Hooper washing machine.
Hooper washing machines are sold in three different shops.

| Washing Power | Whytes | Clean up |
|---|---|---|
| $\frac{1}{4}$ OFF usual price of £370 | 15% OFF usual price of £370 | £240 plus VAT at $17\frac{1}{2}$% |

Find the difference between the maximum and minimum prices Sam could pay for a washing machine.

*Edexcel*

# 36 Conversion graphs

You will learn
- how to use and draw a conversion graph

## A Using a conversion graph

This graph can be used to convert between miles and kilometres.

For example, the dotted line shows that 12 miles is about 19 km.

**A1** Use the graph to convert
   (a) 20 miles to km
   (b) 27 miles to km
   (c) 8 miles to km
   (d) 17.5 miles to km

**A2** Find 35 kilometres on the vertical scale of the graph. Use the graph to convert 35 km to miles.

**A3** Use the graph to convert
   (a) 40 km to miles
   (b) 24 km to miles
   (c) 10 km to miles

**A4** You can't use the graph to convert 50 miles to km, because the 'miles' scale doesn't go up to 50.
How could you use the graph to help you convert 50 miles to km?

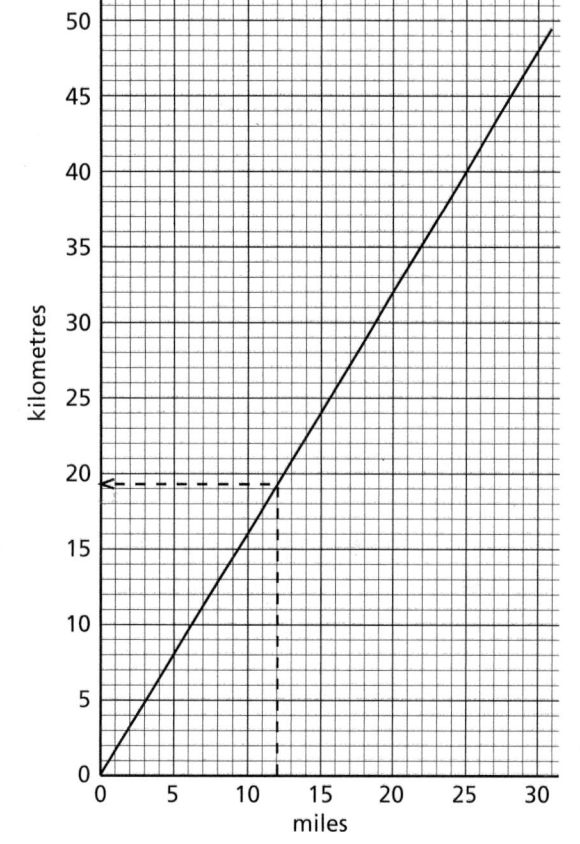

**A5** Use the graph to help you convert
   (a) 100 miles to km
   (b) 75 miles to km
   (c) 60 km to miles
   (d) 100 km to miles

**A6** The distance from London to Cambridge is 55 miles. How much is this in kilometres?

**A7** This graph can be used to convert between pints and litres.

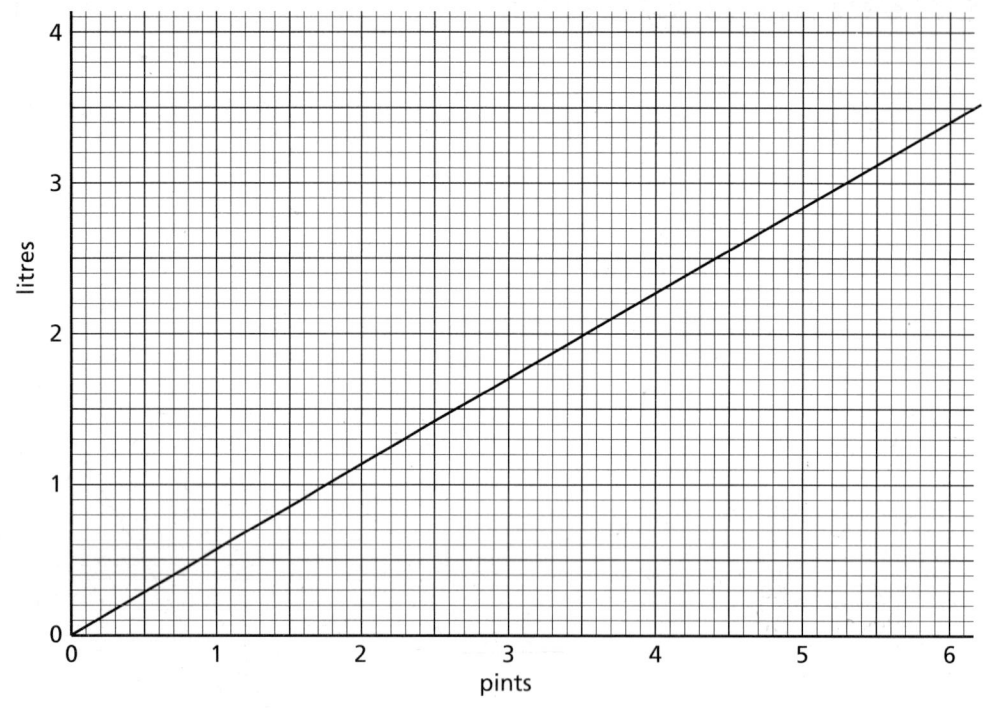

(a) Use the graph to convert
  (i) 4.5 pints to litres
  (ii) 2.8 pints to litres
  (iii) 1.7 pints to litres
(b) Use the graph to convert
  (i) 3 litres to pints
  (ii) 1.5 litres to pints
  (iii) 0.9 litres to pints
(c) Use the graph to help you convert 15 pints to litres.

**A8** (a) Use this conversion graph to convert
  (i) 4 pounds to kilograms
  (ii) 5.5 pounds to kilograms
  (iii) 2.4 kg to pounds
  (iv) 0.9 kg to pounds
(b) Use the graph to help you convert
  (i) 12 pounds to kilograms
  (ii) 10 kilograms to pounds

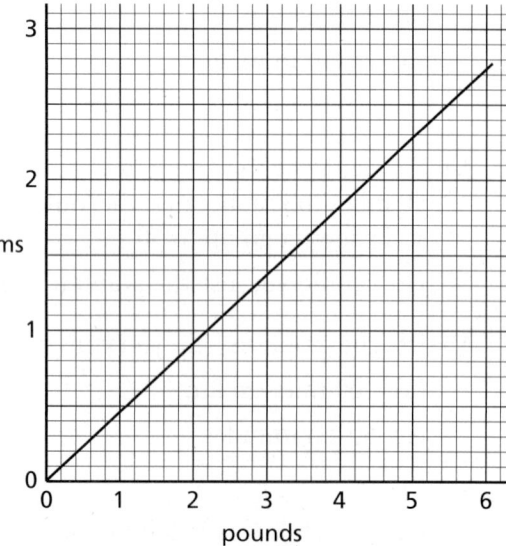

## B  Drawing a conversion graph

You need sheet P187.

**B1** Ships' speeds can be measured in knots.

This table shows speeds in knots and in kilometres per hour.

| Speed in knots | 0 | 5 | 10 | 15 | 20 | 25 |
|---|---|---|---|---|---|---|
| Speed in km/h | 0 | 9 | 18 | 27 | 36 | 45 |

(a) Plot the points from the table on grid A on the sheet.
Draw the straight line through the points.

(b) Use your graph to convert

(i) 17 knots to kilometres per hour

(ii) 39 kilometres per hour to knots

**B2** This table shows areas in square miles and km².

| square miles | 0 | 10 | 20 | 30 | 40 | 50 |
|---|---|---|---|---|---|---|
| km² | 0 | 26 | 52 | 78 | 104 | 130 |

(a) On grid B draw a conversion graph.

(b) Use the graph to convert

(i) 37 square miles to km²    (ii) 85 km² to square miles

**B3** This table shows volumes in cubic feet and m³.

| cubic feet | 0 | 50 | 100 | 150 | 200 | 250 |
|---|---|---|---|---|---|---|
| m³ | 0 | 1.4 | 2.8 | 4.2 | 5.6 | 7.0 |

(a) On grid C draw a conversion graph.

(b) Use the graph to convert

(i) 220 cubic feet to m³    (ii) 5.2 m³ to cubic feet

**B4** An airport shop shows its prices in pounds sterling (£) and euros (€).
A compact camera costs £25 or €40.

Compact camera  £25   €40

(a) On grid D mark the point (25, 40).
The conversion graph must start at (0, 0) because £0 = €0.
Draw the straight line from (0, 0) through (25, 40).

(b) Use your conversion graph to find the missing prices on these tickets.

(i) Digital watch  £17.50   €……

(ii) Make-up bag  £……   €35

(iii) Perfume  £……   €19

**B5** You need sheet P188.

The following table shows how °Celsius can be changed into °Fahrenheit.

| °C | −5 | 0 | 5 | 10 | 15 | 20 | 25 | 30 | 35 |
|----|----|----|----|----|----|----|----|----|----|
| °F | 23 | 32 | 41 | 50 | 59 | 68 | 77 | 86 | 95 |

(i) Use the above information to draw, on grid E, a conversion graph for changing °C to °F.

Use your graph to   (ii) change 80°F to °C   (iii) change −10°C to °F      WJEC

---

**Test yourself with these questions**

You need sheet P188.

**T1** This conversion graph is for dollars ($) to pounds (£).

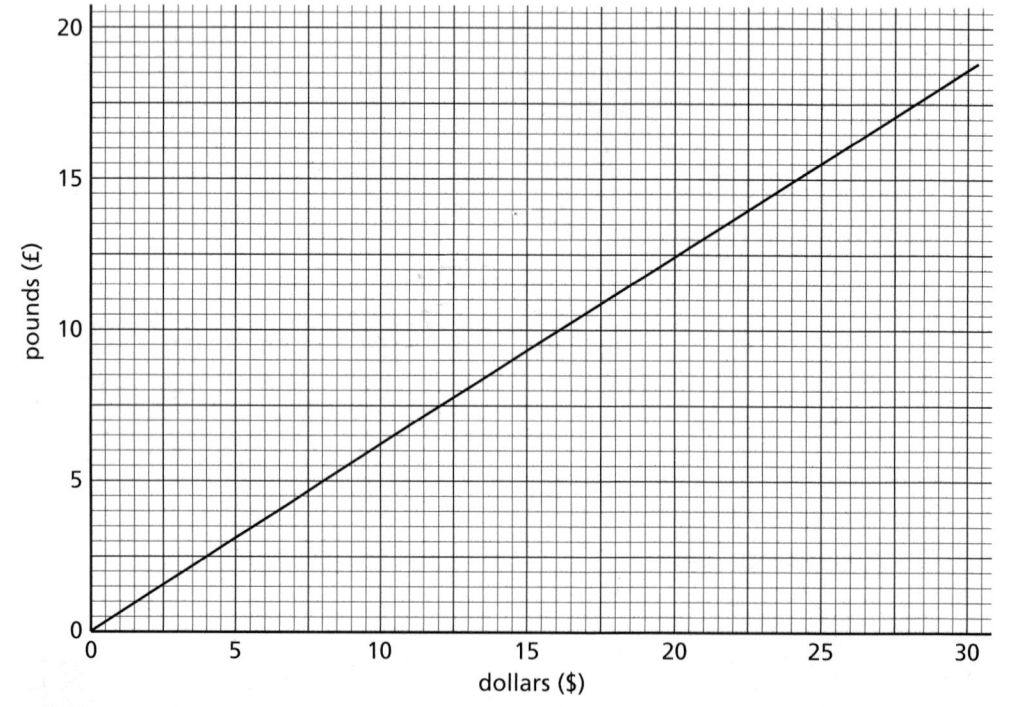

Use the graph to

(a) change £5 into dollars ($)   (b) change $17 into pounds (£)      OCR

**T2** Jack knows that £1 is equal to 1.4 Euros and that £5 is equal to 7 Euros.

(a) Plot this information on grid F in order to produce a conversion chart.

(b) (i) **Use your graph** to estimate how much £2.60 is worth in Euros.

(ii) Jack has 80 Euros.
How much is this worth in pounds (£)?      AQA 2003 Specimen

# Review 4

1. Two fair spinners, numbered from 1 to 4, are spun.
   The numbers shown on the spinners are multiplied together to give a score.
   
   (a) Copy and complete this grid to show all the possible scores.
   
   (b) Find the probability that the score is
   
   (i) 9
   
   (ii) greater than 8
   
   (iii) even

   |  | 1 | 2 | 3 | 4 |
   |---|---|---|---|---|
   | 1 |  |  |  | 4 |
   | 2 |  |  |  |  |
   | 3 |  |  | 6 |  |
   | 4 |  |  |  |  |

   Second spinner across top, First spinner down side.

2. Calculate these, giving your answers to 2 decimal places.
   
   (a) $\dfrac{2.42 + 1.68}{0.28}$
   
   (b) $\dfrac{25}{3.25 - 1.42}$
   
   (c) $5.22 + 1.64^2$

3. Describe fully the transformation which maps shape A onto
   
   (a) shape B
   
   (b) shape C
   
   (c) shape D

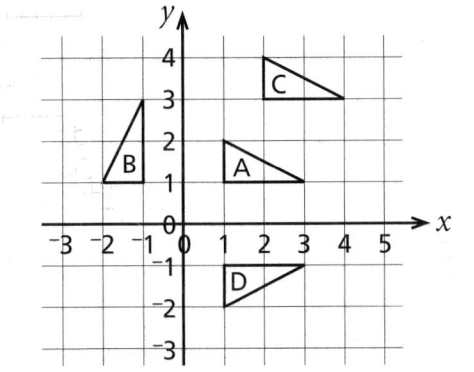

4. Michelle is making curtains.
   She needs 1.4 m of material for each curtain.
   
   (a) How much material does she need to make 4 curtains?
   
   (b) Michelle bought a piece of material 6 m long.
   How much material has she got left after making the 4 curtains?

5. Solve these equations.
   
   (a) $\dfrac{p}{3} = 0.6$
   
   (b) $4r - 1 = r$
   
   (c) $4 = 12 + 2s$

6 Work these out.
   (a) $\frac{1}{4} \times \frac{1}{8}$
   (b) $\frac{1}{2} \times \frac{3}{4}$
   (c) $\frac{1}{4} \div 2$
   (d) $\frac{1}{3} \div 3$

7 (a) Make an accurate drawing of the triangle shown in this sketch.
   (b) Measure and write down the length BC.

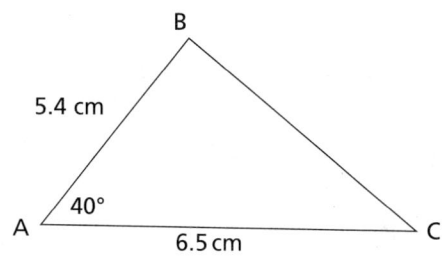

8 A radiator costs £28.40 plus VAT at a builder's merchants. George buys 5 of these radiators.
   Calculate the total cost including VAT at 17.5%.

9 A shop reduces all of its prices by $\frac{1}{4}$ in a stock clearance sale.
   What is the sale price of a table costing £320 before the sale?

10 This diagram shows the position of a lighthouse (L) and a boat (B).
   (a) Measure the bearing of the lighthouse from the boat.
   (b) Measure the bearing of the boat from the lighthouse.

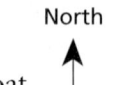

11 Solve these equations.
   (a) $3(e - 2) = 15$
   (b) $f = 4(5 - f)$
   (c) $2(3g + 4) = 12$

12 This conversion graph is for Canadian dollars ($) to pounds (£).
   (a) Use the graph to
       (i) change £50 into dollars ($)
       (ii) change $150 into pounds (£)
   (b) Use the graph to help you convert £150 into dollars ($).

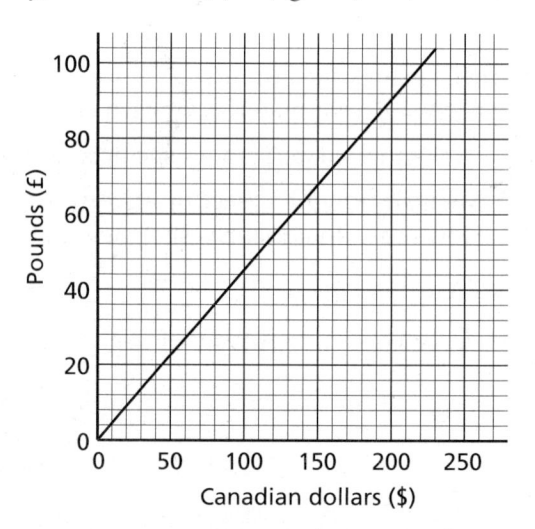